# 100 Places in Spain
*Every Woman Should Go*

# 100 *Places in Spain Every Woman Should Go*

PATRICIA HARRIS

TRAVELERS' TALES
AN IMPRINT OF SOLAS HOUSE, INC.
PALO ALTO

Travelers' Tales and Solas House are trademarks of Solas House, Inc.,
Palo Alto, California. travelerstales.com | solashouse.com

Art Direction: Kimberly Nelson Coombs
Cover Design: Kimberly Nelson Coombs
Cover Photo: Patricia Harris
Interior Design and Page Layout: Howie Severson/Fortuitous Publishing
Interior Photos: Patricia Harris
Author Photo: David Lyon
Production Director: Susan Brady

Library of Congress Cataloging-in-Publication Data

Names: Harris, Patricia, 1949- author.
Title: 100 places in Spain every woman should go / Patricia Harris.
Other titles: One hundred places in Spain every woman should go | Hundred
    places in Spain every woman should go
Description: First edition. | Palo Alto : Travelers' Tales, an imprint of
    Solas House, Inc., [2016]
Identifiers: LCCN 2016021829 (print) | LCCN 2016023099 (ebook) | ISBN
    9781609521196 (paperback) | ISBN 9781609521202 (ebook) | ISBN
    9781609521202 (epub)
Subjects: LCSH: Spain--Guidebooks. | Women--Travel--Spain--Guidebooks. |
    Women travelers--Spain--Guidebooks.
Classification: LCC DP14 .H35 2016 (print) | LCC DP14 (ebook) | DDC
    914.604/84--dc23
LC record available at https://lccn.loc.gov/2016021829

First Edition
Printed in the United States
10 9 8 7 6 5 4 3 2 1

*For David*

# Table of Contents

Introduction                                                                xiii

SECTION I
HEARTLAND: MADRID & CASTILLA                                                    I

1. Sense of Place                                                              3
   *Plaza Mayor, Madrid*
2. The Collector's Eye                                                         6
   *Carmen Thyssen Selections at the Museo Thyssen–Bornemisza, Madrid*
3. Choc Around the Clock                                                      10
   *Chocolatería San Gines, Madrid*
4. Shadow to the Throne                                                       13
   *Monasterio de las Descalzas Reales, Madrid*
5. The Word on the Streets                                                    16
   *Barrio de las Letras, Madrid*
6. If the Shoe Fits                                                           19
   *Shopping for Shoes in Chueca, Madrid*
7. I Am Woman                                                                 23
   *Highlights of the Museo Nacional del Prado, Madrid*
8. A Winter's Feast                                                           28
   *Gastrofestival Madrid*
9. Timeless Cry Against War                                                   30
   *Guernica at the Reina Sofía, Madrid*

10. Where the City Blooms                              33
    *Great Parks of Madrid*
11. Stitches of Time                                   37
    *Real Fábrica de Tapices, Madrid*
12. Just One More Bite                                 40
    *Madrid Food Tours*
13. Echoes of Antiquity                                44
    *Archeological Museum, Madrid*
14. ¡Ole! ¡Ole!                                        48
    *Flamenco at Casa Patas, Madrid*
15. Faith and Will                                     51
    *The Trail of Isabel I of Castilla and León*
16. Within the Walls of Faith                          55
    *Santa Teresa of Ávila*
17. Built to Last                                      58
    *The Aqueduct of Segovia*
18. Dreaming in Stone                                  61
    *Carved Buildings of Salamanca*
19. Big Red                                            64
    *Victoria Benavides and Tinta de Toro*
20. Visions of Heaven and Hell                         67
    *La Colegiata, Toro*
21. In the Name of the Father                          70
    *Victoria Pariente and the Wines of Rueda*
22. Shining Through                                    73
    *Catedral de León*
23. Spain's First Power Couple                         76
    *El Cid and Jimena Díaz, Burgos*

SECTION II
EL NORTE: LA RIOJA & GREEN SPAIN 81

24. The French Connection 83
*Marqués de Riscal, La Rioja*

25. Hope Flies 87
*The Nesting White Storks of Alfaro*

26. Wayside Rest 90
*Santo Domingo de la Calzada*

27. A Mad Dash 93
*Pamplona and the Running of the Bulls*

28. Speaking in Tongues 97
*Monasteries of Suso and Yuso*

29. Power of a Perfect Outfit 100
*The Cristóbal Balenciaga Museum, Getaria*

30. The Guggenheim Effect 103
*Life in Bilbao, A City Saved by Art and Architecture*

31. Off the Rack 107
*Women in Spanish Fashion*

32. A Father-Daughter Culinary Dynasty 110
*Dining at Restaurant Arzak, San Sebastián*

33. A Spanish Movable Feast 114
*Eating Pintxos, San Sebastián*

34. Buried Magic 117
*Prehistoric Cave Art, Cantabria*

35. Green Spain 120
*Driving and Hiking in the Picos de Europa*

36. The Unsung Star of *Vicky Cristina Barcelona* 124
*Celtic City of Oviedo*

37. Galicia's Joan of Arc 127
*The Tale of María Pita of A Coruña*

38. Step by Step      130
  *Pilgrimage on the Camino de Santiago*
39. New Jerusalem     134
  *The End of the Road at Santiago de Compostela*
40. On the Edge      138
  *The End of the World at Fisterra*
41. Making a Splash     141
  *Spain's Top Spots for Water Sports*

SECTION III
LA MANCHA & MOORISH SPAIN   145

42. Eyes of the Artist     147
  *Toledo, as Seen by El Greco*
43. Written on the Walls    152
  *The Ceramics of Talavera de la Reina*
44. Flights of Fancy     155
  *Abstract Art in the Mountaintop Aerie of Cuenca*
45. Learning the Art of the Stripper 159
  *The Saffron Rose Festival, Consuegra*
46. Room for the Night    163
  *Some Great Spanish Paradors*
47. Rome Remains     167
  *The Ancient Colonial City of Mérida*
48. Excess of Splendor    171
  *Sevilla's Massive Gothic Cathedral*
49. Of Cigars and Arias    174
  *In the Footsteps of Carmen, Sevilla*
50. Spanish Rhythms     177
  *Museo del Baile Flamenco, Sevilla*
51. A Slippery (and Delicious) Slope 180
  *The Olive Oil Workshop, Sevilla*

52. Our Lady of Hope                                        183
    *La Macarena, Sevilla*
53. The Fringe Effect                                       186
    *Shopping for Shawls, Sevilla*
54. Duquesa for the Ages                                    189
    *Living Large in the House of Alba, Sevilla*
55. Another Side of Sevilla                                 192
    *Barrio de Triana*
56. Marriage of Styles                                      196
    *The Alcázar of Sevilla*
57. Park of the Princess                                    199
    *Parque de Maria Luisa, Sevilla*
58. The Most Evil Man Who Ever Lived                        203
    *Don Juan in Sevilla*
59. The Intimacy of Women                                   206
    *Baths of Andalucía*
60. Fino and Finesse                                        209
    *Sherry Culture, Jerez de la Frontera*
61. Practice Makes Perfect                                  214
    *Real Escuela Andaluza del Arte Ecuestre, Jerez de la Frontera*
62. Easter on the Beach                                     217
    *Salt on the Tongue, Sanlúcar de la Barrameda*
63. By the Sea, By the Beautiful Sea                        221
    *Cádiz, the First City of Western Europe*
64. The Thrill of the Drive                                 225
    *Crossing the Mountains of Andalucía's White Towns*
65. Living on the Edge                                      229
    *The Daring City of Ronda*
66. Jet Set Playground                                      232
    *Riches of Marbella*
67. New Act for an Ancient City                             236
    *Reinvention Keeps Málaga Fresh*

68. Cradle of Genius                                    239
     *Picasso in Málaga*
69. A Museum of Her Own                                  243
     *Museo Carmen Thyssen, Málaga*
70. Traces of the Wind                                   246
     *El Paraje Natural Torcal de Antequera*
71. Private Lives                                        248
     *Fiesta de los Patios de Córdoba*
72. Morning Prayers                                      251
     *La Mezquita, Córdoba*
73. Last Stronghold of a Lost Empire                     254
     *La Alhambra and El Generalife, Granada*
74. Lorca and the Dark Heart of *Duende*                 258
     *Huerta de San Vicente, Granada*
75. The Art of the Deal                                  261
     *Shopping in Granada*
76. Song and Dance of the Gypsy Zambra                   264
     *Cueva de María la Canastera, Granada*
77. Village to Village in the Berber Foothills           267
     *Walking in the Alpujarra de Granada*


SECTION IV
NORTH BY NORTHEAST: CATALAN SPAIN                        271

78. First Love Lives On                                  273
     *"Los Amantes de Teruel"*
79. From the Beach to the Palm Forest                    277
     *Alicante and Elche*
80. The Perfect Plate of Rice                            280
     *Biking to L'Albufera and Eating Paella in Valencia*
81. Light My Fire                                        284
     *The Fallas Festival, Valencia*

82. Jewel of the Gold Coast 287
    *The Roman City of Tarragona*
83. Wine, Women, and Song 291
    *Catalan Palaces of Wine and Music*
84. Living in a Masterpiece 295
    *Modernista Homes in Barcelona*
85. Walking Barcelona 299
    *Three Promenades to Remember*
86. A Wedding and a Wine Bar 303
    *Basílica de Santa Maria del Mar and La Vinya del Senyor, Barcelona*
87. Portrait of the Artist as a Young Man 306
    *Picasso in Barcelona*
88. Dancing on the Plaza 310
    *Barcelona's Barrí Gotic on Sunday*
89. A Vision to Behold 313
    *La Sagrada Familia of Antoni Gaudí, Barcelona*
90. The Magic Mountain 316
    *Treasures of Montjuïc, Barcelona*
91. Temples of Food 320
    *The Heartbeat Markets of Barcelona*
92. The Most Important Meal of the Day 323
    *Five Breakfasts in Barcelona*
93. Hand of La Moreneta 326
    *The Shrine of Montserrat*
94. Among the Legends 329
    *The Storied City of Girona*
95. Mad Love 333
    *Salvador and Gala Dalí, Figueres, Cadaqués, and Púbol*
96. Running Without the Bulls 337
    *Women's Marathon in Palma de Mallorca*
97. Keeper of the Gate, Keeper of the Flame 340
    *The Pilar and Joan Miró Foundation, Mallorca*

98. Suffering for Art, Like Good Romantics                344
     *George Sand and Frédéric Chopin in Valldemossa, Mallorca*

99. Mallorca's Literary Love Nest                         348
     *Ca N'Alluny, the Home of Laura Riding and Robert Graves*

100. Sun on the Skin                                       352
      *Nude Beaches in Spain*

*Index*                                                   356
*Acknowledgments*                                         364
*About the Author*                                        366

# Introduction

About ten years ago, I had an epiphany in the back room of Casa Patas, a flamenco club off Madrid's Plaza Tirso de Molino. It was 2 A.M., and the flamenco troupe was packing it in after its second set. Unshaven young men with long black ponytails and half-open white shirts put down their instruments, while the dancer cast aside her block-heeled shoes and crossed her legs to massage her feet. A waitress strutted from table to table taking orders, as two men in the back of the room picked up their guitars and launched into a fiery duet.

I checked my watch: It was still early by Madrid standards—and by my own standards when I'm in Spain. I turned to my husband and smiled. We had plenty of time to stop at our favorite spot for a cup of thick, dark hot chocolate before we made our way back to the hotel. Oh, and did I mention it was Tuesday morning after a Monday night out? Mind you, back home in Cambridge, Massachusetts, I probably would have been asleep, cozy in my bed, by 11 P.M. But in Spain, I get a second wind for the *madrugada*, as they call the hours before dawn, and embrace the local passion for life, contempt for sleep, and penchant for the two-hour lunch.

I make my living writing about travel, food, and art, which means—in theory, at least—that the whole world is open to me. My friends can't understand why I return to Spain again and again, year after year. Sure, it's a big country with a lot of ground to cover.

But it's more than that. Simply put, as I realized that early Tuesday morning, I like the person I become in Spain.

Like many life-altering decisions, my interest in Spain began with no hint of the consequences. In junior high school my modest rebellion was choosing to study Spanish rather than the more popular French. I've never quite mastered the proper trill while rolling my r's, but I fell in love with the music of the Spanish cadences nonetheless. And I loved the stories that unfolded as my grasp of the language grew. I was charmed by the sweet donkey Platero, enchanted by the befuddled yet chivalrous Don Quijote, and in awe of the fiery Carmen. I hardly knew what to make of the fierce queen who was equal partner with her husband in wresting Spain from the Moors and who had the vision to launch Columbus on his first voyage of exploration. (In my textbooks, Isabel's less noble acts—the Spanish Inquisition and the expulsion of the Jews—were overlooked in favor of the period of high-rolling prosperity that she helped to usher in.)

When I finally made it to Spain, everything about the country—from Córdoba's flower-bedecked patios to Madrid's raucous Puerta del Sol and Barcelona's bustling Rambles—was bigger, brighter, and more vivid than my wildest imaginings. Getting to know a country is like falling in love. The first time is a giddy experience, and each succeeding date reveals another nuance. For the women who already share my passion for Spain, I hope I can guide you to some new experiences. For those who are embarking on their first blind dates, I'm excited to introduce you to a country that has stolen my heart.

Spain is a land where all of a woman's senses are suddenly and inexplicably heightened. For this book, I have tried to choose places where I hope you will taste, smell, see, hear, and touch some of the same things that linger in my memory. They have become yardsticks against which I measure the rest of the world.

When I name them, the sensations flood back with total recall—the springtime scent of orange blossoms in the Alcázar of Sevilla, the salty-lipped taste of sherry in Sanlúcar de la Barrameda, the arc of a rainbow over a range in the Picos de Europa, the thrum of motor scooters on narrow stone streets, the luscious glide of a silk shawl against bare skin, the hush of a cave where red dust outlines the hand of an artist from 40,000 years ago, the penetrating heat of the naked sun, the burble of water in desert fountains, the endless blue of a cloudless January day in Madrid, the keening wail of a flamenco singer, the aroma of hot olive oil and the sizzle of shrimp as they hit the pan.... Spain is not just a country to see, it is a full-immersion experience.

The more I thought about it, I also realized that Spain's deep, abiding machismo is one of the things that makes the country so alluring—both to men and to the women who love them. The country is arguably the best place for women to get a handle on what makes men tick, whether it's a rascal playwright priest, the most celebrated artist of the twentieth century, or the ultimate womanizer, Don Juan.

But it also takes a strong woman to thrive in such a masculine world. Spanish history and culture are full of women who are as formidable as their male counterparts—María Pita, who thwarted the English invaders in A Coruña, or Gala Dalí, one of the art world's most domineering muses. Women continue to break barriers in Spain. They stand as equals with male chefs in Spain's radical gastronomy, make indelible marks on the art of flamenco, build wineries and museums, launch the first all-women's marathon in Europe, and even run with the bulls in Pamplona.

On my last trip to Spain before completing this book, I began photographing women as they danced flamenco, rode motor scooters, pedaled bicycles, hiked the ancient pilgrimage route, sat in cafés, drank in bars, studied some of the greatest art ever made, took selfies, and clapped wildly for male flamenco dancers. I looked at the photos often as I wrote. The women were all so strong, so self-assured—and so happy.

If you open your heart and your arms to Spain, I think you will become a different person there. She will be a woman to reckon with.

—PATRICIA HARRIS
CAMBRIDGE, MASSACHUSETTS

# I

## Heartland: Madrid & Castilla

# 1 Sense of Place

## PLAZA MAYOR, MADRID

The first time I visited Spain—in fact, on my very first day in the country—I settled into my room in a fifth-floor *pensión* off Puerta del Sol and hurried off for lunch at Plaza Mayor. It was a ferociously hot midsummer day as I walked out of the cool shadows of Calle Mayor, up the steps, through a big archway, and onto the plaza. The sunlight was dazzling and the super-heated air shimmered above the cobblestones. Practically every seat at every table at every café lining the plaza was taken. Oblivious to the heat, the Spaniards drank beer while the tourists drank sangria. I knew I was in the right place.

There's a Plaza Mayor, or main square, in just about every Spanish city or town. Some are bigger, some more grand, some even a little more colorful. But in Madrid, Plaza Mayor achieves the perfect synthesis of the regal and the popular. Even with children chasing pigeons, street musicians holding forth  under the equestrian statue of Felipe III, and Spiderman and a host of other living statues posing for change, Plaza Mayor remains both stately and yet completely down-to-earth.

The big rectangular plaza—423 by 308 feet—was built on the site of a food market just outside the old city walls. It began to take shape

3

in the early seventeenth century during the reign of Felipe III, which explains why the monarch carrying his royal staff sits on horseback in the center. Juan de Villanueva (1739-1811), the Neoclassical architect who designed the Prado Museum (see Chapter 7), re-invented the plaza in the late eighteenth century after fire had largely destroyed the buildings. Stately three-story structures enclose the space, providing room for shops and restaurants on the ground level and for apartments above. More than 230 balconies give plaza dwellers the best views of the goings-on below.

❋ www.esmadrid.com/en/tourist-information/
   plaza-mayor-madrid

Over the centuries, Plaza Mayor has been the place to attend bullfights, participate in political gatherings, shop for meat and fresh bread, witness hangings, and watch unlucky souls tortured into confessions during the Spanish Inquisition. A remarkably detailed painting of an *auto-da-fé*—as the judgment and punishment of heretics was called—was painted by Francisco Rizi (1614-1685) in 1683. You can see it at the Prado.

Today's lesser artists painting caricatures and those solicitous black-vested waiters bustling from table to table are positively sedate by comparison. Even as tourists snap photos with selfie sticks, the plaza retains a resolutely old-fashioned mien. Whenever I'm in Madrid, I make a point to sit at one of the café tables and once again order a glass of beer and a green salad topped with tuna. I reconnect with the rhythms of the city—and with my younger self who was just starting to get to know a country that would shape the person and the writer I've become. I often think of novelist James Salter writing about how Europe gave him a view of existence: "how to have leisure, love, food, and conversation...."

As a microcosm for Spain, Plaza Mayor did that for me. It is Madrid's still point, the quiet heart around which the arteries of the living city continue to course. It stays ever the same, even as everything around it evolves. For evidence of that change, look no farther than the thoroughly twenty-first century re-imagination of the Mercado de San Miguel, just outside the plaza's portals.

✳ www.mercadodesanmiguel.es/en/

The Beaux Arts market opened in 1916 to provide the neighborhood with a clean, bright food hall on the model of Les Halles in Paris. The handsome structure is the only iron and glass market building still standing in Madrid and looks almost like an old-fashioned jewel box mounted on a granite plinth. It had fallen into terrible disrepair as the neighborhood became ever less residential and had less and less need of a traditional food market. Wisely, it was rescued, repaired, and reopened in 2009 as a chic temple of gastronomy.

I suppose you could stop at Mercado de San Miguel to pick up the fixings for dinner at home, but the market is really a destination for casual dining, mingling, and socializing. Spaniards, by the way, are truly the best plate balancers in the world—they don't have to sit down to enjoy their food. During the day, they might snack on paper cones of fresh potato chips, slices of cured ham, or tapas of roasted Galician octopus. But the market becomes far more glamorous at night when couples sip cava and slurp oysters while they stare into each other's eyes, and larger groups snack on the paella of the day and wash down spinach *croquetas* with beer.

By the way, by "night" I mean until 2 A.M. on the extra-long weekend of Thursday through Saturday. That's the other thing about Madrid: the party keeps going. Leisure, love, food, and conversation, you see, don't have an early bedtime.

## RECOMMENDED READING

*Travelers' Tales Spain* edited by Lucy McCauley

# 2  The Collector's Eye

## CARMEN THYSSEN SELECTIONS AT THE MUSEO THYSSEN–BORNEMISZA, MADRID

Baroness Carmen Thyssen-Bornemisza (born 1943) attributes her passion for collecting art to her late husband Baron Hans Heinrich Thyssen-Bornemisza (1921-2002). She certainly had a great mentor. In 1992, the baron's private art collection—considered one of the best in the world—opened in a renovated nineteenth-century palace between the Prado (see Chapter 7) and the Reina Sofía (see Chapter 9) museums. England, France, the United States, and even Switzerland vied for the paintings, but as the *The Guardian* noted in the baron's obituary, "the pressure of the bedroom decided matters in favour of the birthplace of the baron's fifth wife."

✳ www.museothyssen.org/en/thyssen/home

The baroness augmented the riches in 2004 when a museum expansion opened with two hundred paintings from her personal collection. She began acquiring art in the 1980s and the works on display range from Dutch and Italian painting to German Expressionism and international avant-garde art. (For the Málaga museum containing her collection of nineteenth-century Spanish art, see Chapter 69.)

Although only a small segment of the collection is devoted to portraiture, a few key works reveal the baroness's sharp eye for the female form and her profound empathy for the feminine subject.

*Diana Bathing (The Fountain)* was painted by Jean-Baptiste-Camille Corot in 1869-1870. Although better known for his landscapes, Corot painted about thirty nudes, and found the depiction of the womanly figure to be an artistic and intel-lectual challenge. He wrote that "since this is not a lesson in anatomy, I have to blend, like nature does, the cover of the frame which makes up and supports the body, in order to render only what I feel in front of this flesh." Working with a favorite model, he veiled her palpable sensuality behind a cascade of purifying water. She is the eternal Diana, goddess of the hunt, captured in the intimacy of her toilette.

Treating an ostensibly similar subject, Emile Bernard painted the 1889 *Women Bathing* in his characteristic "Cloisonnism" style of delineating forms with a heavy outline as a metal artist might do with cloisonné enamel or a glass artist with leaded stained glass. Each woman possesses the strength and self-possession of a birch tree at the water's edge. Their faces and the sexual details of their bodies are blurred into anonymity, but the angles of their necks as they fix their hair and towel themselves dry gives them a relaxed camaraderie that animates Bernard's simplified, two-dimensional landscape.

Berthe Morisot's *Reclining Nude Shepherdess* is one of the rare portraits by a woman artist on display. The title, in all honesty, is unfortunate. The work, which Morisot completed in 1891, is a serious study of a young girl approaching womanhood, rather than a pin-up of a nubile shepherdess. Morisot, who had been a student of Corot, renders the foreground and background in soft, Impressionist colors and loose brushstrokes to create a strong contrast to the more naturalistically modeled and shaded contours of the young woman's body. With her hair piled up on her head and her chin resting in her hand, she anticipates Brigitte Bardot of more than a half century later.

*Summer Afternoon* was painted by Emil Nolde in 1903 when he and his wife, actress Ada Vilstrup, were living in a fisherman's cottage on the Danish island of Als. The seaside light and country lifestyle were instrumental in the artist's transition from northern European Romanticism to a more immediate and vibrant style that would later blossom into a kind of revolutionary Expressionism. The woman in the painting, Ane, worked in the painter's household and he recalled her as "in her most tender and beautiful age.... She, that candid daughter of the earth, has probably been the most beautiful and bare expression of real femininity I have ever seen." Nolde chose to capture her not in a portrait or a nude study, but fully clothed with her back to the viewer as she pushes a wheelbarrow along a flower-lined path. He has rendered the landscape with muscular brushwork, but it is Ane's strong presence that animates the world within the frame.

Henri Manguin completed *Model Resting* in 1905 during the period that he shared a studio and a model with friends and fellow artists Henri Matisse and Albert Marquet. As each artist developed his own approach to classical figure studies, Manguin also created this more candid portrait of the model at rest. Wrapped in a robe, she sits in a chair while ignoring the canvas on an easel in front of her and the pile of drawings at her feet. Skillful modeling captures the contours of her body beneath the thin fabric of the robe. Manguin has caught the model—a woman whose job is always to hold a pose—in a rare, off-guard moment.

Childe Hassam painted *The French Breakfast* in 1910 while he and his wife of twenty-five years, Maude, were traveling through Europe so that the artist could study and absorb the sweep of European painting. It depicts the three-week period they spent in a modest hotel in Paris and captures the ease and intimacy of a long-married couple. Bedclothes are piled haphazardly on a chair and the bright red canopy is drawn back from the bed to reveal Maude with her breakfast tray. She is perhaps planning the day ahead, but has not yet put on her public face.

Max Pechstein's 1912 painting *The Bathers* brings together two of his preferred themes: landscapes and nudes. It really should have been titled "Alice and Eve in Paradise." The two solid, rounded female figures rest in the foreground, against a vivid landscape of pine trees, sand dunes, and sky that recalls Pechstein's membership in the Expressionist group Die Brücke. One of the women flourishes a fan, a frivolous reminder of the civilization they have left behind—if only momentarily.

The last work in this brief survey is by Spanish artist Juan Gris, who painted *Seated Woman* in Paris in 1917. Working in the Cubist style, Gris introduced more color to his canvases than Pablo Picasso or Georges Braque, the artists who had pioneered this new way of conveying the complexity of a form in space. Art historians believe that Gris's wife Josette is the subject of this canvas and that she was dressed for a night on the town. Known as a clotheshorse, she probably didn't mind that the angles and folds of her garment tend to obscure her face, making her a woman of mystery.

# Choc Around the Clock

## CHOCOLATERÍA SAN GINÉS, MADRID

Chocolatería San Ginés just might be the most reassuring place in Madrid. It's open around the clock every day of the year. Whenever you walk in, waitstaff in white jackets with high collars are pouring pitchers of hot chocolate into white cups lined up in a row on the bar. All the handles face the same way.

The Spaniards took to chocolate as soon as Hernán Cortez brought the Aztec drink back when he conquered Tenochtitlán, renamed it Mexico City, and made off with everything he could ship home—cacao beans included. The Aztecs ground the beans to a paste and made a bitter drink they called *xocolatl*. Back at home the Spaniards combined cacao paste with sugar (introduced by the Moors) and thickened the hot liquid with flour (introduced by the Romans). The drink encapsulates the history of Spain in a cup.

Spanish hot chocolate is a thick, rich revelation, and the version at San Ginés seems even thicker and richer than most. It is a soothing balm at every hour. Office workers stop at the *chocolatería* for breakfast on their way to work; shoppers laden with bags find San Ginés the perfect venue for a *merienda*, or afternoon snack; and nightowls stumble in after leaving the clubs in the *madrugada*, or the hours just before sunrise. Spaniards did not need twentieth-century scientific studies to tell them that chocolate is a so-called "joy stimulant," and that those who sip chocolate daily are calmer and more content than the misguided souls who deny themselves.

San Ginés sits up an alleyway, the Pasadizo de San Ginés, next to the discotheque Sala Joy Eslava, the most recent occupant of a cavernous nineteenth-century theater building. The little *chocolatería* is halfway between the Puerta del Sol and the Teatro Real. When it opened in 1894, it was an immediate hit with the after-theater crowd.

✳ chocolateriasangines.com

The interior does not seem to have changed since Ramón del Valle-Inclán (1866-1936) immortalized it as the Buñolería Modernista in his 1924 play, *Luces de Bohemia*. A dogleg bar lines two walls at the entry and green banquettes line the others. Black bentwood chairs cozy up to small, marble-topped tables. Wood panels painted a deep forest green rise halfway up the walls and large mirrors bounce the light around to make the room seem bigger than it is. Black-and-white photos chronicle the celebrities who have made their way down the atmospheric alley over the years.

Each table is topped with a shaker of powdered sugar. Another reassuring thing about San Ginés is that you don't have to make many decisions. The proper accompaniment to hot chocolate are *churros*. These ridged sticks of fried dough are extruded in a spiral of a yard or more into hot fat. They're cut into pieces six to nine inches long after they're cooked. Often served at fairs and beach snack bars, the casual treats acquire a certain decorum in the elegant *chocolatería*. Thicker tubes of fried dough, called *porras*, are the only other option. In either case, they should be liberally dusted with sugar before being dunked in the chocolate. It's impossible to get the last of the chocolate from the cup without mopping the bottom with a *churro*.

San Ginés is one of the few remaining traditional *chocolaterías* in Madrid. Many bars and cafés serve hot chocolate and *churros* in the morning and again at tapas time. But few places make their own *churros*, preferring the convenience of reheating some that they buy from a small factory. A reheated *churro* is definitely heavier and tastes more of oil than dough. And I've even seen baristas tear open packets of instant chocolate to make a muddy imitation of the rich, hauntingly spiced drink served at San Ginés. Take the polyphenol joy cited in the research on the benefits of chocolate, and multiply it times three. This is a *chocolatería* that's good for your health, and even better for your state of mind.

# 4 Shadow to the Throne

## MONASTERIO DE LAS DESCALZAS REALES, MADRID

In court portraits, Juana de Austria, the youngest daughter of the Holy Roman Emperor Carlos V, is always dressed in black. It's not particularly surprising since she was a widow at age 18, though in her mature portraits she hardly seems weighed down by grief. The founder of a convent for aristocratic women seems more like someone with better things to think about than the latest in court fashion. More than four and a half centuries later, her convent is still active and you might seek out its quiet confines to contemplate the subtle ways that women can exercise power.

Spain was at the height of its worldwide dominance when Juana was born into the royal family in 1535. Overshadowed by her father and her brother, Felipe II, she wasn't destined to play a bravura role like her famous great-grandmother Isabel I (see Chapter 15). But Juana did carve out her own place in the male-dominated court, proving that it's possible to make a mark without riding off on horseback to finish the job of recapturing Spain from the Moors.

Instead, she was dispatched to Portugal in 1552 to marry her first cousin Prince João. By 1554, Juana had become a widow, given birth to a son (who would become Sebastião I of Portugal), and returned to Spain to become regent while Felipe was married to Mary Tudor, queen of England. She never returned to Portugal and never saw her son again. She did, however, seem to blossom in her role as acting monarch and was regarded as a savvy politician. Having done her bit for strengthening political alliances, she never married again.

Juana was a well-educated patron of the arts and literature, but was most absorbed in the cause of religious reform against the excesses of the Spanish Inquisition. Under the guidance of several religious thinkers, she espoused a path of quiet contemplation and meditation. Some believe that she even made secret vows to the Jesuit order using a false name—a claim that has never been fully proven.

What is undisputed is that in 1559 Juana's regency ended and she established a convent in Madrid for nuns of the order of Poor Clares. The Monasterio de las Descalzas Reales—or "barefoot royals"—was a haven for aristocratic women and seat of Juana's power. The twenty or so nuns who live here today come from much more modest circumstances than Juana and her contemporaries, but they occupy a convent that feels like a museum. The contemplative order allows tours led by secular guides. A visit reveals how skillfully Juana wove together her faith and aristocratic bearing, and managed to reconcile her lavish surroundings with the order's vows of poverty.

✻ www.patrimonionacional.es/en

In finding a home for the convent, Juana literally returned to her roots by purchasing the palace where she had been born. The former home of her father's treasurer exudes wealth and power with its marble-columned courtyard, elaborate Moorish-style tile and decorative plasterwork, and grand staircase where murals of Spanish kings mix with others of saints and angels. The fine artwork brought by Juana and other noble women fit right in. But it was possible to live simply amid such splendor. The walls of the nuns' former dormitory are warmed by a series of Flemish tapestries woven from cartoons by Rubens, but look closely on the floor and you'll see tiles that outlined each nun's minuscule sleeping area.

Juana kept her own apartments in the convent and took an active role in educating members of the royal family, including Felipe's young wife, Isabel de Valois, and their two daughters, spreading her influence one woman at a time, one country at a time. Infanta Isabella Clara Eugenia became archduchess of the Spanish Netherlands, while her sister Catalina Micaela was duchess consort of the French region of Savoy.

A female artist painted the most perceptive portrait of Juana. Sofonisba Anguissola, the court painter to Isabel de Valois, captured Juana at the height of her powers in 1561. Her wavy hair is tucked into a cap and her face is framed by a lacy white ruff that emphasizes her strong chin. A ribbon around her neck holds a cameo of Carlos V. Juana's right arm rests on the shoulder of a young girl, presumably under her tutelage and destined for a religious life.

In 1573 Juana died at El Escorial, the more imposing and austere monastery and palace built by Felipe II as a retreat and burial place for the Habsburg royal line. Juana, however, lies at rest in the convent she created, in a chapel which many believe marks the spot where she was born.

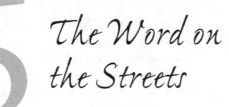

# 5 The Word on the Streets

## BARRIO DE LAS LETRAS, MADRID

No one disputes that Félix Lope de Vega y Carpio (1562-1635) was one of the most famous writers of Spain's literary Golden Age. In fact, more than 300 of his plays survive of an estimated 1,500 that he claimed to have written. While many of his most popular works dealt with impossibly complicated affairs of love and honor, nothing in his body of work ever quite rose to the high drama (and low comedy) of his own life.

Lope played all the parts from hero to buffoon. He was a sailor in the ill-fated Spanish Armada, married twice, and was often sued for libel. An infamous *mujeriego,* or womanizer, he fathered at least fifteen children by several different women—some of whom were other men's wives—yet proved to be a dutiful and loving father to many of his offspring. At age fifty-two, he joined the priesthood, but continued his multiple love affairs until his final lover died when Lope was seventy.

After returning from eight years of banishment for libeling a former lover who had spurned him, he bought a house in Madrid between the Trinitarian convent and the main outdoor theater of the time. He lived there from 1610 until his death. Today the house is embedded among later buildings and opened as a house museum in 1935, the third centennial of the writer's death.

Guided tours are by reservation but worth the trouble because it's a rare chance to see an early Madrid house. Felipe II had only made the city Spain's capital fifty years earlier, and this neighborhood near the crest of the ridge on which Madrid is built was just being constructed when Lope de Vega moved in. Behind the modern facade remains a rare early seventeenth-century house, complete with its small courtyard where the original granite well still stands next to an orange tree. The house is on three levels, and the tour covers them all. But four rooms really define this charismatic author who clearly had a way with women as well as a golden tongue. Some of the furnishings are said to have belonged to Lope de Vega and were held for centuries in the Trinitarian convent where his daughter Marcella by actress Micaela Luján eventually became Mother Superior.

✳ casamuseolopedevega.org/en

There is, of course, the book-lined study, where he wrote furiously. A desk stands near the unusually large window and a portrait of Lope de Vega hangs on the wall. The books, most bound in vellum, are seventeenth-century volumes on loan from the Spanish National Library. The museum calls the adjacent room the "ladies drawing room," but with its seating on large cushions on the floor, where women would sit cross-legged, it bears an uncanny resemblance to a Moorish harem. Next to it is the small bedchamber where Lope de Vega died. There is a window in the wall opposite the bed so that he could look into the chapel and watch another priest celebrate the Mass when he was too ill to do it himself. It was the story of his life—a man in bed torn between women on one side and God on the other.

Ironically enough, the Casa de Lope de Vega is on Calle Cervantes, named for *Don Quijote* author Miguel de Cervantes Saavedra (1547-1616), who spent his last nine years in a house about a hundred yards away. The Cervantes house was long ago replaced by another building, but the spot is marked with bronze plaques and a bust of the author. The prevalence of such markers suggests that the whole neighborhood was crawling with writers over the years, and some of the streets even carry embedded literary quotations in brass.

The so-called Barrio de Las Letras remains a residential district of private homes, small shops, and neighborhood bars. Wander around and you'll eventually come to Plaza de Santa Ana. The east side is dominated by the imposing Neoclassical building containing the Teatro Español, perhaps the grandest of Madrid's traditional theaters. A frieze of busts on the facade honors great playwrights, ranging from Lope de Vega to Federico García Lorca. There is a bronze statue of a young Lorca in the middle of the plaza, dressed in suit and tie and holding a dove. Street musicians often perform just feet away from him. The plaza is one of the city's top tapas destinations and tables spill out into the center from the bars on the north and south sides of the square. Of some modest literary note is the Cervecería Alemana at Plaza de Santa Ana 6, one of many places in Madrid where Ernest Hemingway used to drink and where aspiring American writers still sit at tables in the sunshine, scribbling in their Moleskines.

# 6 *If the Shoe Fits*

## SHOPPING FOR SHOES IN CHUECA, MADRID

I live in a small condominium with little extra storage or display space, so I long ago decided that I could only buy practical things when I travel. In addition to foodstuffs (which are quickly eaten), I find it impossible to resist shoes—which can be stylish and practical at the same time.

Shoe designer Mare Espinal agrees with my decision. "All women in the world want the best closet full of shoes," she told me the last time I stopped in her shop, By Mare Shoes (Calle Augusto Figueroa 12). Born in Manhattan to parents from Latin America, Espinal came to Madrid to study public  relations and was still a student when she created her brand in 2011. She launched her seventh collection in 2015 and operates a retail shop in the hipster neighborhood of Chueca.

"This is the street of the shoes," said Espinal, and she's right. It seems like every other store on Calle Augusto Figueroa sells shoes—everything from inexpensive everyday styles to gorgeous and timeless designs from some of Spain's top brands. More to the point, most shops offer the previous season's merchandise at discounts of up to 50 percent. If you are lucky enough to wear the sample size 37 (U.S. size 6 1/2), you might get even greater discounts and find more unusual, one-of-a-kind designs.

Whenever I'm going to be in Madrid, I set aside an afternoon for checking out the merchandise on Augusto Figueroa. I'm hardly alone: The street is usually full of girlfriends toting big bags and cajoling each other into buying just one more pair.

Espinal's shop is by far the most fashion-forward and her shoes are truly works of art. She does design sneakers, wedges, and boots, but high heels with a signature fuchsia sole are her passion. "High heels are really important for us," she said. "A girl looks fantastic with high heels, very elegant, but not sexy." We're not talking just any high heels. "You can get shoes with 11-12 centimenter heels [4.3-4.7 inches] anywhere on the street," Espinal said dismissively. "I have 14-15 centimeter heels [5.5-5.9 inches], but I design them on a platform to be more comfortable."

I'm rarely in the market for even 11-12 centimeter spikes, let alone Espinal's skyscrapers. But I like her philosophy that "a black dress or pants and a great pair of shoes are all a girl needs." With that in mind, I almost always find something I love as I browse along Calle Augusto Figueroa.

If I'm looking for something casual that's a step up from a canvas espadrille, I head to Pons Quintana at number 33. The Menorca-based company was founded in 1953 and is still run by the family. As in many shops, the new, full-price merchandise is in the front, so I usually avoid temptation by heading quickly to the back for the discounts. Pons Quintana made its name by fashioning shoes from woven strips of high-quality leather. The patterning gives the shoes a playful look and the flats are cool, comfortable, and classy for summer. Accents of woven leather also dress up a pair of winter boots.

Caligae Muestrarios at number 31 never disappoints when I want a statement shoe. The shop carries the posh Farrutx brand, founded in 1982 on Mallorca, and known for elegant, sophisticated style. But if ever a collection of shoes could be called vivacious, it would be those designed by Chie Mihara, who founded her footwear line in 2002. She often bases her designs on flamenco style, incorporating blocky heels and ankle straps that give the shoes tremendous stability as well as style. Then she embellishes them with fringe, colored and patterned leathers, small wings, initials, or ironic bows. Some of the designs are so elaborate—or such takeoffs on school girl or nun shoes—that they border on fetishistic.

It's always worth veering off onto some of the side streets, where up-and-coming designers often get a toehold in the neighborhood and some better established designers have set up shop to get in on Chueca's youthful cachet. On my last visit I discovered Rebeca Sanver on Plaza Vázquez de Mella 10. José Juan Sanchís Busquier founded the company in 1987 to commemorate the birth of his daughter—and if she gets an unlimited choice of shoes, she is one lucky lady. I fell hard for a gorgeous pair of lace-up ankle boots in a black-and-white floral pattern.

Between them, sister shops Ambar and Rue St. Honoré, which face each other across Calle Augusto Figueroa at numbers 14 and 21, respectively, provide a terrific overview of trends in European footwear design. They both carry a variety of makers, from the urban streetwear of FLY London (manufactured, by the way, in Portugal) to the strappy Italian sandals, ballet flats, moccasins, and androgynous lace-ups of Lilimill. For something entirely different, they also carry Papucei. Angela Vasiliu was only in her twenties when she launched the company in a shoe manufacturing town in her native Romania. Featuring leathers with deeply saturated colors and complex textures, each handmade pair of Papucei shoes or boots has a darkly romantic Goth quality.

The shops also have great twists on traditional footwear. If I want an espadrille with a little more edge, I check out styles with high, sculptural platform heels from Paloma Barceló. And the Spanish company Hispanitas is known for its eponymous version of the classic ballet slipper. They're wonderfully comfortable and easy to pack. I also like the company's motto: "Joy is a choice."

What woman doesn't get a fresh spring in her step from a new pair of kicks—not to mention joy in her heart?

# 7

## I Am Woman

### HIGHLIGHTS OF THE MUSEO NACIONAL DEL PRADO, MADRID

Created with the holdings of the Spanish royal families, the Prado has a world-class collection of European art from the twelfth through the early nineteenth centuries. It's tempting to try to see everything, but the museum is best known for its superb collection of Spanish art, including the largest holdings of the great masters El Greco, Velázquez, and Goya. For a first visit, at least, it's best to start with the Spanish works. The monarchs were very loyal to their favored painters, so you'll have an unusual opportunity to follow artists over the course of their careers.

The Prado also has a wonderfully enlightened admissions policy. For the last two hours of every day, the museum is free. Rather than devoting a full day to a visit, which can tax both the eyes and the feet, I try to stop in every afternoon when I'm in Madrid. I explore one or two galleries, or look at all the works by a particular artist. Then I head off to tapas.

Whether you plan to power view or take it slow, here is a small selection of pieces that shed light on women and notions of femininity. The Prado, in fact, owes its existence to the persuasive powers of a queen.

That monarch, María Isabel de Braganza (1797-1818) married her uncle Fernando VII (1784-1833) in 1816, and died from complications of childbirth only two years later. Despite her short reign, she left a remarkable legacy. She is credited as the power behind the creation of the Royal Museum of Paintings and Sculpture, now the Prado. It opened in 1819 in a building designed by Neoclassical architect Juan de Villanueva. Fernando charged court sculptor José Álvarez Cubero (1768–1827) with creating a likeness of the queen for the Prado. The marble sculpture, *María Isabel de Braganza, Queen of Spain,* was completed in 1827. Dressed in a belted tunic, she rests comfortably in a chair decorated with images of castles, lions, and lilies. The Neoclassical style suits the woman who is sometimes called "La Reina del Prado."

❋ www.museodelprado.es/en

Images of the Virgin Mary are almost ubiquitous in the Prado galleries and, indeed, throughout Spain. One of the most unusual is the *The Virgin and the Souls of Purgatory* completed in 1517 by Pedro Machuca (1490-1550). In an act of compassion, the Virgin grasps one breast while the baby Jesus grasps the other. They direct her milk toward Purgatory, hoping to extinguish the flames and ease the suffering of the souls who languish there. The subject seems to have slipped from favor by the end of the sixteenth century, but Machuca (also the architect of the palace for Carlos V at the Alhambra in Granada) had studied in Rome and helped introduce the classical Renaissance style to Spain.

Diego Velázquez (1599-1660) had an amazing ability to capture the spirit of the monks who often posed for him. But he also turned his penetrating eye to *The Nun Jerónima de la Fuente.* Born to a noble family in Toledo, Jerónima (1555–1630) became a Franciscan nun and ultimately Mother Superior at the convent of Santa Isabel in her hometown. Velázquez painted her in Sevilla in 1620 as she was about to set sail for the Philippines, where she was to found a convent in Manila. She was sixty-six years old and Velázquez did not hesitate to convey the effects of age in her face and hands. But her intense gaze and firm grip on the crucifix in her right hand show a woman at the height of her power and conviction.

The subject of the Immaculate Conception was so popular with Spanish painters—particularly during the Baroque period—that curators at the Prado hold that studying the depiction of the Virgin over time is one of the best ways to trace the evolving notions of feminine beauty. Bartolomé Esteban Murillo (1617–1682) was the acknowledged master of this treatment of the Virgin. He painted the subject at least twenty times, and of the five versions in the Prado, *The Aranjuez Immaculate Conception* from 1675 reflects the strength and sensitivity of his mature style. As the Virgin rises to the heavens, she stands on a crescent moon and is bathed in otherworldly light.

You won't miss *Las Meninas.* Diego Velázquez's 1656 depiction of the court of Felipe IV is probably the most viewed painting in the museum. But do take special note of it if you plan to visit Barcelona. Picasso's fifty-eight-canvas homage to the painting—and to its central figure, the Infanta Margarita—is the centerpiece of his museum in that city (see Chapter 87). The Infanta may be the most famous little girl in art history. Born in 1651, she was betrothed as a child to her uncle Leopold I, Holy Roman Emperor, and Velázquez often painted her so that the future in-laws could watch her growth. But Velázquez elevated the mere act of portraiture to a feat of psychological insight and artistic innovation. Weighted down by her elaborate dress, the Infanta is surrounded by maids of honor and two dwarfs. Her father and mother, Mariana of Austria, are reflected in a mirror, but the painter's own self-portrait in front of the easel is more prominent. It's almost as if he knew that he had created a touchstone of Spanish art.

"If at the beginning of the modern period there existed an artist who explored in depth and variety the universe of the feminine, this artist was Goya," wrote former Prado director Fernando Checa Cremades in a catalog for an exhibition of Goya's images of women. Francisco de Goya (1746–1828) was equally adept at capturing innocent young girls frolicking outdoors as depicting crones, witches, and prostitutes. But his portraits of aristocratic women afforded some of his best opportunities to explore character. You'll find many in the galleries, including _Queen María Luisa on Horseback_ from 1799. Queen María Luisa de Parma (1751-1818) was known for her strong personality and the artist conveys her self-assurance as she wears the uniform of a colonel of the Guardia de Corp. The painting was a complement to a similar image of her husband, Carlos IV (1748-1819), but tellingly, she sits on a horse given to her by Manuel Godoy, the sometimes prime minister who was rumored to be her lover.

Godoy was said to have enjoyed the favors of many noble women, including the Duquesa de Alba. For some time, the Duquesa was thought to be the model for one of Goya's most famous and sensuous paintings, _La Maja Desnuda,_ painted before 1800. There is no false modesty about this image. Comfortable in her nudity, the model lifts her hands behind her head to raise her bosom and Goya has made the curve of her abdomen into her pubic area the focal center of the work. The painting hung in Godoy's private study where he and his friends could enjoy images deemed titillating by the Spanish Inquisition. Tastes have changed, and the nineteenth century's softcore porn became instead an emblem of Spanish womanhood. Between 1800 and 1805, Goya revisited the subject with the same model, now believed to be another of Godoy's mistresses. _Maja Vestida_ recapitulates the pose and the direct gaze. Her white gown, cinched with a sash at the waist, follows the contours of her body. The brushwork of the second painting is more lively and less exacting—as if he were rushing to finish.

The renowned Spanish actress María Guerrero (1867-1928) was one of the most widely painted women of her day. Her friend Joaquin Sorolla (1863-1923) captured her in 1906 at the peak of her fame. *The Actress María Guerrero as La Dama Boba* depicts her in one of her most popular roles as Finea in the comedy *La Dama Boba* by Lope de Vega (see Chapter 5). Secure in his belief that his technique rivaled that of Velázquez, Sorolla was certain that the painting would end up at the Prado. He employed a loose but confident brushstroke to capture the drape and sheen of her costume and the magnetism of her gaze. María's husband, the actor Fernando Díaz de Mendoza, is seated in the background as Finea's teacher, Rufino. The couple founded a theater company and made a huge impact on the development of the Spanish stage by premiering almost one hundred and fifty works. After her death, the Madrid building that is now the home of Spain's National Drama Center was named for her: the Teatro María Guerrero.

## RECOMMENDED READING

*Goya Images of Women* edited by Janis A. Tomlinson

8   *A Winter's Feast*

## GASTROFESTIVAL MADRID

My friends are always surprised when I tell them that January is one of the best times of year to spend in Madrid. The skies are blue. It might rain twice. Overnight temperatures drop near freezing, but they rise to sweater weather by lunchtime. And, speaking of lunchtime, it's the season when Madrid goes a little crazy about food culture.

Madrid Fusion has taken place for years at the end of January or sometimes the beginning of February. Although this annual summit meeting of the top chefs from around the world has done plenty to cement Spain's leadership in European cuisine—they're pretty sure that they've put France in the shade—it didn't do much for ordinary Spaniards. Madrileños mostly had to read about the talks, technique demonstrations, and philosophical arguments the next day in *El País*.

People demanded more, so the Madrid City Council and Madrid Fusion obliged. In 2010 they joined forces to launch the three-week Gastrofestival Madrid. It typically takes place during the last two weeks of January and the first week of February.

If you ever doubted that food permeates every aspect of Spanish culture, look no further than the program for the festival. Bars and restaurants are obviously involved, but museums, art galleries, markets, and lecture halls get into the act with everything from food-themed tours of special exhibitions to food- and wine-themed art shows to food-themed fashion shows and fashion-themed menus at cafés inside designer boutiques. Several public food markets hold tastings, cooking classes, and workshops. The Conde Duque cultural center offers gastronomically themed concerts. (In 2016, composers scored musical pieces based on the recorded sounds of neighborhood residents cooking favorite recipes.) Food-themed films are screened throughout the Gastrofestival, sometimes combined with a tasting. If your Spanish is good, there are also gastronomically themed theater pieces and literary walking tours. Honestly, you can see almost all of Madrid through the tines of a fork.

And that's just what you do between meals.

A small number of top restaurants offer special dining events (usually at one hundred euros and up before wine). Even better, about one hundred seventy restaurants offer three-course festival menus that highlight their house specialties. Most of these cost less than thirty euros and include wine or beer, taxes, and service charge. A few shoot a little past that mark, but often include a fourth course.

The worst thing about Gastrofestival Madrid is that there aren't enough meals in the day to try everything I'd like to. My strategy is to eat the special menu for lunch and walk a lot afterwards, then spend the evening indulging in another festival program called Degustatapas. Each of about ninety bars and restaurants around the city offers a specialty tapa with a glass of Mahou beer. The price is minimal, so chefs rise to the occasion to show how creative they can get with tapas on a tight budget. Most recently the set price was three euros for the beer and tapa combo. You always get more than your money's worth.

As Spaniards might say, *¡Que rico!*

❉ www.gastrofestivalmadrid.com

# 9

## Timeless Cry Against War

### *GUERNICA* AT THE REINA SOFÍA, MADRID

Even for the prolific Pablo Picasso (1881-1973), completing an eleven-foot by twenty-five-foot canvas in just over a month was a remarkable feat. But he was driven by moral outrage to conceive and paint *Guernica*, one of the seminal works of art of the twentieth century and arguably the most powerful anti-war statement of all time.

After a long odyssey, Picasso's masterpiece resides in the Museo Nacional Centro de Arte Reina Sofía, the Madrid museum that opened in 1990 to show such Spanish masters as Picasso, Joan Miró, Salvador Dalí, and Juan Gris in the context of their international contemporaries. But *Guernica* stands alone, almost outside of time and trends in modern art. As much an experience as a painting, its vision is so visceral that any art historical analysis pales.

✳ www.museoreinasofia.es/en

Although he spent most of his adult life in France, Picasso cherished his identity as a Spaniard in exile. About a year after the start of the Spanish Civil War, he was asked to create a painting for the Spanish Pavilion at the 1937 International Exposition in Paris. Besieged by the Nationalist forces under General Francisco Franco, leaders of the Second Spanish Republic hoped to rally international support for their democratically elected government. With

material and strategic support from Nazi
Germany, the Nationalists had already
seized almost half of Spain.

Some of Picasso's art of the period
made his antipathy for Franco clear, but
the artist was nonetheless slow to commit
to the project. Even once on board, he
appeared to be contemplating a larger-
than-life image of a subject that had already captured his imagination: the relation of artist and model in the studio.

Everything changed on April 26, 1937, when the German
Luftwaffe, in support of the Nationalists, dropped 100,000
pounds of explosives on the Basque town of Gernika. Attempting
to obliterate the historic home of Basque freedom was a crude act
of symbolism conducted with calculated disregard for noncomba-
tants. More than sixteen hundred people were killed or wounded
and 70 percent of the town was reduced to rubble. News reports
reached France the next day, and by May 1, Picasso had made the
first small pencil sketches of his ultimate masterpiece. He applied
the final brushstrokes to the canvas only thirty-five days later on
June 4. His muse and lover, the Surrealist artist and photographer
Dora Maar, documented the evolution of the imagery in a series of
masterful photographs.

Picasso drew from the well of Spanish bullfight imagery that
had fascinated him since childhood, including both the impassive
bull and a screaming horse. A woman with a lamp—an image he
used in other paintings of the period—appears to be observing the
scene, or perhaps shedding light on the horrors. Death and suffering stretch across the canvas in a frieze: a slain warrior, a woman
holding a dead baby, human heads screaming in pain, agony, and
disbelief. And this entire capsule of universal suffering and horror
is rendered in shades of gray, black, and white.

At the close of the Paris exposition, *Guernica* traveled to other European capitals to raise support for the Republican cause and for Spanish refugees. On May 1, 1939, it arrived in New York and spent most of the next four decades at the Museum of Modern Art. Picasso himself never returned to Spain.

After Franco's death in 1975 and the establishment of a constitutional monarchy in 1978, conditions were right to return *Guernica* to Spain. The town of Gernika made an unsuccessful bid for the painting, but Gernika had its best revenge by rebuilding as a sleepy, normal town far from the centers of power and population. (The scars of war are healed; Gernika is worth visiting mainly for its medieval Basque history.) So *Guernica* the painting came to Madrid, initially to an annex of the Prado. It was unveiled to the Spanish people, fittingly enough, on October 25, 1981, the centenary of Picasso's birth.

## RECOMMENDED READING

*Picasso's Guernica: History, Transformations, Meanings* by Herschel B. Chipp
*Guernica: The Biography of a Twentieth-Century Icon* by Gijs van Hensbergen

# 10 *Where the City Blooms*

## GREAT PARKS OF MADRID

Shortly after Felipe II (1527-1598) moved the Royal Court to Madrid in 1561 he brought a bit of countryside to the city by ordering the planting of *allées*, or avenues, of trees in the monastic retreat just east of the gates. Centuries before the "green" movement, the king set Spain's new capital on the right path. Today, Madrid ranks among Europe's greenest cities, as measured by number of trees and area of green space per inhabitant.

Madrileños use that precious space well. Every neighborhood has at least a pocket park where kids kick soccer balls, someone sits on the grass leaning against a tree to read a book, old men reminisce on a bench while they smoke cigars, someone inevitably chatters animatedly on his or her phone, and someone else basks quietly in the sun. The city has some grand public parks as well, and perhaps aside from tapas bars, they are the places to see Madrileños at their relaxed best.

On Sundays, it seems that every family heads to the Parque del Buen Retiro, or simply El Retiro. But the 308-acre park, close to the Puerta de Alcalá and the Museo del Prado, can absorb them all. Originally a royal retreat, El Retiro opened to the public in 1767 and came under city ownership a century later.

It really is a democratic space. Older gentlemen face off across chessboards. Brightly dressed women offer to tell your fortune. Children ride patient ponies—or plunk down to watch a puppet show—methodically moving their hands from potato chip bag to mouth while never taking their eyes off the action.

Of course, traces of royal pomp still exist. A formal French-style garden, or *parterre*, with broad straight pathways and sculpted shrubbery was constructed during the reign of Felipe V (1683-1746). The formal entry path from the Puerta de Alcalá, the Paseo de la Argentina, is often called the "Paseo de las Estatuas," because the walkway is punctuated with statues of kings. It's the backdrop for some of almost every Madrileña's wedding pictures (even if she was married across town).

The park's most impressive royal memorial, however, is the grand semicircular colonnade on the edge of an artificial lake. Its centerpiece is a massive equestrian statue of Alfonso XII. Where nobles once staged mock naval battles, Alfonso now surveys families enjoying outings in rowboats.

Some of the most charming features of the park were added after it became public. The Palacio de Cristal, a marvelous confection of glass set in an iron framework, was built in 1887 to display flora and fauna from the Spanish colony of the Philippines. These days, the Reina Sofia Museum (see Chapter 9) mounts temporary exhibitions in the light-filled space (as well as in the 1884 Palacio de Velázquez, also built as an exhibition hall).

The early twentieth-century Rosaleda, or rose garden, has a surprise lurking amid its bright and fragrant blooms: the dark bronze *Fuente del Ángel Caído*, or *Fountain of the Fallen Angel*, by Ricardo Bellver. Installed in 1922, this rare public monument to Lucifer was inspired by Milton's *Paradise Lost* and its twisted, tortured forms recapitulate the whole tradition of Mannerist expression in Spanish art.

El Retiro is big enough that you can find a peaceful spot to ponder the struggle between good and evil or simply escape from the rush of the city. But if quiet contemplation is what you seek, the Real Jardín Botánico is much more conducive.

The garden was created in 1755 by Fernando VI (1713-1759) to explore botany around the world. The original garden of about 2,000 plants was placed on the banks of the Río Manzanares, but it was relocated to its present location at the Plaza de Murillo next to the Museo del Prado in 1781 during the reign of Carlos III (1716-1788). The great Neoclassical royal architects Francesco Sabatini and Juan de Villanueva designed the graceful stepped terraces that host plants from the Americas, Europe, and the Pacific. Today, the twenty-acre garden contains about 90,000 plants and flowers and 1,500 trees, altogether representing 5,000 species.

❊ www.rjb.csic.es

Something blooms almost all year in the Botanical Garden, but the orderly terraces are especially resplendent in spring when masses of tulips and roses scent the air and almonds, peonies, and rhododendrons burst into bloom. Every city needs a place where its citizens can chart the seasons by the flora, marking February with the bloom of camellias and crocuses, welcoming autumn with the ripening scarlet globes of pomegranates. The garden can be perused slowly, reading each label and imagining how the plant might fit into the landscape back home—or passed through swiftly, letting yourself be swept up in a rush of color, shape, and scent.

In contrast to the traditional garden landscapes of El Retiro and the Botanical Garden, the newest and most ambitious urban green space, the Madrid Río, is designed primarily as a place to play. Located on the west side of the city below the hill of the

Palacio Real, the 400-million-euro project opened in 2011. With seventeen playgrounds and about eighteen miles of paths shared by pedestrians and cyclists within its 300 acres, it has become a favorite for active sports. Madrid conjured the three-mile linear park along both banks of the Río Manzanares by burying part of the busy, congested M-30 roadway and building above it.

The long straightaway path that follows the river canal is great for cyclists and joggers alike, and dedicated sporting areas accommodate skateboarders, football players, wall climbers, and rowers. But there's nothing mandatory about breaking a sweat. It's just as pleasurable to take a leisurely stroll, stop to enjoy the gardens and a cool drink from a refreshment kiosk, and even laugh at the whimsy of the urban "beach" with jets and sprays of cool water that take the sting out of summer's heat.

Even old Madrid up on the hill looks better from Madrid Río, especially from the two ingenious new footbridges over the water. The Andorra bridge branches off in a graceful Y-shape, but the Arganzuela footbridge, which looks like swirls of metal ribbon coiled into a tube, is the most striking. It's one of the best vantage points to admire the monumental beauty of the early eighteenth-century Baroque-style Toledo bridge with its nine arches and rounded supports. Time your visit for late in the day to watch the sun set over the river and darkness gather across the plains of La Mancha.

# 11
## Stitches of Time

### REAL FÁBRICA DE TAPICES, MADRID

You'll probably catch glimpses of Madrid's tapestry-making tradition during your sojourns through the city. Galleries 90 through 94 of the Museo Nacional del Prado (see Chapter 7) have sunny oil paintings by Francisco de Goya (1746-1828) of hunting scenes and of ladies and gentlemen picnicking outdoors, flying kites, or dancing by the banks of the Río Manzanares. Hardly the most upbeat of artists, Goya nonetheless created them as models for tapestries to be woven at the Real Fábrica de Tapices, or Royal Tapestry Factory. That workshop also created the thick, rich carpets that you can't miss if you treat yourself to tea at the Hotel Ritz. The stately property was opened in 1910 at the behest of Alfonso XIII so that Spain could boast hotels at least as grand as those in other European capitals.

It was a similar sort of royal rivalry that led to the creation of the Real Fábrica de Tapices in Madrid in 1721. For those with money and power, tapestries were the ultimate in decorating. Hung on the large walls in cold, drafty palaces, monasteries, and noble homes, they added warmth and color and were instant status symbols. By the fourteenth century, Paris and Flanders had emerged as the most important manufacturing centers. During the century-plus (1581-1713) that Spain controlled the so-called Spanish Netherlands, there was a steady flow of prized tapestries back to the Iberian peninsula.

Felipe V wasted little time establishing Spain's own weaving center after he lost the Spanish Netherlands to Austria in 1714 in the War of Spanish Succession. Almost three centuries later, the tradition of fine craftsmanship is carried on primarily by a tight-knit sisterhood of women who still create beauty knot by knot.

To be fair, there are a few men among the thirty or so weavers, all of whom barely lift their eyes from the looms in front of them when small tour groups come through. To see this living history at work, make your way to the red brick building not far from the Atocha train station that has housed the Real Fábrica since 1889.

✴ www.realfabricadetapices.com/#/eng

The lobby and entry hall give a quick overview of the genre. One of the standout tapestries in the hallway is a scene of the martyrdom of San Esteban, designed by the Italian Renaissance artist Raphael and woven in Flanders. When the Real Fábrica was first established, it was headed by a master tapestry maker from Antwerp and the mostly Flemish weavers often worked from Flemish and Italian designs.

But the workshop soon began to develop a more colloquial Spanish style. Between 1775 and 1793 Goya, who became painter to the royal court in 1779, painted sixty-three models for tapestries for the royal residences of El Escorial and El Pardo. Several watercolor cartoons made from Goya's oil paintings hang in the lobby.

The Real Fábrica may have established its reputation on the quality and originality of its tapestries, but carpets are also an important part of the artistic output. Tours begin in the carpet workshop where a line of five to six weavers stands at eighteenth- and nineteenth-century looms where the work is wound on thick round wooden trunks about the size of a telephone pole. They face the front of the carpet-in-progress and build it knot by knot. Working from a graph-like, full-size cartoon of the finished design, they fasten a knot for each square of the graph, using merino wool from Toledo over the cotton warp that forms the skeleton of the carpet. The weavers work in a rhythm, completing one line and moving on to the next. They move easily in unison like old married couples completing each other's sentences—not surprising since most of them have stood side by side at these antique looms for twenty-five years or more. Even with the synergy of each weaver knowing the crew's motions in her bones, it takes about a week to complete a square meter of carpet.

In the tapestry room next door, weavers sit at smaller individual looms, facing the reverse side of the image with only a mirrored reflection of their work to guide them. They copy small sections of the full drawing onto the warp with graphite and then exercise their own artistic judgment to select the colors of wool to execute the design. A tapestry in process may have hundreds of spindles, each with a different shade of yarn, hanging off the back of the piece.

"This is an artistic, intellectual activity," a guide recently told my tour group. "The quality of the finished piece depends on the weaver's skill and taste to select the colors." They use different shades to create modeling of the images, and control the tightness of the knots to produce slightly different reflective textures. A tapestry that is merely a rote repetition of the cartoon can look as mechanical as a paint-by-numbers landscape. A tapestry woven by a master has the electric presence of an oil painting. The work is painstaking. Most weavers take eight months to weave a single square meter.

Most of the current weavers began their training as teenagers and the Real Fábrica, which became a quasi-public foundation in 1996, operates a school to train new generations of artisans to carry on the venerable traditions. After all, the symbolic value of finely woven textiles remains undiminished. Kings, queens, presidents, and titans of industry will always need the weavers' deft touch to soften and transform the otherwise quotidian wall or floor.

# 12 *Just One More Bite*

## MADRID FOOD TOURS

One of the best things about travel is learning about a place, plate by plate. When I'm heading to a new city, I seek suggestions from friends—and friends of friends—for their favorite restaurants and bars and markets and for the dishes and local specialties that I shouldn't miss. But sometimes my circle of acquaintances comes up short. So the next best bet is often a gastronomically inclined guide who can introduce me to the flavors of a place, orient me to its dining rhythms, and then point me on my way.

That's what Lauren Aloise had in mind when she founded Madrid Food Tours in 2012. It was a huge undertaking for a young American who had grown up in a food-loving Massachusetts family with parents of Polish and Italian heritage. After college, she moved to Sevilla to work as an English-language teaching assistant. She had been in Spain only a week when she met her future husband, a Spaniard from Cádiz. When the couple moved to Madrid for the energy and opportunities of a bigger city, she hit on the idea of a business that would combine her love of food with her studies in tourism and hospitality.

She also realized that Madrid was the perfect location for an overview of the tastes of Spain. "Madrid is the melting pot city of Spain," she told me as we sipped glasses of wine and shared a small cheese platter in the back room of Casa Gonzalez, one of her favorite hangouts. "It's a planned capital. Everyone came here from other parts of Spain—and they all brought their food traditions."

Aloise and a small corps of guides lead three different tours that introduce visitors to traditional foods, colorful restaurants and taverns, and a variety of food vendors. Each tour lasts from three-and-one-half to four-and-one-half hours—with so many foods to taste that participants won't want another meal any time soon.

Visitors to Spain are particularly fascinated with the tradition of the tapas hop, a way of life that seems to prove poet Diane Ackerman's observation that of all the senses, "taste is largely social." So it's no surprise that an early evening outing to several tapas bars—combining history with tasting and sipping—is the most popular tour. Just for the record, Aloise says that any woman should feel secure even if she is alone in a tapas bar during the traditional early evening hours. "It's uncomfortable for anyone not familiar to shove in to be served," she says, "but there is nothing weird about being alone. It's more likely that you will be ignored than hit on."

I was most intrigued by Aloise's food-centric tour of the Huertas neighborhood, one of the city's oldest and most historic. Located just off Puerta del Sol, it's filled with atmospheric restaurants and bars, but has also captured the attention of some of Spain's top chefs—including Sergi Arola—looking for a place to launch a casual eatery.

The tour also gives visitors a sense of what it might be like to live in a Madrid neighborhood. "It's like a day in the life of a Madrileña," says Aloise. The eating and shopping are "not that far off from what someone would do in a couple of days."

The group might begin with *churros* and rich hot chocolate at aptly named Chocolats (Calle Santa María 30), one of the few places in the city, besides Chocolatería San Ginés (see Chapter 3) that still makes its own *churros*. If you have any doubt, just sit at the counter and peek into the kitchen where *churros* bubble in a big pot of hot oil. Nearby Mantecería de A Cabello (Plaza de Matute 13), one of the oldest grocery stores in the city, is the place to taste jams, honeys, and olive oils. "They have everything a Spaniard would have in their pantry," says Aloise.

A stop at a small potato chip factory is usually a revelation for Americans who are accustomed to chips from a convenience store bag, which typically taste more of salt than anything else. The fresh chips are usually a little thicker and have a pronounced potato flavor with a pleasant overtone of the oil in which they're cooked. A small artisanal bakery offers the tour group slices of traditional Galician cheesecake made with *tetilla*, a tangy but creamy cow's milk cheese shaped into small cones with a nipple on top. (The name translates as "small breast.")

Casa Gonzalez (Calle León 12), a cheesemonger and ham shop with a history, is one of Aloise's neighborhood favorites. As a group samples a few cheeses (such as Cabrales, a blue cheese from Asturias) the guide explains the family story.

"The grandfather of the current owners founded the business in the 1930s," says Aloise. "Socialists used to meet in the back room and the grandfather was jailed for eight years. The women of the family kept the business going."

These days, that same back room is a good place to return in the early evening for wine by the glass with some cured ham, a selection of raw milk sheep and goat cheeses, and maybe some red peppers stuffed with squid. The tables will most likely be filled with neighborhood regulars.

"People in Madrid live in the street and don't socialize at home," says Aloise, who points out that Casa Gonzalez is a great meeting spot because it offers more wines by the glass than most Madrid establishments.

One of the highlights of the Huertas tour is a stop at Mercado Antón Martín, one of Madrid's traditional neighborhood food markets. It has such a variety of vendors that the group might compare Spanish-style roast pork with Italian porchetta and sample such staples of Spanish cuisine as olives, pickled anchovies, cured ham, and perhaps beef cheek. "The butcher will even dissect a cow's head," says Aloise, noting that Madrileños prize offal and organ meats.

"When I moved to Madrid, the market was half empty," Aloise recalls. "Now it's filled with a lot of new vendors." It's part of a citywide trend to revive old markets that are so central to neighborhood life. Some, like Mercado San Miguel (see Chapter 1), have even become late-night social scenes.

Aloise is thrilled with the market's resurgence, which, in some ways, parallels her own trajectory. From her modest start in Madrid, she has joined with a partner, renamed the business Devour Spain, and branched out to include tours in Sevilla, Málaga, and Barcelona. After all, visitors also need to taste *salmorejo*, *espeto malagueña*, and *pa amb tomate*.

✳ www.devourspain.com

✳ spanishsabores.com

# 13 Echoes of Antiquity

## ARCHEOLOGICAL MUSEUM, MADRID

A pair of very womanly winged sphinxes flanks the door to the Museo Arqueológico Nacional, which traces the story of habitation on the Iberian peninsula from prehistoric times to the mid-nineteenth century. The museum reopened in 2013 after a top-to-bottom renovation, and your eyes will pop at the beautiful displays of objects that encourage us to imagine those long-ago lives. Now and then, we can even call them by name.

✳ www.man.es/man/en/home

Isabella II founded the museum in 1867 to bring together the royal collections of archeological, ethnographic, and decorative arts objects. Perhaps it's just coincidental, but it's striking to see how often the anonymous artists and artisans turned to the female form for comfort or bounty—and how often women were venerated, at least by their own families if not always by the larger community.

The collection ranges from a monumental sixth-century B.C. tomb with decorative reliefs of a fertility goddess to the fifteenth-century A.D. carved alabaster sarcophagus of a noble woman. But some of the most significant—and frankly most affecting—pieces date from the Iron Age cultures of first millennium B.C. to Roman Spain (first century B.C. to fifth century A.D.). If you have time to visit only one gallery—which I don't really recommend—you should head straight to Gallery 13 on the first floor. It holds one of the museum's greatest treasures, the carved limestone bust of the Dama de Elche, dating from the Iberian culture of late fifth century to early fourth century B.C. The image of a fine lady was discovered outside the town of Elche (see Chapter 79), south of Valencia in eastern Spain in 1897, and brought to Madrid after four decades at the Louvre in Paris.

Even stripped of her polychrome painting (although her lips still look berry-sweetened), there is something arresting about this woman whose eyes are slightly downcast, but who wears an elaborate headdress and jewels with aplomb.

Travel writer Jan Morris imagined her best in a delightful description in her book *Spain*: "She is a formidable dame: a broad-shouldered, rosy, heavily built woman, slung about with amulets, with an elaborate cartwheel headdress and a general air of no-nonsense, as if she is about to tell a recalcitrant nephew to pull himself together, or ask some wilting cousin where on earth she bought that frightful dress."

In the gallery, the Dama de Elche is surrounded by seated and standing women in more stylized postures, such as "offerant," or figure presented to a deity. The Great Lady Offerant, a limestone carving from the third century B.C., was found in Albacete in south-eastern Spain. Also richly coifed and adorned with jewelry, she holds a vessel in her hands as she most likely prepares to be presented to a deity to mark her passage from childhood to womanhood.

Yet another passage is represented by the Dama de Baza, a limestone carving from the first half of the fourth century

discovered in a necropolis in the province of Granada. This figure
of a seated woman, in a nearby gallery, was used as a cinerary urn
and it's tempting to assume that she had been well loved by her
family. In death, she is elegantly dressed, sits on a winged throne,
and holds a pigeon in one hand to seek protection in the next
world.

In the museum's skylit central courtyard, carved marble statues
from Spain's Roman era almost seem to glow from within when
sunlight filters down on them. Among the collection of sculptures
of the main ruling dynasties of the Roman empire are several
images of Livia (58 B.C.–A.D. 29), the wife of emperor Augustus
who was subsequently deified by her grandson, the emperor
Claudius. History records her as a savvy and trusted adviser to her
husband, as well as a perhaps somewhat scheming mother who
made sure that Tiberius, her son by an earlier marriage, became
emperor on the death of Augustus. In one image found in Baena,
in Córdoba province, she holds a cornucopia to show her power to
provide bounty and prosperity to her subjects.

It's notable how often jewelry conveys the status and power of
the ancient women who wear it. If adornment through the ages is
of special interest, you will find case after case of jewelry, including many pieces that would not be the least out of place today. But
the most moving pieces are small assemblages that seem to have
been carefully accumulated by one woman—her personal statement of taste and style. The objects found in a woman's tomb
from first to third century A.D. Roman Spain seem to have been
plucked right off a dressing table: several small glass and clay
unguent jars, a tiny gold ring, a bronze bracelet and brooch, and
a big gold earring.

A similar tomb of the young Roman-era woman Agele bears
this inscription: "Agele, in the flower of her twentieth year, first

among women in conduct and beauty. This place was reserved for the bones of the ill fated girl.... May you rest in this eternal home, Agele, unharmed, and may the light earth settle softly upon you."

Read that inscription and she lives again in her spoken name.

## RECOMMENDED READING

*Spain* by Jan Morris

# 14 *¡Ole! ¡Ole!*

## FLAMENCO AT CASA PATAS, MADRID

Every woman will have her own Spanish epiphany—that moment when she realizes that the country has gotten under her skin and maybe even changed her in some way.

As I wrote in the Introduction to this book, mine came late at night at the flamenco club Casa Patas. It's hard to say when yours will hit since it's not something you can force. It will come upon you when you're least expecting it. The only thing to do is keep an open mind and let Spain sneak up on you.

In the meantime, if you are in Madrid, there is no better place to spend an evening than at Casa Patas. Flamenco is so much more than simply an art form, although it is a great one full of raw emotion and passion. It's also a way of life, and Casa Patas is one of the few places where outsiders can peel back the curtain on the whole flamenco culture.

Flamenco was born around a Gypsy campfire and grew up in the bars and back rooms of Andalucía. It fell into disfavor during the Franco years. During the Civil War, the Nationalists had slaughtered Gypsies by the hundreds, and the dictator considered flamenco and its practitioners anarchic and subversive. A few touristic shows and underground clubs kept flamenco alive during those grim years. Finally, in the 1980s, flamenco burst back onto the

scene, with Madrid at the forefront of its revival and even renaissance. In a way, the music followed a parallel track to La Movida,
the no-holds-barred movement of artists and filmmakers that
brought Madrid back to life. Certainly La
Movida's slogan *"Madrid nunca duerme,"* or
"Madrid never sleeps," is apt for flamenco,
where shows might start at 10:30 P.M. or
later and go on into *la madrugada,* as the
Spanish call the hours between midnight
and dawn.

Casa Patas was founded in 1985 by afi-
cionados of what was then hailed as "nuevo flamenco," a new wave
that brought elements of jazz, blues, salsa, and other world music
into an expanded definition of the music and art form. "Nuevo"
has become the new norm, and Casa Patas has become its high
temple in Madrid.

❋ www.casapatas.com

Unlike most flamenco *tablaos* (as the nightclubs are called),
Casa Patas does not have a regular troupe of beautifully costumed
performers who knock out the same show twice a night. Instead, it
presents about three hundred performances a year by about a hundred different groups of artists. The lineup is a mix of established,
sometimes famous performers with promising up-and-comers. In
either case, there is always a buzz of anticipation in the crowd.

Casa Patas occupies an 1880s building in Lavapies that's exceed-
ingly modest compared to the club's outsized reputation and
impact. The front of the building is given over to a bar and restaurant, which begins to fill up a couple of hours before the first performance of the night. It's never a good idea to opt for a "dinner
show" at a *tablao,* where you'll eat a fixed menu before or during the
performance. But at Casa Patas, a good meal before the show is the

best way to warm up for the main event. For one thing, Casa Patas is a proper restaurant, with great classic dishes such as ratatouille-like *pisto* with fried egg, artichokes with red peppers and diced ham, and *albóndigas*, or meatballs, in spicy paprika sauce.

It's also a real scene. More than a dozen hams hang above the long copper bar on one wall and black-and-white photos of performers cover every available inch of wall space. The soundtrack is flamenco and it gets louder and louder as performance time nears. Nobody is bothered by the volume. Everyone just yells louder. Men in black shirts with long ponytails grab a drink at the bar before they disappear into the back.

The long, narrow performance space is so intimate that I almost wish that Spain hadn't outlawed smoking in bars and restaurants. It cries out for a haze of smoke. There's a stage in the corner at one end with tables on two sides. Sit in the front row and the ruffles of a skirt may brush against your glass of wine when the dancer really gets going. Sit way down on the left and you may see a dancer release the tension in his or her body and slump in a chair against the wall during a short break from the stage.

The stage is only big enough for a small group—a singer, guitarist, percussionist, and one or two dancers. But that is more than enough as the lights go down and the music begins. The musicians strike a chord and fall quickly into a rhythm, the singer lets out an anguished lamentation that raises the hair on everyone's neck. The dancers stare each other in the eye, with more dare than longing. He fixes her with a gaze and claps. She answers with her hips. And the crowd nods in agreement.

# 15 *Faith and Will*

## THE TRAIL OF ISABEL I OF CASTILLA AND LEÓN

By all counts, Isabel I should never have been queen. She was sandwiched between an older half-brother and a younger full brother, which meant that the order of succession was stacked against her. But after the sudden, unexplained death of her brother Alfonso in 1466 and the death of her half-brother Enrique eight years later, she was, in fact, crowned Queen of Castilla and León. She was twenty-three years old and assumed control of the largest kingdom on the Iberian peninsula.

Isabel also hit the jackpot in the arranged royal marriage lottery. At her coronation, she had already been married for five years to her cousin Fernando, heir apparent to the kingdom of Aragón. Married within weeks of meeting, Spain's first power couple had a real love match, a true physical and intellectual bond. They ruled equally, though Isabel's larger realm often gave her the upper hand. In between unifying and forging modern Spain, she also managed to give birth to six children. Spain had never before seen a woman so freely able to exercise her intellect and ambition.

Historian and biographer Peggy Liss contends that "Europe had no queen as great until the advent of England's Elizabeth I."

Isabel still fascinates people today because it's so difficult to grapple with her legacy. In 1492—the signature year of her reign—"Los Reyes Católicos" completed the reconquest of Spain at Granada and set the country on the path of empire and riches by financing Christopher Columbus's first voyage of discovery. But that same year, the monarchs also decreed that all Jews be expelled from Spain, an act of intolerance that would haunt the country for centuries.

Isabel's life, says Liss, is "a story of conjugal love, familial warmth, and ambition to excel, as well as a cautionary tale for the ages, having to do with the use to which are put extraordinary reserves of will, resolution, and courage."

There seem to be few places in Spain where Isabel did not touch down during her thirty-year reign. But if you want to follow her footsteps as you contemplate the uses and abuses of power, here are a few touchstones.

Isabel was born in 1451 and grew up in Castilla, a flat dry land where frontier fortresses top every hill. She spent much of her childhood in the Alcázar in Segovia. Situated on a rocky outcrop at the confluence of two rivers, it was one of the more elegant and easily defended royal residences. In a scenario worthy of a soap opera, Isabel was part of the entourage of her sister-in-law and the queen consort, Juana of Portugal, second wife of Enrique IV. The poor man is better remembered as Enrique the Impotent, a sobriquet that explains the questionable paternity that always dogged Juana's daughter. She was also named Juana, but often called "La Beltraneja," in reference to her suspected father.

When Enrique died in 1474, Isabel moved quickly to fend off any pretenders to the throne. Dressed in mourning, she attended a funeral mass at the church of San Miguel on Segovia's Plaza Mayor. When the last benediction was spoken, she re-robed in noble finery, stepped out the portal of San Miguel, and ascended a makeshift platform. Before the city, she was crowned Queen of Castilla and León.

A mural in the Alcázar captures the occasion. In fact, Isabel grew up in the castle-fortress surrounded by similar such trappings of royalty and destiny, and a visit lets you ponder the all-encompassing sense of history that shadowed her childhood. The Hall of Monarchs contains a frieze of carved polychrome statues of every Spanish ruler from the semi-mythical eighth-century Pelayo onward (see Chapter 35). They are seated on golden thrones, as if they had achieved a sort of earthly apotheosis. It was the young princess's room of family portraits.

Isabel had little time to bask in her new power. Almost immediately, Afonso V of Portugal agreed to marry his niece "La Beltraneja" and declared her Enrique's legitimate heir. Isabel and Fernando spent almost two years fighting off a Portuguese power grab. After the last major battle, they entered the medieval walled city of Toledo in January 1477, reportedly riding hand in hand through the Moorish-era Bisagra gate and celebrating mass at the Gothic cathedral. For the first time, Isabel wore a magnificent golden crown encrusted with pearls, rubies, and diamonds.

Toledo's cathedral, seat of the primate of Spain, has suffered over the centuries from perhaps too much royal or noble attention. The main altar commissioned by the Catholic Kings is cluttered with other statements of power and politics. But when you visit the cathedral, forget the pomposity of the statuary and the anti-communist rhetoric of several memorials and pay closest attention to the carved choir stalls, which commemorate the triumph of the Catholic Kings over the Moors in Granada. The emotionally powerful images of knights in prayer are a reminder that church and state were largely synonymous in late medieval Spain and that Isabel was guided as much by faith as by political instinct.

In 1482, Fernando and Isabel began the campaign to conquer the kingdom of Granada, the last Moorish stronghold on the Iberian peninsula. Isabel held up her end as the warrior queen, an equal partner in planning strategy, mustering troops and financial support, and handling the logistics of keeping the army fed and healthy. She often joined Fernando in camp, but also spent time in the Alcázar in Córdoba.

Ordered built by Alfonso XI in 1328, about a century after Córdoba was recaptured, the Alcázar is more military fortress than sumptuous palace. Even as the quest for Granada was joined, Columbus lobbied Isabel for support for a westward voyage of discovery. Although it's not certain where the monarchs met with the explorer to give him the final go-ahead, Córdoba is a likely spot. A statue amid the fountains and greenery of the Alcázar garden commemorates the event.

But nothing rivals the couple's triumphant entry into Granada on January 6, 1492, after accepting the keys to the city from Boabdil, the last Moorish ruler, several days earlier. In a decade, the monarchs had completed the seven-century crusade to return Spain to Christian control—a struggle begun by the pantheon of Isabel's ancestors on the walls in Segovia.

It's hardly surprising that the monarchs chose to be buried in Granada. They lie at rest in the Gothic-style Royal Chapel behind Granada's grand Renaissance cathedral. Isabel died first, on November 26, 1504, and Fernando followed her on January 23, 1516. Her unadorned coffin is surprisingly tiny for a woman who still seems, somehow, larger than life.

## RECOMMENDED READING

*Isabel the Queen: Life and Times* by Peggy K. Liss

# 16 *Within the Walls of Faith*

## SANTA TERESA OF ÁVILA

Approach Ávila from the arid western plain across the Río Adaja, and you will be greeted by one of the most iconic sights in Spain: the great stretch of high stone walls with a dozen defensive turrets that surround the hilltop medieval city. Standing up to 39 feet tall, those walls were begun in 1090 and created an impenetrable bastion that was never conquered by force. Even the cathedral forms part of the defensive wall. Recognized as a UNESCO

World Heritage site, the walls are partially open for visitors to walk the ramparts, eye to eye with the storks that nest on the nearby rooftops.

Ávila was also the home of Teresa Sánchez de Cepeda y Ahumada (1515-1582), best known to posterity as Santa Teresa de Jésus or simply as Teresa of Ávila. This Carmelite nun was a mystic and theologian who shook the very foundations of faith and power. An easy woman to admire, she was perhaps harder to like and yet impossible to ignore. As Simone de Beauvoir wrote, her life and writings "rose to heights that few men have ever reached." De Beauvoir further noted that Teresa, like Joan of Arc, went her appointed way "with an intrepidity unsurpassed by any man."

Born to a large family, some of whom were Jewish converts to Christianity, or *conversos,* Teresa spent key portions of her childhood, youth, and mature years in Ávila. She is so much a part of this compact historical city that Ávilanos simply refer to her as "La Santa," or The Saint. In a way, it's not surprising since so many touchstones of her life remain.

The church and Convent of Santa Teresa were built between 1629 and 1636 on the site of the house where Teresa was born, and they preserve the little garden where she wrote in her autobiography that she loved to play with her siblings. But Teresa's focus even then was more on the next world than this one, as she ran off at age seven with her brother Rodrigo, both of them seeking martyrdom in distant Moorish lands. (They only got as far as the crossroads just beyond the Roman bridge over the Río Adaja before their uncle dragged them back.)

The vaulted burial crypt of the Barefoot Carmelite convent has been converted into a museum dedicated to Teresa, who co-founded the order with fellow Ávilano, San Juan de la Cruz. The museum deals principally with Teresa's extended influence—the convents she founded and the cult of her theology, particularly its spread in Latin America through the influence of her brothers. More telling than all the accomplishments, however, are copies of some of her correspondence with Juan de la Cruz. Her penmanship is bold and without pretense, yet at points rushed in her seeming impatience to let her thoughts be known.

At the age of twenty, Teresa took the habit at the Carmelite Monastary of La Encarnación, located a short walk outside the city walls from the gates next to the cathedral. It was then a wealthy convent, where some sisters lived in considerable comfort in private rooms with fireplaces. She eventually became prioress and a small museum includes a statue said to have spied on the nuns when Teresa was away on business and tattled on their sins when she returned. More evocative of the saint, however, are the *locutorios,* or conversation rooms, where, by her own account, she and Juan de la Cruz were inflamed with the passion of their mystical union with Christ.

In perhaps the most famous passage in her autobiography, Teresa describes an angel plunging a large golden dart through her heart and into the depths of her body: "He left me all on fire with great love of God," she continued. The passage inspired Gian Lorenzo Bernini to sculpt the hypersexualized statue of the encounter, *The Ecstasy of Santa Teresa,* in 1647-52 for Santa Maria della Vittoria in Rome.

Finding life at La Encarnación far too cushy and secular, Teresa hatched the idea for a reformed order, the Barefoot Carmelites. Inspired partly by the Barefoot Franciscan order founded by Juana de Austria in Madrid in 1559 (see Chapter 4), Teresa's nuns would take severe vows of poverty and spend their lives in cloistered meditation and prayer. In 1562, the first Barefoot Carmelite institution, the Monastery of San José, opened on the outskirts of Ávila when four novices took vows under Teresa's more severe rule.

Another small museum at San José displays artifacts such as the saint's saddle that she rode all over Spain founding seventeen Barefoot Carmelite convents. A re-creation of her cell shows a narrow bed with a log for a pillow and a window where she sat to write, penning her final masterpiece, *Camino de Perfección* (Way of Perfection). Her description of the four stages of prayer—meditation, quiet, repose of the soul, and finally perfect union with God—remains the keystone of Roman Catholic mysticism. Enter the tiny convent church, and you may hear but not see the cloistered nuns singing their prayers in an unbroken 350-year lineage from the time of Teresa.

✳ www.avilaturismo.com

# 17

## *Built to Last*

### THE AQUEDUCT OF SEGOVIA

The seal of Segovia, the proud city where Isabel was crowned queen in 1474 (see Chapter 15), is uncluttered by the usual Castilian castles and lions. It draws its identity instead from its ancient Roman aqueduct. Segovia is unimaginable without the towering arches that carry the waterway into the city, so its seal simply displays those arches on a shield topped by the royal crown.

Segovia sprawls across a steep, wedge-shaped hill at the junction of two rivers about 65 miles (100km) northwest of Madrid. The Romans considered its location strategic, since it stood about halfway between the major cities of Caesaraugusta (Zaragoza) and Ermita Augusta (Mérida). At the end of the first century A.D., Roman engineers constructed the aqueduct to slake the thirst of the growing city. It delivers water from the Río Frío at the base of the Sierra Guadarrama to the city about 9 miles (14km) away. What seems simply a logical solution was actually a marvel of engineering. The 24,000 granite blocks in the aqueduct and its arches are held in place by counterbalancing forces—no cement or mortar necessary.

✳ visitsegovia.turismodesegovia.com

The construction was state-of-the-art stuff in those days, and Sextus Julius Frontinus, Rome's water commissioner at the end of the first century A.D., was proud of it. He called aqueducts "the most solemn testimony of the Empire." They were, he pronounced, monuments to Rome's reach across Europe. Traces of Roman aqueducts remain in Sevilla, Toledo, Merida, and Calahorra, but Segovia's is "one of the most intact Roman aqueducts in Europe," as the World Monuments Fund puts it.

It is revered as a towering achievement of early civil engineering—conceived and built so well that it carried water to the thirsty city for about twenty centuries. While it had to have been a sight for early Roman eyes, Frontinus was most concerned with practicality, once comparing Rome's aqueducts to "the idle Pyramids or the useless, though famous works of the Greeks."

But modern sensibilities do not necessarily consider beauty and function to be mutually exclusive. It is quite possible to view the Segovia aqueduct as a marvelous piece of environmental art and its designers and builders as worthy forerunners of Christo, Andy Goldsworthy, and Robert Smithson. Intentional or not, Segovia's aqueduct enhances and transforms its urban setting.

From its source in the foothills, the aqueduct ran both underground and on the surface as an enclosed stone channel. Most of those outlying portions were replaced in the twentieth century by pipe. The famous section of the waterway is the final elevated portion. The covered stone water trough emerges from the ground on the east end of the city to be carried 2,388 feet on ever-higher arches until it pierces the city walls.

Those 166 arches mounted on granite ashlars march down from the hillside with the majesty of giant, long-legged camels.

At the Plaza Azoguejo, the two-tiered arches reach more than ninety-three feet into the sky, and they are the signature architecture of Segovia. Beheld through the frames of those towering stones, Segovia almost seems reduced to a dollhouse city on a hill. The shapes of those towering arches must have haunted the city's builders. Along the late medieval streets, the buildings bear an arch here, an arch there. Finally, at the Plaza Mayor, narrow rounded arches define the building arcades. Segovia is a Spanish city, but its stones still speak Latin.

# 18

## Dreaming in Stone

### CARVED BUILDINGS OF SALAMANCA

Perched on the high ground of the north bank of the Río Tormes, the great, blocky buildings of Salamanca glow like El Dorado when the low sun strikes them at dawn and again at sunset. But that golden aura is only one of their delights. The mica-flecked local sandstone from which much of the city was built yields so easily to the chisel and mallet that it seems to have inspired stone carvers to new heights of artistry and imagination.

The city unfolds from the medieval core of one of Spain's most prestigious universities, and the 30,000 students—about 15 percent of the entire population—lend the center a purposeful, energetic vibe. But to give Salamanca its due, you need to do something the students rarely do—look up from your digital screen and practice the art of truly seeing what stands before you. We all get caught up in the nagging insistence of instant communication. On the other hand, Salamanca's often anonymous stone carvers, many of whom worked centuries ago, were incising messages for the ages. Grant Salamanca the proper time and attention, and you will find that the city is as engaging as a graphic novel.

✳ www.salamanca.es

The University of Salamanca inhabits about one-quarter of the old city and it's a good place to begin a day of focused wandering and looking. The University was founded in 1218 and the so-called "doorway to heaven," or entrance to the original college, was completed in 1534. It's the very definition of "Salamanca Plateresque," a style that emulates in stone the fine detail of the silversmith's art. Forever linking the state and the church, carvings include the "Reyes Catolicos," Fernando and Isabel holding a single scepter and an image of an unidentified pope addressing two cardinals. You'll also find the heads of Venus and Hercules and the double-eagle insignia of Holy Roman Emperor Carlos V, grandson of Fernando and Isabel and Spain's king at the time.

Eminences aside, the most famous figure on the facade is one of the smallest. The image of a frog perched on a human skull is said to represent sin, but has taken on new meaning over the years. Students like to think that spotting the frog will guarantee good luck in their exams, which might explain why frog merchandise is ubiquitous. The stone frog, by the way, is about two-thirds of the way up the doorway on the right.

It's only about a two-block walk to the Catedral Nueva, the tallest building in the city and one of Spain's last great Gothic structures. It was begun in 1513 and shares a wall with the more modest Romanesque-style Catedral Vieja, which is known for its fifteenth-century carved polychrome altarpiece of fifty-three scenes depicting the life of Christ. But the devout didn't have to enter the sanctuary to "read" some of the most compelling stories of their faith. Scenes of the Nativity, the Adoration of the Magi, and of Christ on the cross were carved on the main facade of the Catedral Nueva.

✳ www.catedralsalamanca.org (Spanish only)

These days, Puerto Ramos—the west door of the Flamboyant Gothic-style cathedral—garners more attention than the main facade. Half a millennium ago, stone carvers crafted a moving scene of the entry of Jesus into Jerusalem, but over the years, the searing sun and dusty west winds took their toll on the building's most exposed surface. During a 1992 restoration of the doorway, modern artisans embraced Salamanca's sense of whimsy by adding carvings of an astronaut floating in a space suit, a stork carrying a branch in its beak, and a gargoyle-like monkey eating an ice cream cone. Nestled among carved leaves and vines, the anachronistic interlopers can be hard to find. Fear not—there's always a panhandler or two more than eager to point them out for a small consideration.

My favorite Salamanca stone carvings are well enough hidden that they almost seem like a secret. They reside in the 1533 central patio and cloister at the Convento de las Dueñas, a quick stroll from the cathedral. Although the Dominican order is cloistered, one sister meets the public to take admission fees and direct visitors to the two levels of columned arcades surrounding a grassy courtyard and fragrant rose garden. At first glance, it seems one of the sweetest and most tranquil spots in the city. But take a second look. The capitals on the upper gallery conjure the sacred and the profane: griffins and angels, leering devils and menacing Moors, winged horses and flying goats. Magic is afoot here, and good and evil are locked in eternal combat. If there was ever a place to meditate on the state of your soul, this is it.

This is the life the sisters have chosen—a life of withdrawal from the world of the flesh and submission to the world of the spirit. And here they stay. You, however, will eventually return to modern Salamanca, to your modern cares and concerns, but you will bring with you a whiff of roses and a fresh set of eyes to behold the city before you, golden in the day's dying light.

# 19 Big Red

## VICTORIA BENAVIDES AND TINTA DE TORO

The Elias Mora winery is named for an old man in San Román de Hornija who was willing to take a chance on a visionary young woman winemaker. Name aside, there's no mistaking that this is a woman's operation. From the carmine-rose color of the winery building to the graphic splashes of red and pink that lead from room to room and floor to floor in the business end of the facility, Bodegas Elias Mora bears the unmistakable stamp of Victoria Benavides and her sensuous embrace of color and drama.

The winery and the woman are in the vanguard of the D.O. Toro wine district along the Duero River east of Zamora and west of Tordesillas in Castilla y León. When Benavides built her winery in 2000, most Toro wines still had a reputation as big, alcoholic brutes. But like Manuel Fariña of Bodegas Fariña, who was instrumental in establishing the Toro appellation in 1987, Benavides believed in the potential of the region's native grape, *tinta de Toro*. It is usually classified as a clone of tempranillo, but has evolved in viticultural isolation for so many centuries that it has its own distinct flavor profile.

An agricultural engineer who trained to make wine in Bordeaux, Benavides fell in love with Toro when she was working at the region's enological station. But as a woman whose family was not in the wine business, she was locked out of buying local grapes, let alone buying vineyards. So she settled on a small slice of the Toro district—ancient parcels in and around the village of San Román de Hornija—and pleaded her case in person. Finally, in the village's senior center, she met retired winemaker Elias Mora, and convinced him to sell her an allotment of grapes from his vineyards.

She named her first wine for him, and when she built her winery, she named the entire operation Bodegas Elias Mora. Toro is difficult country for growers, where it is a struggle to wrest the grapes from the stony soil. The community tends to be very close-knit. It is a place where loyalty begets loyalty.

✳ www.bodegaseliasmora.com

"I believe in the people of the village," Benavides says. She still makes wine from the parcels of Elias Mora, and as word of the quality of her wines spread, other parcels have come her way—either for sale or as grape contracts. "We look to preserve these small parcels," she explains. "Some of them were more than eighty years old when we started here. Now they are approaching one hundred."

In all, Bodegas Elias Mora owns about 30 acres of vineyards, but Benavides and her crew make wine from sixty parcels spread out among 173 acres. Toro has made wine since the Romans, and escaped the phylloxera plague that decimated most of Europe's vines. As a result, it is a rare area where the vines are not grafted to American rootstock. While some growers are trellising their vines in the French style, Benavides tends to stick with growing them the way they've been cultivated here for two thousand years—short bushes on thick trunks with deep roots burrowed into the stony soil in search of moisture.

The diversity of parcels is very important to Benavides. "Exceptional and big wine must be complex," she explains. "The complexity comes from the subtle contributions from many parcels and many different clones."

With a total production around 200,000 bottles (roughly 17,000 cases), Elias Mora is not exactly a boutique winery, but Benavides prefers to keep production limited. The winery only operates at about two-thirds capacity, but she would rather lavish time and attention on making great wines than on making a lot of wine.

Even the entry level Viñas Elias Mora, with its bright raspberry and violet notes, spends more time in oak than is typical of young Toro wines. Her flagship Elias Mora Crianza, aged a year in a mix of French and American oak, shows a huge range of subtle flavors, including blackberries, anise, warm spices, and even a hint of menthol. Grapes from the oldest vineyards are used to produce Gran Elias Mora, which represents a selection of the best barrels from those old parcels. Only produced in exceptional vintages and in batches of 6,000 barrels or fewer, it tastes of concentrated ripe fruit, violet, and anise with a velvet feel in the mouth.

"This is my soul," Benavides says.

She admits that she probably helped blaze a trail for other women in the Toro region. Although female winery owners are still rare, "nowadays, it is not a problem to be a woman winemaker in Spain," she says. Certainly not in Toro. Nearly sixty *bodegas* now belong to the D.O. Toro appellation, and many, including Bodegas Elias Mora, welcome visitors for tours and tastings by advance reservation. Unlike other parts of Spain, more than half their winemakers are women.

✳ www.dotoro.com

# 20 *Visions of Heaven and Hell*

## LA COLEGIATA, TORO

Approaching Toro on the back roads from the west, the city makes instant sense. It sits high on a sandy hill above a sharp bend in the Río Duero ("the river that loves wine"). It has controlled traffic on the water since the Middle Ages. The fertile river plain is half planted in feed corn, half in the gnarled grapevines of *tinta de Toro*, a local grape famous since Roman times. Toro's ancient walls come to a point at the hulking eleventh-century fortress, and the skyline is dominated by the double-decked dome of its main Romanesque church, La Colegiata.

Santa María la Mayor, or La Colegiata, is as powerful a civic symbol as the aqueduct of Segovia or La Giralda of Sevilla. Even one of the region's top winemakers, Bodegas Fariña, names its wines after the church. I have always imagined that the people of Toro—all 10,000  of them—are probably very well behaved. After all, the sculptural adornment of the church includes one of the most graphic representations anywhere in Christendom of the rewards of heaven and the agonies of hell.

The masterpiece of the entire church complex is the original west entrance, the Portada de la Majestad, or Door of Majesty. The church was begun in 1170, and the doorway was carved sometime in the thirteenth century in that distinctly Castilian Romanesque style that has an emotional directness missing in other sculpture of the same era.

The carvers, identified by scholars as members of the family of Maestro Mateo, the genius behind the sculptures of the cathedral at Santiago de Compostela (see Chapter 39), worked their way into the lessons with a sweet rendering of the Virgin Mary receiving her celestial crown and de rigeur portraits of Old Testament prophets and assorted bishops and abbots. A row of musicians contains such detailed depictions of their instruments—flute, harp, lyre, bagpipes, dulcimer, hurdy-gurdy, bowed *vihuela*, and so on—that it has been an important source document for historians of music. But the joy of music gives way quickly to vivid portraits of saints and martyrs with the instruments of their martyrdom—St. Catherine with her wheel, St. Lawrence with the grills on which he was roasted.

The suffering of the martyrs is almost trivial compared to the souls consigned to hell in the Last Judgment scene that tops the doorway. Naked and terrified, they march to hell where they are greeted by Satan. The horrors multiply as the frieze continues with the torments of the damned—being boiled alive in cauldrons, being hung and dismembered, being devoured alive by demons, and so on. Little is left to the imagination. By contrast, the chosen are welcomed into the Gates of Paradise by Saint Peter and their faces are radiant with a giddy joy that contrasts with the silent screams of the damned.

That certainly would have made me behave.

The sculptures were finished and painted by Domingo Pérez, who signed his name on the lintel and identified himself as court painter of Sancho IV, who reigned from 1284-1295. In the 1400s, a church expansion enclosed the Portada de la Majestad, which then served for many years as an altar. Because the sculptures were protected from sunlight and wind, much of the original polychrome has survived.

✳ www.turismotoro.com

The town fans out from La Colegiata, widening as it moves back from the fortified wall above the river. It quickly becomes clear that wine is Toro's main business, and as you walk the streets, note the windows at sidewalk level. These are actually openings for chutes to the cellars. They were used to dump grapes into the stone rooms below, called *lagars,* where the owners would make their wine for the year. In many cases, the cellars have a wider footprint than the houses, stretching under the streets and often connecting to the neighbors. These underground passages proved useful during periods of warfare, which afflicted Toro about once a generation until modern times. No one makes wine in town these days—that's all moved to modern facilities in the countryside.

The other local sights are just a few—one of the oldest wooden bullrings in Spain, the offices of D.O.C. Toro, where you can get a list of wineries that can be visited by appointment, and some handsome Baroque gates to the city that have outlasted the walls they once breached. Somehow I always end up in the marvelously Castilian Plaza Mayor, where limestone columns support huge wooden lintels for the arcades around the public space. I find an outside table and, almost without asking, a few plates of snacks, a bottle of Toro red, and some glasses magically appear.

Now that's a vision of heaven.

# 21 In the Name of the Father

## VICTORIA PARIENTE AND THE WINES OF RUEDA

Stop at any bar in the dusty village of Rueda about 25 miles (40 km) southwest of Valladolid and you can quench your thirst with a cold glass of verdejo. The crisp white wine is the quintessential expression of place. The verdejo grape originated here and flourishes in the stony soil. No one makes wine from it with quite the power and

elegance as Victoria Pariente, whose success with verdejo catapulted the grape from relative obscurity to a place of prominence on Spanish wine lists. It also made her an enological rock star.

It was a grape her father had taught her to love. When she was growing up, her parents owned a bar-restaurant and her father had about fifteen acres of verdejo vineyards

from which he made white table wine. Although the Rueda region was the first in Castilla y Leon to gain D.O. (*denominación de origen*) status in 1980, "the wine was very rustic," says Pariente. "He sold it in the restaurant and a little around Rueda and north around Burgos." But when her father died suddenly after the 1997 harvest, "I decided to run his vineyards and make my own wine." That next fall, she made her first 15,000 bottles.

Pariente was hardly a novice when she launched Bodegas José Pariente, the winery she named as a tribute to her father. Having studied chemistry and enology in Madrid, she was working for the Castilla y León wine research station in Rueda when her father was stricken. That background gave her insight into the potential of the grape her father had loved.

✳ www.josepariente.com

"With that 1998 vintage, I began my adventure in the world of wine," she explains. She quit the government lab and hasn't looked back. When she started, she was one of the rare women making wine in Spain, and she was one of the even smaller number of women who owned their own wineries. Winemaking has since opened up as a career to women in Spain. Winery ownership—not so much.

She has expanded her vineyards to about 120 acres and also buys grapes from other growers. "With good grapes we can make good wines," she says, explaining why she and her viticultural staff even oversee the contract vineyards during the growing season. Some of the parcels are as much as eighty years old and about half the vineyards are planted "bush style," allowing the leaves to shade the roots and prevent evaporation. Without wire trellising to support the vines, the grapes must be picked by hand.

Bodegas José Pariente has grown incrementally over its first two decades, and the winemaking operations are now concentrated in a large facility that sprawls on a rise beside the road between Rueda and the even smaller village of La Seca. The winery building opened in 2008, and is clearly divided between the labs and offices with big windows at one end, and thick-walled industrial winery on the other. (It is one of more than twenty *bodegas* on Rueda's wine route that can be visited by prior reservation.) Pariente's annual production now tops 700,000 bottles but takes up less than half the physical plant. There is clearly room to grow.

The wine that Victoria Pariente made in 1998—the Jose Pariente Verdejo Varietal—remains the flagship of the *bodega*. It is a crisp, floral wine with hints of anise in the nose and pronounced pear, apple, citrus, and even pomegranate on the palate. It is my favorite all-purpose white table wine made in Spain—and the favorite of many restaurants and wine bars as well.

But Pariente did not stop with that singular achievement. She makes a barrel-fermented verdejo, sourced from old vines and fermented for a year in French oak with regular stirring of the lees. The resulting wine is spectacularly elegant, with spicy aromas, intense fruit, and an ethereal smokiness. She also makes a small amount of *cuvée especial*, which is sourced from some of the oldest traditional vineyards in one small plot in La Seca. Taking advantage of a technological innovation, it is fermented in egg-shaped concrete and tile vessels where the shape and temperature gradients create a steady circulation of the lees within the wine. The result is an extremely smooth, very complex verdejo with pronounced minerality and the ability to age almost like a red wine.

Pariente is not sure that women are necessarily better winemakers than men, but she does believe that they make wine differently. "We have another kind of sensitivity to the wine, another feeling," she says. "We feel all the details—and we take care of them."

Appropriately enough, her daughter Martina Prieto Pariente has joined the firm as a winemaker. She is exploring red wines made with tempranillo grapes from Toro, Cigales, and the Ribera del Duero, as well as garnacha de Toro, and garnacha de Ávila—regional variants of the grenache grape introduced to the area by Cistercian monks nearly a thousand years ago.

Victoria Pariente's husband and son are also involved in the family wine business. "They handle the paperwork," she says.

✳ www.rutadelvinoderueda.com/en

# 22 *Shining Through*

## CATEDRAL DE LEÓN

I decided long ago not to let unpleasant weather spoil my travels. It can't be sunny every day, and if I'm unprepared for rain, I figure it's the opportunity to buy a pretty new umbrella. But there is one place where sunshine is essential, and I'm not talking about a beach resort.

To get the full effect, the Catedral de León must be visited on a sunny day when light pours through its windows. A highlight for pilgrims walking the Camino de Santiago (see Chapter 38), the cathedral sits on the Camino Frances, which begins in France just across the Pyrenees from Pamplona. I'm sure the pilgrims are happy to sit in the pews to rest their aching feet and weary shoulders, but the church provides a spiritual uplift as important as its physical respite.

Entering the pale stone Gothic cathedral through one of the three carved stone portals on the west facade is like walking into a rainbow. No other Gothic cathedral prepares you for the experience.

Begun in 1255 on the site of two previous cathedrals built over ancient Roman baths, the Catedral de Santa María de Regla opened for worship in 1302 and was largely completed by the late sixteenth century. Like the contemporary Burgos cathedral, it was modeled on northern French Gothic cathedrals of the same period, thanks largely to the close connection of their patron king, Alfonso the Wise, to the court of Louis IX of France.

In contrast to the squat Romanesque fortress cathedrals of much of Spain, these early Gothic cathedrals strain toward the sky with forms that resemble a flickering flame. León's master builders were following the ideas promulgated about a hundred years earlier at the Abbey of St-Denis near Paris, that sunlight flooding through stained glass allowed worshippers to experience the Divine Light of God. Drawing on innovations at St-Denis and the Reims cathedral, the León builders constructed massive flying buttresses to hold up walls that were almost more glass than stone.

In fact, they pushed the idea farther than any other builders in Europe. The cathedral boasts 125 stained glass windows, most of them created from the thirteenth through fifteenth centuries. As if the soaring, ribbed vaults of Gothic cathedrals weren't amazing enough, León brought maximum light to the potentially dark interior. Stone is at a minimum. The light streaming through more than 19,000 square feet of stained glass fills the cathedral with pure color.

There is really nothing to do but sit and let it envelop you. Divine or not, the light is a wonder, both mesmerizing and uplifting. I almost feel sorry for the talented artists and historic figures who are overshadowed by the play of light and color. The fifteenth-century, carved-walnut choir stalls, for example, are among the oldest in Spain and a thirteenth- or fourteenth-century statue of the pregnant Virgin Mary is a touching image of hope and innocence. Laid to rest here are the patron saint of León, San Froilán, a Benedictine monk who helped revive monastic life after the Reconquista, and King Ordoño, whose defeat of the Moors in 917 made León the capital of a powerful medieval kingdom.

In fact, León's first king was crowned in 911—more than a century and a half before the rival kingdom of Castilla was established. Hence the Leonese brag of having twenty-four kings before Castilla ever existed. Since it's such a sunny day, you might as well stroll around the old city center and seek some of them out. The pantheon, or burial vault, of the kings of León is beneath the Basilica de San Isidoro, a handsome Romanesque church. Eleven kings, even more queens, and assorted other nobles are entombed amid a forest of columns topped with Visigothic capitals and beneath a ceiling painted with twelfth-century murals of Biblical scenes and court life. I visited the first time with a sense of duty, expecting a dreary and depressing cellar of tombs. To my surprise, it proved to be an unusual and moving evocation of medieval León.

The cathedral and the basilica constitute the main landmarks of León, but I never miss a chance to enjoy the famous charcuterie of the region. The nearby mountains are almost as famous for their air-dried hams as the mountains of Andalucía, and the Leonese version of chorizo is prized for its spice balance. Most famous of all is *cecina*—smoked, salted, and air-dried beef. A plate of *curados surtidos,* or assorted charcuterie, and a cold beer are a perfect way to soak up the atmosphere on the plaza outside the cathedral.

✳ www.leon.es

# 23 *Spain's First Power Couple*

## EL CID AND JIMENA DÍAZ, BURGOS

A visit to the city of Burgos should start at Plaza de Mío Cid, with it's larger than life-size statue of Rodrigo Díaz de Vivar (1043-1099). The stirring monument captures Spain's national hero, popularly known as El Cid, astride his equally renowned war horse Babieca. The horse surges forward as El Cid brandishes his sword. His long beard and cape swirl in the wind. It's a fittingly dynamic image for the fierce warrior who is lionized in the *"Cantar de Mío Cid."*

The twelfth-century epic poem, the first written in the Spanish language, is ostensibly about its hero's military exploits as the Christian rulers of northern Spain began the centuries-long campaign to regain control from the Moors. But the themes of honor among men and a warrior's love of his wife and family have echoed down through the ages. The anonymous scribe who told the tale of El Cid invented an almost impossibly romantic archetype—the man who was tough and fearless toward the enemy, but soft and tender toward his loved ones.

El Cid was born in the town of Vivar northwest of Burgos, and the big city, once the capital of the kingdom of Castilla, has claimed him as its own. In 1919, the remains of El Cid and his wife Doña Jimena (1046-1116) were interred in the cathedral, where any tour of Burgos should conclude. In October, the city puts on a medieval festival, the Fin de Semana Cidiana, complete with jousting tournaments and an artisan market.

✳ turismoburgos.es (Spanish only)

El Cid spent his youth in the court of Fernando el Magno (the Great) and became military commander to Fernando's son, Sancho II of Castilla in 1065. In addition to campaigns against the Moors, El Cid assisted Sancho in his efforts to seize León and Galicia from his brothers. Things took a bad turn for El Cid in 1072 when Sancho died without legitimate heirs and one of the adversarial brothers was crowned Alfonso VI of León and Castilla.

El Cid threw in his lot with the new king, but Alfonso was understandably leery about the knight's true allegiance. In 1074, El Cid married a relative of Alfonso in what may have been a test of his loyalty. As it turned out, El Cid and Doña Jimena seemed to have had a genuine connection. In signing his marriage contract, he famously wrote, "I, Rodrigo, with my wife, affirm what is written above." The act of granting his wife equal say was unprecedented at the time.

When El Cid was finally forced into exile by Alfonso in 1081, the *"Cantar de Mío Cid"* recounts his tearful farewell to his family. Working for the Moorish rulers of Zaragoza in their battle against other Moorish taifa kingdoms, El Cid established himself as such a powerful force that Alfonso had no choice but to bring him back to court in 1086. El Cid seized control of the city-state of Valencia in 1094 and had a tearful reunion with his wife and with daughters María and Cristina.

The family happiness was undermined, however, when the daughters married brothers who turned out to be of low character.

Shamed for cowardice, the knights took revenge by beating their wives and abandoning them on the side of the road. In the epic poem, El Cid rode to the rescue. The sons-in-law were eventually routed in a duel with his soldiers, and the noble hero found more honorable husbands for his daughters.

There is no historical evidence to support the subplot of the evil sons-in-law, but the historical record is clear that El Cid ruled Valencia until his death in 1099, when Doña Jimena took control. She was forced to abandon the city in 1102 when Alfonso made the strategic decision not to defend it against the Moors. She is presumed to have lived out her life in or around Burgos.

From the Plaza de Mío Cid, walk past the nineteenth-century Teatro Principal and follow the Paseo del Espolón, a pathway with colorful gardens and orderly rows of plane trees. You can enter the old city through the ceremonial Arco de Santa María. One of the medieval city gates, it was remodeled in the sixteenth century to resemble a castle with two towers. Take your time wandering the pedestrian streets, where you'll probably cross paths with pilgrims on their way to Santiago de Compostela (see Chapters 38 and 39). The streets are lined with shops and restaurants, many serving the local version of garlic soup with bread and egg, called *sopa Doña Jimena*.

All streets eventually lead to the Catedral de Santa María. The large cathedral was begun in 1221 and, like the cathedral in León (see Chapter 22), recapitulates the northern French Gothic style in Spain. Work continued on and off until the mid-sixteenth century, adding the bell towers and some of the elaborate ornamentation. The walkway around the cathedral rises on one side so that viewers get an unusually close look at some of the upper level carvings. Constructed over a three-hundred-fifty-year span, the cathedral chronicles the evolution of Gothic art in its paintings, stained glass windows, carved choir stalls and tombs, and elaborate reredos.

✳ www.catedraldeburgos.es

On observing the cathedral, Felipe II (1527-1598) is said to have exclaimed that it seemed "more the work of angels than of men." Most impressive is the 164-foot vaulted dome at the center of the Latin Cross. On clear days, rays of sunlight stream through the stained glass and down onto the red marble tombs of El Cid and Doña Jimena in their place of honor directly beneath the dome.

## RECOMMENDED READING

*The Song of the Cid* by Anonymous, translation by Burton Raffel

# II

*El Norte:*
*La Rioja &*
*Green Spain*

# 24 The French Connection

## MARQUÉS DE RISCAL, LA RIOJA

The Hotel Marqués de Riscal looks for all the world like a giant puddle of shiny silver, gold, and pink ribbons curling up among the vineyards of its eponymous estate. It's as if architect Frank Gehry wrapped up his second building in Spain and tied it with a big bow. Opened in 2006, the hotel is the  centerpiece of the City of Wine, a complex created by one of the area's top producers to bring wine tourism to La Rioja in much the same way as Gehry's startling Guggenheim Bilbao museum building drew people from near and far to that once-floundering industrial city (see Chapter 30).

✳ www.hotel-marquesderiscal.com/en

That's not to say that La Rioja was suffering the sort of decline that had dogged Bilbao. Located in northeast Spain along the Río Ebro, La Rioja has long been Spain's flagship wine region. The thick plantings along both banks of the river are protected from the drying Atlantic winds by the high ridges of the Sierra de Cantabria, while warm and moist winds from the Mediterranean ensure the sweetness of the grapes. The Romans may have introduced wine-making, but the French put the area on the map in the nineteenth century when Bordeaux winemakers crossed the Pyrenees in search of fertile territory free from the phylloxera infestation that was ravaging their beloved vines.

It wasn't such a big move for Spaniard Guillermo Hurtado de Amézago (1794-1878), who had escaped Spain's political turmoil by settling in Bordeaux in 1836. The fifth Marqués de Riscal, he returned to La Rioja in 1858 when he inherited vineyards and winemaking facilities in Elciego after the death of his sister Marceliana. History does not record that the Marqués displayed any interest in making wine when he lived in Bordeaux, but once back on Spanish soil he seems to have thrown himself into making Marqués de Riscal into a powerhouse brand in enological circles.

Setting the standard for La Rioja's eventual wholesale adoption of French wine culture, Hurtado supplemented the indigenous tempranillo grapes with Bordeaux and Burgundy varietals—cabernet sauvignon, pinot noir, merlot, cabernet franc, malbec, semillon. He trellised them in the Bordeaux manner, fermented on the stems in large wooden vats, and aged his reds in small casks of French oak. It was a fully successful translation of Bordeaux wine culture into northern Spain. In 1862, he bottled his first wines, establishing Marqués de Riscal as a pioneer of Rioja wine-making.

These days, Marqués de Riscal is a pioneer of wine tourism in Spain, where the California model of open tasting rooms has yet to take root. At the City of Wine, the tasting is but a prelude. All the sensory pleasures implied by a good bottle of wine are there for the taking.

Winery tours must be reserved in advance and follow the process from the vine to the bottle. The highlight is the "cathedral," a wine cellar that holds 8 million bottles dating back to 1862. Only forty-three lucky couples get to spend the night in Gehry's play-ful hotel. The interior is more restrained than the voluptuous exterior, but it nonetheless takes its cues from the curve of the building. What must tipsy guests make of the tilted walls and oddly shaped windows, with views of the vineyards, the surrounding countryside, and the little town of Elciego?

The outdoor terrace of Bistro 1860, sheltered from the sun by the unfurling ribbons of the titanium roof, offers a commanding view. It looks across the valley and all the way to Elciego's low blocky buildings huddled around the twin stone towers of San Andrés, the town's sixteenth-century church. The fresh air and view are fit for a marquesa, even if it means forgoing the Michelin-starred plates served in the formal Restaurant Marqués de Riscal.

❈ www.marquesderiscal.com

La Rioja would not enjoy the cachet it has today without the influence of the French, whether the tire company restaurant reviewers or the winemakers. To pamper its women guests, Marqués de Riscal aligned with the French again to bring a Spa Vinothérapie Caudalie to the City of Wine. About two decades ago, the Bordeaux-based winery and spa pioneered the concept of Vinothérapie after the felicitous discovery that the antioxidant properties of the grape—particularly the pips and skins and other byproducts of winemaking—can soothe and invigorate the skin. How convenient that wine coun-try compost is the key to banishing crow's feet!

Caudalie is very particular about where it opens new spas, but Marqués de Riscal was as natural a fit as the original Caudalie spa at the Smith Haut Lafite wine estate in Bordeaux. Twisted grape vines hang on the walls of the indoor pool where chaise longues all face the neat rows of vines. Grapes find their way into all kinds of treatments from the cleansing merlot body wrap to the honey-and-wine wrap for dry skin. The ultimate in relaxation is the Barrel Bath—a soak in a deep tub filled with a swirl of exfoliating grape marc and featuring (naturally) a vineyard view.

Add a glass of the house Gran Reserva and you'll have all you need to soothe body, mind, and soul.

## 25 *Hope Flies*

### THE NESTING WHITE STORKS OF ALFARO

At the end of every February, the people of Alfaro begin to antici-
pate the return of the European white storks for the breeding
season. The population of the stately baroque town at the southern
tip of the Rioja wine region swells as the roughly 10,000 human
residents are joined by up to 200 nesting pairs of *cigüeñas* and their
boisterous young. The messy nests of branches and sticks cover just
about every flat surface on the Iglesia Colegiata de San Miguel, the
seventeenth-century baroque church on the Plaza de España—the
town's main square.

You'd never know it by the squawking, squabbling, and flying
feathers in Alfaro, but storks—the birds associated in folklore with
bringing new life—became increasingly threatened as their preferred hunting grounds of wetlands, meadows, and grazing land
shrank during the last half of the twentieth century. Collisions
with power lines have also taken a toll. But according to the nature
conservation foundation EuroNatur, Spain is one of the countries
where white storks are staging a comeback. The rookery on San
Miguel is by far the world's largest urban concentration of the
endangered species. Alfarans watch like anxious grandparents as
each generation of birds hatches, matures, and eventually leaves the
nest. To me, the cycle is hope in action.

✳ www.alfaro.es (Spanish only)

It's almost impossible not to be cheered by the sight of the immense white birds with their long necks, long red beaks, long red legs, and broad wings outlined with black feathers. Despite a wingspan of six and a half to seven feet, the gawky storks are slow fliers. They make their way from their winter feeding grounds in central Africa and Morocco by gliding on the warm thermals across the Strait of Gibraltar and up Spain's western border with Portugal. Solitary nests and small clusters of nests top chimneys, bell towers, and abandoned Roman ruins throughout the western province of Extremadura.

But nothing compares with the avian crowd in Alfaro, where elbow room, so to speak, is at a real premium. The male storks arrive first and set about refurbishing old nests with fresh twigs and grass—or building new ones if their previous spot has been usurped or destroyed. The females come along later. Storks are monogamous for the season, though pairs may stick together over the years out of force of habit, always returning to the same nest. The two birds take turns with the five-week task of incubating the clutch of up to five eggs.

Once the young hatch, the church of San Miguel assumes a busy, animated majesty as the adult storks come and go in an almost constant hunt for food. The black bills of the downy chicks always seem to be open and waiting. Sometimes a mature bird will add a soundtrack to the action by throwing its head back and clattering its bill in a rising and falling staccato rattle.

At about two months old, the chicks have grown their flight feathers and begin to literally test their wings in anticipation of the late-August departure for their African wintering grounds The city has even built an elevated Mirador de Cigüeñas, or overlook, next to the church to let the humans watch as the birds reach for the sky. Day to day, nest to nest, the chicks hop, hop, hop and then furiously flap their wings before flopping back into the sticks. Exhausted, they rest, and then repeat. Up, up, up...and back down. When a bird finally achieves liftoff and becomes airborne for the first time, it is truly a joy and a privilege to behold. Hope, indeed.

# 26 *Wayside Rest*

## SANTO DOMINGO DE LA CALZADA

The town of Santo Domingo de la Calzada began hosting a livestock and agricultural fair about a thousand years ago and traditions die hard in these parts. Every December, the town turns the clock back a millennium and welcomes visitors to La Concepción festival, where they can forget the twenty-first century—at least for a weekend. The old city is transformed into a giant medieval market with traditional crafts, music, dance, falconry demonstrations, jousting tournaments, and even re-enactments of medieval weddings. There is, of course, plenty of food—and plenty of wine. Santo Domingo de la Calzada is located in La Rioja, Spain's most celebrated wine region.

It's also one of the most welcoming spots along the so-called French Route of the Camino de Santiago, or Way of St. James. Pilgrims who still have about 342 miles (550 km) to their final destination of Santiago de Compostela (see Chapter 39) can swap their hiking boots for sandals and spend the night in this little town that is a time capsule of faith and site of one of the most enduring legends of the Spanish Catholic church.

The town is named for Santo Domingo de la Calzada (1019-1109), the shepherd turned hermit who was born Domingo García. Frustrated in his efforts to take vows as a monk, he dedicated his life to improving the pilgrimage route to Santiago. He cleared paths, built a bridge, and most significantly, established a hostelry for pilgrims on the site of the town that now bears his name. The Romanesque building with a magnificent lobby of rough stone walls, arched doorways, and wooden ceiling beams is now the town's *parador*.

My friend and fellow travel writer Patti Nickell, from Lexington, Kentucky, was drawn to the region by the quality of its wines, but quickly became fascinated by the way that past and present mingle so smoothly. "Spain is deeply rooted in the past," she says, "and nowhere is that more apparent than in La Rioja. In Santo Domingo de la Calzada, you can really sense the presence of the twelfth-century pilgrims that the saint took in."

The twenty-first-century pilgrims are in evidence as well. After picking up Compeed blister plasters at the pharmacy and waiting their turn at the town's only coin-operated laundry, most of them head to the cathedral. Practically next door to the parador, it was begun in 1158 and has retained its Gothic look through centuries of enlargements and renovations. It was even fortified in the fourteenth century when wars between the kingdoms of Castilla and Navarra threw the region into turmoil. The facade, completed in the eighteenth century, includes a sculpture of Santo Domingo with the scallop shell of St. James over his head and a shepherd's crook in his right hand.

❊ www.english.catedralsantodomingo.es

He is depicted again on the ornate fifteenth-century mausoleum that stands right inside the entrance and holds the saint's remains. But a much more humble structure commands all the attention. High up on one of the walls, a small cage holds a hen and a rooster, which, as my friend Patti says, attest "to the power of miracles."

A young woman set the miracle in motion, but, alas, her motives were anything but pure. A serving girl at a local inn became enamored of a young pilgrim who was spending the night with his family. When he rebuffed her advances, she hid a silver cup in his pack so that she could accuse him of theft. Punishment was swift and harsh in those days and the young man was sentenced to death by hanging. His devastated parents continued to Santiago de Compostela. On their return route, they found their son alive—but still hanging from the gallows. He had been brought back to life, he said, by Santo Domingo. His overjoyed parents rushed to the mayor's house and arrived as he was about to eat dinner. He was less than pleased to be interrupted and dismissed the news by telling them that their son was as dead as the rooster and hen in his pot. As if on cue, the two birds leapt up and began to crow.

The birds of honor, who do often crow during Mass, are swapped out every few weeks and the town even has a ditty to recall the event: *Santo Domingo de la Calzada, cantó la gallina después de asada.* Less mellifluous in English, it translates as "Santo Domingo de la Calzada, where the chicken sang after being roasted."

It's something for the pilgrims to ponder as they leave the storied town and continue on their way. If they are smart, they have packed some of the town's signature pastries in their backpacks, either the *milagros del santo* shaped like a chicken or the more elaborate *ahorcaditos,* which feature a puff pastry shell filled with almond cream and topped with another piece of pastry in the silhouette of the hanged man.

✻ lariojaturismo.com/en/community/larioja

# A Mad Dash

## PAMPLONA AND THE RUNNING OF THE BULLS

"It is very Spanish to juxtapose gaiety and the threat of tragedy in a single fiesta," food and travel writer Penelope Casas (1943-2013) once wrote. A Greek-American married to a Spaniard, Casas made sharp observations about Spanish culture and the Spanish psyche as she traipsed about the country recording its foodways and recipes. More than most outsiders, she understood what makes Spaniards tick.

In her characterization of the nexus of joy and fear, Casas was referring to the Fiesta de San Fermín held each July 7-14 in Pamplona, the capital of the northern region of Navarra. The festival

ostensibly honors the city's patron saint and was made famous in the English-speaking world through Ernest Hemingway's 1926 novel, *The Sun Also Rises*. The whirlwind week includes a religious procession, parades with giant-headed figures, singing, dancing, fireworks, and lots of eating and drinking. In simple, clipped prose, Hemingway captured the sense of abandon—that feeling of anything goes—that the festival inspires even in those who only watch from the sidelines. Unsurprisingly, the author most savored the unbridled machismo of the festival's signature event, the *encierro*, or running of the bulls through the streets each morning to the bull-ring where they will meet the matadors—and their deaths—later in the day. Whatever your opinion of the institution of bullfighting, the *encierro* taps into the primitive fight-or-flight adrenaline rush that Spaniards savor.

Hemingway's characters more than once grumble about the day-trippers who usurp their favorite café tables, although the crowds in the 1920s were probably nothing like the million or so people who now descend on Pamplona for the fiesta. As you might guess, you should confirm hotel reservations far in advance or plan to join backpackers camping out in the parks and plazas.

The running of the bulls starts at 8 A.M each morning after the runners have prayed to San Fermín for their safety. The traditional dress of white shirts and slacks with red waist sashes and scarves makes for quite a spectacle. About 2,000 people run on week-days, while the numbers swell up to 3,500 on the weekends. Once banned, women are now allowed to join men on the route.

Riley J. Ford, a writer from southern California, was twenty years old when she ran the *encierro* with her eighteen-year-old sister. She wrote about the experience in her novel *Carpe DiEmily*.

"We scouted the bulls the night before," she recalls, "then got up a couple of hours early to do stretching exercises as if we were running a marathon. As beginners we were at the front of the pack," while experienced runners ran closer to the bulls, or "on the horns."

Waiting for a rocket to signal that the bulls were out of the pen, "was one of the scariest moments of my life," says Ford. "I didn't know what was going to happen. Will the bull charge me? Will I trip and fall and be trampled by other runners?"

Ford recalls the surge of testosterone in the largely male pack as the runners took off. "The crowd was deafening," she says. "We followed the leaders and eventually entered the dark tunnel that leads to the bullring. It was so narrow it was terrifying. When we made it into the sunshine of the ring, we had a feeling of complete exhilaration."

Almost thirty years later, Ford says, "I'm a suburban mom now. But when I mention that I ran with the bulls, people look at me differently."

✳ rileyjford.com

Though it must seem much longer as six bulls and eight steers breathe down your neck, the route covers roughly a half-mile through narrow streets lined with barricades to protect spectators. The fleet of foot can cover the distance in under four minutes. Each year there are a few hundred (usually) minor injuries; the city is quick to point out that the last time a runner was killed by a bull was in 1995. "There is a risk involved, but that's also part of the fun of it," says Ford, who hopes that her preteen daughters someday have the chance to run the *encierro*.

When San Fermín concludes for the year, Pamplona reverts to a lovely, quiet city that serves as the seat of government for Navarra, an important wine-shipping center, and a major stop on the Santiago pilgrimage route. It is worth marveling at the high French-style vaults of the Gothic cathedral and seeing the beautifully modeled carvings on the sepulcher of Navarran king Carlos III (1361-1425) and his queen, Eleanor of Castilla (1363-1416), then spending an hour at the Museo de Navarra admiring the Roman mosaics and the faded Gothic frescoes—some of the most powerful in Spain.

Probably the best way to see Pamplona, though, is to trace the route of the *encierro*. The corrals where the bulls are held are near the museum, and the route flows more or less downhill from there. It follows Calle Santo Domingo past the public market and city hall on the Plaza Consistorial, before veering left onto Calle Mercaderes. Within a block, the route makes a dangerous 90-degree right turn onto Calle Estafeta. If you are not being chased by highly annoyed bulls, this is the place to shop for tacky souvenirs emblazoned with bulls. Calle Estafeta is the longest straightaway of the *encierro* so runners and bulls alike get up quite a head of steam. A broad plaza on the right, Plaza del Castillo, used to be a venue for bullfights, but since 1922, Pamplona has had a dedicated bullring, a slight left jog at the bottom of Estafeta. Seating more than nineteen thousand spectators, it's hard to miss. In recognition of the best publicity Pamplona has ever received, there is a bust of Hemingway by the entrance.

✳ www.turismodepamplona.es

But if you really want to channel Don Ernesto and his first wife Hadley when they discovered Pamplona in 1923 (or Jake Barnes and Lady Brett Ashley in *The Sun Also Rises*), sit down for a drink at the stupendous Art Deco-style Café Iruña on Plaza del Castillo. The elegant bar calls itself "rincón de Hemingway," or "Hemingway corner," and with a little imagination, you can almost smell the testosterone over the aroma of gin.

## RECOMMENDED READING

*The Sun Also Rises* by Ernest Hemingway

*Discovering Spain, An Uncommon Guide* by Penelope Casas

*Carpe DiEmily* by Riley J. Ford

# 28 *Speaking in Tongues*

## MONASTERIES OF SUSO AND YUSO

If the sixth-century hermit San Millán (473-574) sought to escape from the world and settle closer to heaven, he certainly chose the right place. From the little La Rioja town of San Millán de la Cogolla that was named for him several centuries later, the narrow and winding road up the slope of Mont San Lorenzo is a demanding drive, even on modern asphalt.

That's where the Monasterio de Suso rose on the site of the saint's rustic hermitage shortly after his death. Far removed from the rest of humankind, this remote community of faith would ultimately become a crucible of the Spanish language. It is now abandoned, and the voices of modern visitors bounce off the stone walls as if to conjure speech from long ago. The monastery is most renowned as what UNESCO calls "the birthplace of the modern written and spoken Spanish language," first rendered as Castilian and Basque margin notations on Latin text. Moreover, Gonzalo de Berceo, the first named poet writing in Castilian Spanish, was born nearby and received his early education—and likely his love of language—from the brothers at the monastery.

The Monasterio de Suso also became an important early pilgrimage site and a detour for those on their way to Santiago de Compostela. (By tradition, San Millán joined Santiago in slaying Moors at the Battle of Simancas in 939.) By the middle of the eleventh century, the monks had outgrown their mountain retreat and moved down to the valley, where the new Monasterio de Yuso was constructed and the remains of San Millán were reinterred. The monastery remained under Benedictine rule until government confiscations in the nineteenth century closed it. Reopened in the twentieth century, Yuso is now an Augustinian community.

✳ www.monasteriodesanmillan.com (Spanish only)

Visits to both monasteries are strictly by guided tour, with separate tickets for each. (A bus takes visitors from Yuso to Suso, though many choose to walk back down.) It is enlightening, even rather jarring, to see how the trappings of monastic life have evolved. Much of Suso was literally carved out of the mountainside, representing a rough-hewn limestone manifestation of a simple, even fanatical faith. From an architectural standpoint, it more closely resembled the restrained pre-Romanesque churches at Oviedo (see Chapter 36) rather than the sprawling, farm-like Cistercian monasteries just a few miles east in Navarra.

By contrast, Yuso is comfortable and refined. Only the walled keep dates from the original eleventh-century construction, while the rest was built between the sixteenth and eighteenth centuries. The Baroque cloister with its fine vaulted ceilings demonstrates a faith that has come into its own with a secure expression of beauty and power. The sacristy of the striking sixteenth-century church holds the monastery's most valued possessions. Along with the usual fine paintings, hand-carved furniture, ancient frescoes, and a golden altar are the books. The volume of Gregorian chants alone weighs 176 pounds. The monastery's library also contains the first verses known to be written in Castilian Spanish.

Like pilgrims of yore, today's travelers often treat the monasteries as a detour from the road between Logroño and Burgos. They may be drawn to the architecture, where history is written in every stone. Or they may want to pause before the ancient texts to marvel at the power of the written word. But it takes more than a brief stop to divine the spirit of the place and to embrace the rhythm and remove of the contemplative life.

Because the monastic community has contracted over the years, an unused building within the keep was renovated and opened in 1995 as a small hotel, La Hostería de San Millán. Like the Spanish *paradors* (see Chapter 46), it offers travelers the opportunity to stay the night in a place steeped in history and decorated accordingly with dark wooden furniture and polished wood floors. The twenty-five rooms are comfortable and affordable. More to the point, they are in San Millán, so you can appreciate the quiet of the keep after the tourists leave, or walk the surrounding trails lost in your own thoughts.

✳ www.hosteriasanmillan.com (Spanish only)

The hillside above the monastery is planted with vineyards—this part of Rioja Alta has grown the finest garnacha and tempranillo for nearly a thousand years. As night falls, stars wink on in clusters in the dark sky. Settle in for dinner at In Vino Veritas, the hotel's gastrobar, with a glass or two of the Monasterio de Yuso red. Rise before morning prayers to see the sun come up over the vineyards. What if every day for the rest of your life were like this? What if the cowl-like hills around San Millán were the bounds of your world? So close to heaven, so far from care....

# 29 *Power of a Perfect Outfit*

## THE CRISTÓBAL BALENCIAGA MUSEUM, GETARIA

Cristóbal Balenciaga (1895-1972), the couturier dubbed by Christian Dior as "the master of us all," came into his own in the understated but elegant Paris couture house that he opened after moving to the city in 1936. But he was born and was first drawn to the intimate world of women's fashion in the big-shouldered fishing village of Getaria on the Basque coast only 15 miles (25 km) west of more glamorous San Sebastián.

For all his success in Paris, Balenciaga never truly abandoned Spain and was laid to rest on a hilltop above town. As if his grave were not enough, the city firmly staked its claim on its native son with a sweeping glass museum building designed by Cuban-born architect Julián Argilagos. When the Cristóbal Balenciaga Museoa opened in 2011, British *Vogue* reported that "the height of Spanish society" turned out for the event—some in their vintage Balenciagas.

It's hard to imagine what the reserved designer would have thought of all the fuss, though he probably would not have been surprised that his clothes were holding up well and still gave their wearers a timeless panache. Balenciaga never granted an interview during his years as a couturier. Moreover, he never even took a victory lap on the runway after his shows, even though *Vogue* editor-in-chief

Diana Vreeland once described the debuts of his collections as so intoxicating that "one fainted—it was possible to blow up and die."

Son of a fisherman, the little boy grew up watching his seamstress mother make clothing for private clients. One of the most important was the Marquesa de Casa Torres, who summered in the area and sponsored young Cristóbal for an apprenticeship in San Sebastián. (The new museum is grafted onto the side of the Palacio Aldamar, the nineteenth-century family villa of his patroness.) As a designer uniquely skilled in sewing, cutting, and draping, Balenciaga dressed everyone from jet-setting socialites to movie stars such as Marlene Dietrich and Lauren Bacall and such cultural icons as Grace Kelly, the Duchess of Windsor, and Jacqueline Kennedy.

When he closed his couture house in Paris in 1968, many considered it the end of a particularly glamorous era. The clothing, photographs, and film clips in the museum help to bring that golden age back to life, when wealthy American society women kept apartments in Paris for their dress fittings.

But what's truly wonderful about Balenciaga is that he did not consider *haute couture* the province solely of the young and thin. On the contrary, he had a very generous attitude toward the female body. "The women he really liked to dress...were oddly enough small, plump, and middle-aged," wrote Mary Blume in *The Master of Us All: Balenciaga, His Workrooms, His World*. "Their roly-poly bodies told him how to confer, or to enhance, beauty."

You have to love a designer who made women feel good about their bodies. For that reason alone, it's worth a pilgrimage to this dramatic museum, also situated on the high ground above the working port.

✳ cristobalbalenciagamuseoa.com/Ingles.html

The museum's collection of 1,600 pieces is the largest in the world and enables curators to trace Balenciaga's trajectory as an artist who trusted his own instincts and sense of invention. The clothing in the permanent exhibition changes annually so that the pieces will remain in good condition, while temporary exhibitions help round out Balenciaga's vision.

The evening wear and wedding gowns are, of course, the show-stoppers. One of the most iconic is the silk-and-tulle wedding gown trimmed in ermine that Queen Fabiola wore for her 1960 marriage to King Baudouin of Belgium and donated to the museum. (A Marquesa de Casa Torres herself, the Queen was descended from Balenciaga's first patron.)

Balenciaga was at the top of his game in the 1950s, when he introduced a number of dress silhouettes such as the now-ubiquitous sheath, the sack dress, and the baby doll, one of his most playful designs. In the process, he liberated women from snug waistlines and gave us the ease and elegance of a more forgiving line.

As a young woman in Paris, author Blume was befriended by Florette Chelot, Balenciaga's top *vendeuse* or saleswoman, and was able to secure a few pieces at bargain prices. "You knew that despite your imperfections you were, thanks to him, perfect," she later wrote.

Now that is power dressing at its most sublime.

### RECOMMENDED READING

*The Master of Us All: Balenciaga, His Workrooms, His World* by Mary Blume

# 30 *The Guggenheim Effect*

## LIFE IN BILBAO, A CITY SAVED BY
## ART AND ARCHITECTURE

Architect Frank Gehry probably never thought about soccer balls when he decided to sheath his undulating, fish-shaped museum in titanium, a silvery metal that gleams in the sun and clings to the building's impossible curves. Aesthetics aside, the famous titanium skin is also strong enough to withstand the soccer balls that local kids bomb against it—or at least those who aren't too busy hurtling their skateboards down the stairs and ramps of the outside terraces.

If the young Bilbainos know that an international panel of critics surveyed by *Vanity Fair* anointed the Guggenheim Bilbao as the most important piece of architecture since 1980, they are clearly unfazed.

When I arrived in Spain's fourth largest city in the early evening, I immediately made my way to the museum, much as a religious pilgrim would head to the cathedral. It's not such a crazy notion. The "Guggenheim effect" of economic revival through landmark architecture has become an international article of faith since the museum opened in October 1997. About a million foreigners travel to Bilbao every year to take in the iconic landmark on the banks of the Río Nervión and to see first-hand how culture can help turn a city around. The kids were a wonderful wake-up call that art is not an abstract concept, but rather part of everyday life.

The adults of Bilbao seem equally nonchalant about their city's international reputation. As I settled into a café table at a nearby plaza, everyone was sipping wine and tapping their feet to a jazz combo as they watched Spandex-clad runners stride down the riverfront path, dwarfed by the museum's looming mass. I had thought there might be a lot of pressure living in a city that has become a cultural phenomenon, but Bilbainos take it in stride.

That's not to say that they don't relish telling the tale of how grim their once-proud industrial city had become. By the 1980s, the shipbuilding and steel industries that had made Bilbao an economic powerhouse had collapsed, leaving behind a poisoned river, double-digit unemployment, and decaying dockyards. Bilbao and the Basque regional government improved transportation and cleaned up abandoned industrial sites along the river. They placed their biggest bet on culture—spending more than $100 million to partner with New York's Guggenheim Museum, which was looking for satellite locations.

Gehry's building rose in just four years and was an instant sensation. With its soaring ceilings and skylit central atrium, the Guggenheim Bilbao is a magnificent cathedral to contemporary and modern art. It's also a gigantic sculpture that has brought art onto the streets and into the everyday life of the city.

Jeff Koons's forty-three-foot-tall topiary sculpture "Puppy" may be even more popular than the celebrated museum building. When curators planned to remove it from the museum plaza, schoolchildren were so distraught that the Guggenheim made it a permanent fixture. Covered in seasonal flowers, it features in every tourist's souvenir photos and serves as a sweet counterpoint to darker, more aggressive works such as Yves Klein's *Fire Fountain* of dancing jets of fire, air, and water or Louise Bourgeois's *Maman*, a thirty-foot-high sculpture of a mother spider. Honestly, I find the Bourgeois piece a little creepy, but cyclists zip blithely through *Maman*'s legs as they pedal the new four-mile (6.4 km) riverfront path that links the Guggenheim to Bilbao's medieval city, intent no doubt on a rendezvous at one of the tapas bars beneath the arcades on the 1826 Plaza Nueva.

The Guggenheim showcases a glittering array of international artists, but Spanish art has not been neglected in the museum or the city. Valencian architect Santiago Calatrava installed one of his signature sail-like pedestrian bridges to connect the new walkway to the far side of the river. And about a third of the artists in the growing Guggenheim collection are Basque, which is decidedly not the same thing as Spanish (just ask any Basque).

The older, less flashy Bilbao Fine Arts Museum has a much better handle on the full sweep of the Basque artistic tradition. Founded in 1908, its galleries are filled with Spanish and Basque works that range from starkly beautiful Gothic madonnas to expressive renderings of shipyard workers that call to mind the tenor of the city in pre-Guggenheim days. The Fine Arts Museum may have more competition for visitors now, but it has also benefited from the Guggenheim effect. It was expanded in 2001 with an airy addition by Basque architect Luis Maria Uriarte.

The people of Bilbao claim that every modern architect with serious ambition either has or wants a building in their city and the tourist office offers walking tours of the bold architecture and sculpture that have followed in the wake of the Guggenheim. The impulse was already in the air. Bilbao's new subway system, designed by Sir Norman Foster, was built 1988-1995. Bilbainos adopted it with zest—they even call the glass hoods over the entries *fosteritos*.

Following Gehry's catalytic example, Argentine architect César Pelli, best known for the twin towers of Kuala Lumpur, created the forty-one-floor Iberdrola Tower office skyscraper, the tallest building in Basque country and another riverfront landmark. Even French designer Philippe Starck got into the act. His remake of a 1909 former wine storage facility into a cultural and athletic center marked his debut as an architect. The brick, iron, and concrete Modernist building was rejected by Gehry as the site for the Guggenheim. But Starck, a lifestyle guru better known for furniture and interior design, created the space that perhaps best sums up the city's new attitude.

Opened in 2010, the Askuna Zentroa features a gallery and concert hall on the lowest level. The ground floor is intentionally dark to provide couples romantic trysting spots amid a forest of columns that support brick and glass cubes that contain a public library and a state-of-the-art gym. There are, of course, restaurants and bars. There's also a rooftop swimming pool with a glass floor. Gazing upward at the swimmers floating in ethereal silhouette, I knew just how to create my personal Guggenheim effect. I headed to the roof, ordered a drink, and stretched out on a lounge chair by the pool. A Bilbaino would do no less.

✳ www.bilbaoturismo.net

## RECOMMENDED READING

*Frank O. Gehry: Guggenheim Museum Bilbao* by Coosje Van Bruggen and Frank O. Gehry

# 31 Off the Rack

## WOMEN IN SPANISH FASHION

Rosalía Mera was the richest self-made woman in the world when she died in 2013 at age 69. *Forbes* estimated her worth at about $6 billion—not bad for a woman of humble origins born in the Galician capital of A Coruña. She dropped out of school before she reached her teens, began making clothing, and founded a little shop called Zara with then-husband, Amancio Ortega, in 1975.

The pioneer of instant response to sartorial trends, Zara became ubiquitous in Spain and abroad. Even those who are fatigued with the shortcomings of "fast fashion" find the success of Mera and the company she helped found to be a reminder that Spain is a major player in the modern fashion world. Here are some other women who have made Spain and style synonymous. Look for their brands in stand-alone boutiques and department store counters all over the country.

Also born in Galicia, Purificación García (b. 1952) is a true woman of the world. She grew up in Montevideo, Uruguay, studied textile engineering in Canada, and began making and selling clothing while living on the island of Mallorca. After settling in Barcelona, the largely self-taught designer presented her first collection in 1981. Her upbeat and even whimsical style was received with open arms by Spanish women looking to break out of the bland uniformity of the Franco years.

❋ www.purificaciongarcia.com/cz

In 1998, García formed a partnership with three brothers of Spanish fashion designer Adolfo Dominguez to design ready-to-wear clothing and accessories for both women and men. Her graceful updates on classic style remain fresh and uncluttered and her bags and purses have proved enduringly popular. In 2001, García published her first book, *Tener Estilo*, which, alas, has not been translated into English. But García has often spoken about her approach to style, which does not involve flashing the most expensive brand names. And, contrary to Coco Chanel, she believes that good fashion sense can be cultivated—even in those to whom it does not come naturally. Having style, she says, "is knowing how to walk, how to move, how to cross the street, how to kiss a child...."

Maybe it's the weather of "green Spain," but something about the north seems to breed fashion designers. In 2006, sisters Uxia and María Dominguez (who carefully guard their ages) opened their first Bimba & Lola store in Bilbao, only about 50 miles (80 km) west of the museum of Spanish fashion legend Cristóbal Balenciaga in Getaria (see Chapter 29). Clearly fashion runs in their blood. They are the nieces of Adolfo Dominguez and worked in their father's clothing distribution business before branching out on their own. They named their brand for their dogs and chose a greyhound as their logo—which pretty much defines their playful approach to fashion. Their sporty, largely affordable pieces are feminine, modern riffs on boarding school style—squarely targeted at an audience of worldly millennials willing to spend a few extra euros to stand out from the crowd.

❋ www.bimbaylola.com/cms

There's no missing a woman dressed by Madrid-based designer Ágatha Ruiz de la Prada (b. 1960), whose unrestrained use of color

and graphic shapes has characterized her work since her first collection in 1981. Known as one of the most visible design figures in
La Movida, the exuberant movement of creativity that exploded in
Madrid in the 1980s, she is like the hippie seamstress who refused
to grow up—and why should she? She seems to keep her finger on
the pulse of changing taste. Yet her pop sensibility has remained
in the design DNA of her company even as it has grown and she
has branched out from women's clothing to menswear, children's
clothing, ceramics, shoes, housewares, sunglasses, watches, umbrel-
las—and just about anything else to which she can affix her signature
heart (or her name).

✳ www.agatharuizdelaprada.com

For her, dull is a cardinal sin. "What leaves me stunned is that
theoretically, fashion changes every six months," she once said,
"and yet everyone dresses the same."

Not if she has her way.

# 32
## A Father-Daughter Culinary Dynasty

DINING AT RESTAURANT ARZAK,
SAN SEBASTIÁN

There's so much to like about San Sebastián on Spain's Bay of Biscay coast. It's been a favored beach resort since the late nineteenth century, when Queen Regent Maria Cristina made it her summer residence. About 30 miles (48 km) southwest of France's more self-consciously chic Biarritz, San Sebastián managed to enter the twenty-first century with much of its Belle Époque grace intact.

✳ www.sansebastianturismo.com/en

It all begins, of course, at the beach. Playa de la Concha, a sublime mile-long crescent of soft white sand and slow rolling waves anchored by rocky headlands, is one of the best Atlantic beaches in Europe. Unlike newer high-rise beach developments, its shores are lined with nineteenth-century Neoclassical buildings erected when the city rebuilt itself after near total destruction during Spain's war with Napoleon. The result is a setting that's guaranteed to make you feel glamorous even as you stroll the beachside promenade in flip-flops while licking a dripping ice cream cone. Every September, the film world's A-listers tread this same path as they make their appearances at the San Sebastián International Film Festival, launched in 1953 to boost the city's profile and give people something to do when it gets too cold for swimming.

✳ www.sansebastianfestival.com

But what's truly great about San Sebastián is that its residents love to eat. Make that live to eat. In this city of appreciative and discriminating diners, you'll find great, inventive food at modest prices (more on that in the next chapter). And if you want to splurge on a once-in-a-lifetime meal, you will not be disappointed. That's just what my husband and I decided to do when we put ourselves in the hands of legendary chef Juan Mari Arzak and his daughter and co-chef Elena Arzak at their eponymous family restaurant.

"Food has always been very important here and nobody knows why," Elena said when she and her father chatted briefly with us before heading into the kitchen to oversee lunch for a room full of eager diners. "Most of our customers are local," she said. "They save and come here once or twice a year. They need it. They want to see what we are doing."

In the 1970s, Juan Mari and fellow Basque chef Pedro Subijana fomented a culinary revolution by applying the sensibilities of French Nouvelle cuisine to the hearty peasant and fishing village dishes of the Basque country. In the process, they catapulted "new Basque cooking" to the forefront in Spain and soon entered the pantheon of avant-garde European gastronomy. Suddenly San Sebastián was on every foodie's radar.

We could feel the buzz of excitement as we took our seats in the simply furnished modern dining room. We had half expected a reverential hush in this three-Michelin-star temple of gastronomy, but the room was alive with talk and laughter as couples, families, and groups of friends relished their Basque birthright of good food—or more accurately, course after course of great food too surprising to ever imagine, but somehow just right.

Juan Mari and Elena spend at least a day a week in the restaurant's research kitchen perfecting new dish ideas from concept to execution. "We use conventional foods in our cooking, but try to use up-to-date technique that somehow transforms them," Elena said. "That enables us to create plates that no one else has yet imagined." True to their word, the "low-tide monkfish" that came to our table was a mock sea floor with a small monkfish loin, spherified red pepper that looked like caviar, and piquillo pepper "coral." The muddy ocean floor, it turned out, was a savory cream of clams. For one dessert (there were several), the waitress placed a bowl of warm, honey-flavored "soup" before us, then poured on a colder tart, bright red cherry liquid that immediately broke into a kaleidoscopic fractal pattern. We waited until it was still before we dared dip spoons into the bowls. The Arzaks clearly know showmanship as well as flavor.

✳ www.arzak.info

For all their innovation, the Arzaks have not lost sight of their family's long history of feeding the hungry diners of San Sebastián. Juan Mari's grandparents unwittingly launched a culinary dynasty when they opened a modest wine cellar and tavern in what was then the outskirts of the city in 1897. Juan Mari's mother and Elena's grandmother, Paquita, transformed the restaurant into the go-to place for special celebrations; brides were known to set their wedding dates based on availability of the dining room. Juan Mari took over the restaurant in 1966 and soon turned the tables, so to speak, by making the meal itself the cause of celebration.

Juan Mari trained at a school of hostelry in Madrid, but acknowledges Paquita as his most important influence and her respect for the farmers, fishermen, and foragers as his most valuable lesson. Elena was also inspired by her grandmother, but told us that it was her father who nurtured her early confidence in the kitchen. "Since I was young," she said, "he encouraged me to make plates."

After starting in the family kitchen, Elena honed her skills by studying and working in Switzerland, London, Paris, Italy, and with other top chefs in Spain. But she was destined all along to return home to San Sebastián and to join her father as an equal at Arzak, which she did in 1995. Seasoned by the outside world, she embraced her essential "Basque spirit," as she puts it.

"When we cook, we have tastes in mind," she says. "The Basque code of flavors is unique—it comes from our history, and from the flavors of our childhoods. The Basque food tradition is very strong."

And in very good hands.

# 33 A Spanish Movable Feast

## EATING PINTXOS, SAN SEBASTIÁN

"A woman walks into a tapas bar" is not the set-up for a bad joke. It is, however, something you should plan to do wherever you happen to find yourself in Spain. The tradition of "going out for tapas" is a way of life in Spain—and the country's contribution to casual dining. Your visit will not be complete until you've claimed your place at a bar to enjoy a drink, a small bite of food, and the noisy, lively scene. Once you're in the groove, you may even find yourself doing as other patrons do and letting your paper napkins float down toward but rarely into the trash receptacle by your ankles.

If you've eaten at tapas-inspired "small plates" restaurants outside Spain, you may think that tapas are a meal. Spaniards know better. Tapas are simply little treats that accompany a drink and they are usually consumed while standing up. (Beware of drippy tapas like *patatas bravas,* coated with a thin paprika sauce or anchovies in a puddle of olive oil that can wreck havoc with your wardrobe.) Sometimes a drink will be accompanied by a modest free tapa—a thin slice of potato omelet, a saucer of salty Marcona almonds, or a plate of freshly fried potato chips. A couple of tapas will stave off hunger until the typically late dinner hour, which is why you'll find tapas bars most crowded in the late afternoon and early evening. Spaniards enjoy a tapa and a drink and a chat with the person they are rubbing elbows with at the bar. Then they move on to another spot for a different bite of food and a fresh conversation. Going out for tapas is as much about socializing as it is about food.

One of my favorite cities for a tapas-hop is San Sebastián, where, in typical Basque fashion, tapas have a different name. They're called *pintxos*. The city is flush with Michelin-starred restaurants but the delight in creativity and invention is too great to be contained in a few top kitchens. Even in modest bars, *pintxos* have a certain flair and the most ambitious chefs call them *pintxos creativos*.

On weekends, it seems that all of San Sebastián goes out for *pintxos*. "We are a very social city," Ana Intxausti agreed when she joined me for a late afternoon of tapas hopping. "Our businesses don't need team-building programs. Just give everyone twenty euros and send them to a bar for a *caña* [small glass of beer]."

Intxausti has worked in the wholesale fish industry and shepherded celebrities around the San Sebastián Film Festival. "Even a woman alone is very safe and will have no problems at all visiting *pintxos* bars," she said. "Everybody mingles in the same places—grandparents, children, people with their dogs." But for those who prefer companionship, she has recently begun offering *pintxos* tours for individuals.

✳ Professional Association of Tourist Guides of the Basque Country: www.apite.eu

In many cities, tapas-hopping is a fairly casual activity. But the folks in San Sebastián take it more seriously. "When we go out," Intxausti said, "we don't choose a bar, we choose a food specialty." We could have eaten ourselves silly on Calle 31 de Agosto in the old city. The street is practically lined with bars where smokers spill out onto the sidewalks with food and drink in hand. Spain outlawed smoking in bars in 2012. "Owners of bars complained," Intxausti said, "but we non-smokers are happy."

We began by detouring down side streets until we reached Ganbara Bar-Asador. One look at the overflowing baskets of fresh mushrooms on the bar and I knew what we were in for. We consulted with the cook and settled on a gorgeous plate of sautéed mixed wild mushrooms with a couple of glasses of *txakoli*, the tart white wine characteristic of the Basque coast. Each of the mushrooms had a slightly different flavor. Some were chewy, others soft and buttery. Intxausti approved. "Texture is very important in Basque cuisine."

✳ www.ganbarajatetxea.com

The genius of a tapas-hop is that it gives you a chance to digest between stops. The Basques are legendary fishermen—they were fishing the Grand Banks for centuries before North America was officially discovered—and fresh seafood plays a huge role in Basque cuisine. For delicious fresh fish we stopped next at Restaurante Bernardo Etxea, where we broke the unwritten rule of one *pintxo* per bar. We couldn't resist a *txangurro* (spider crab) salad made with garlicky aioli and a plate of grilled *txiperones* (squid) dusted with smoky paprika.

✳ www.bernardoetxea.com (Spanish only)

The Basques also love grilled beef and Intxausti wanted to make sure I had a taste. For our final stop, we returned to Calle 31 de Agosto and found a place at the bar of Restaurante Gandarias. Soon we were eating small pieces of grilled sirloin on rounds of French bread and topped with green Gernika peppers—one of the essential Basque flavors. "We use the products from all around us very well," Intxausti said as we finished our last glasses of wine.

A Basque would expect no less.

✳ www.restaurantegandarias.com

# 34

## Buried Magic

### PREHISTORIC CAVE ART, CANTABRIA

María Justina Sanz de Sautuola was not yet ten years old when she made a discovery that rocked the worlds of science and art. In 1879 she accompanied her amateur archeologist father, Marcelino Sanz de Sautuola, as he explored the Altamira cave in Cantabria that had been discovered only a decade earlier. When I first learned about her in my high school Spanish class, I pictured María as a bored kid, dragged along into a dark cave when she'd rather be at home playing with her friends. I imagined her wandering around, kicking at the ground—until she looked up and saw paintings of animals on the ceiling. In that instant, she discovered the first prehistoric cave paintings known in modern times.

Other discoveries were to follow, but the beautifully rendered bison, horses, and other animals on the walls and ceiling of the Altamira cave remain some of the finest prehistoric paintings yet unearthed. They are so vivid and accomplished that it took more than two decades of heated debate and research before they were universally acknowledged as authentic. After a visit to the caves, Pablo Picasso famously declared "after Altamira, all is decadence."

I had always assumed that I would see for myself someday, but I waited too long. Bacteria carried in by visitors was causing so much damage to the art that the cave was closed to the public. In 2001, the Museo de Altamira opened outside the village of Santillana del

Mar near the site of the cave. The centerpiece is a full-size replica of the cave, while adjacent museum displays tell the story of the discovery of the cave and fill in details about the Ice Age humans dwelling at the northern edge of the inhabitable world.

✳ en.museodealtamira.mcu.es

I know that Altimira, populated between 22,000 and 13,000 years ago, is too rare a touchstone of early humanity to risk its destruction in just a few generations. And I am the first to admit that the recreated cave and museum are very well executed. But I was still crushed. I didn't want to experience the latest in museum technology and interpretation. I wanted magic. I wanted to reach back across the millennia and stand where people had found shelter at the end of the Ice Age. I wanted to see the images that they had created with their own hands.

Every traveler is disappointed now and then—what matters is how you deal with it. Sometimes you just have to move on. But I was fortunate. The limestone hills of Cantabria are full of caves. With a little research I discovered that seven others—smaller and less famous—are open for tours under the aegis of the Cantabrian government. There's even a website where you can make reservations (see below), which are essential since the number of tours and number of visitors per tour are carefully controlled to protect the caves.

✳ cuevas.culturadecantabria.com/en

I settled on El Castillo, part of a labyrinth of caves about 15 miles (24 km) farther up in the mountains. The route from the village of Puente Viesgo was hard to find and I began to despair until a small sign finally pointed the way. Discovered in 1903, El Castillo shows archeological evidence of use by humans—both Neanderthal and Homo Sapiens—over the last 150,000 years. The art on its walls is the oldest known cave art in the world, some of it dated at 40,800 years before the present.

My group of about ten followed our guide into the depths of the high-vaulted cave where ancient bands of people would gather around a fire. I could see that it was warm, dry, and safe and I could almost picture the reflected firelight flickering on the stone walls. Soon our guide began to point out images with a flashlight beam. One after another, a horse, a deer, and a bison emerged from the darkness. They were all simply, but not naively, drawn. The ancient artists used the contours of the stone to shape the bodies of the animals and make them seem as if they were in motion.

The drawings in El Castillo are not as clustered as those on the walls of Altamira. I had to patiently search them out. But those elusive animals spoke to me across the ages. They were, in fact, magic. Perhaps even more wondrous were the dozens of hands—white outlines surrounded in red pigment—that ran throughout the cave. Four hundred centuries ago people left their mark to claim their home, to make themselves known, or to say, most simply, "I was here."

# 35 *Green Spain*

## DRIVING AND HIKING IN THE PICOS DE EUROPA

Spain has no shortage of mountains—the whole Iberian peninsula is surrounded by them—but my favorite range is probably the Picos de Europa. Declared Spain's first "natural park" in 1918, they are the jagged limestone peaks of the central Cantabrian Mountains that wall off the green north coast from the arid plateau of Castilla y León. The actual peaks average only around 8,500 feet, but their precipitous vertical drop makes them among the country's most dramatic.

The first time I ever traveled through them on the winding N-630 highway from León toward Oviedo, I had to pull over to the narrow side of the road just to admire a double rainbow over the misty green valley that swept down toward the sea. There really is a kind of magic in these mountains. The north slopes are pocked with caves that hold some of the earliest signs of human habitation in Europe (see Chapter 34). A little higher up, those same slopes abound with sheep, goats, and cows whose milk produces some of Spain's greatest cheeses. And higher still is Spain's most romantic patriotic shrine.

To explore the area, I like to start at the Asturian village of Cangas de Onís, which has a Roman bridge, a dolmen archeological site, and a lot of nice bars and hotels to recommend it. (It's also close to Arriondas, a tiny village that, improbably, has three Michelin stars for its two restaurants.)

Just a little over 6 miles (10 km) uphill from Cangas de Onís, "Covadonga" is literally a place name to conjure with—the Spanish equivalent of Valley Forge or the Alamo. By tradition, a Visigothic warlord named Pelayo ambushed a troop of Moorish soldiers in this mountain valley in 722 and sent them fleeing for their lives. Later glorified as the Battle of Covadonga, the skirmish marked the beginning of the reconquest of Spain by the Christians. Pelayo was crowned king of the Asturians, and his descendants became the kings of Castilla, Leon, and Galicia—and ultimately the kings of Spain.

✳ www.cangasdeonisycovadonga.com (Spanish only)

All manner of legends have grown up about the battle and the Christian victory, not least of which is that Pelayo's band carried a banner (or perhaps a small statue) of the Virgin Mary, whose intervention was no doubt responsible for the outcome. What began as a "sacred cave" with a small shrine to the Virgin and a slot tomb in the rock wall for Pelayo's sarcophagus (he died in 737) has been superseded by a complex of buildings centered on the late nineteenth-century Basilica de Nuestra Señora de Covadonga. Unless you are especially devout, steer clear of the enormous church and the busloads of religious tourists in favor of following the one-mile trail up the river valley to the Santa Cueva.

The trailhead along the stream flowing down from Covadonga is at the back of the parking lot across the road from Casa Rural Priena. Since this is the rainy side of the Picos, the landscape is lush and green, despite limestone karst beneath the soil. Butterflies flit through the valley and birdsong fills the air. The path climbs slowly along the stream bank until the foliage parts to reveal a towering waterfall. In the pool at the bottom is a manmade fountain, La Fuente de los Siete Caños, or Fountain of Seven Pipes. Legend holds that whoever drinks from it will marry within the year. On the side of the pool, 101 stone steps lead up the cliff face to the chapel and tomb, moving in their simplicity.

Back at Cangas de Onís, it's an easy half-hour drive east along AS-114 to the village of Las Arenas de Cabrales. Many maps simply identify it as Las Arenas, but the Cabrales designation is an important one. Queso de Cabrales is a protected name for the local blue cheese made from a mix of raw milk from sheep, goats, and cows, inoculated with the penicillium mold, and aged for two to six months in limestone caves. Many farmers along this road make their own version, and some of them sell it at roadside stands. The perfect foil for the local hard cider, Cabrales is one of the most pungent of Europe's blue cheeses. The producers have banded together to create an exhibition center, the Cueva del Queso, in Las Arenas, but I find a cheese plate and cider at one of the village bars introduction enough.

✳ www.fundacioncabrales.com (Spanish only)

Drivers might skip the hard cider, since the drive from Las Arenas to Sotres clings to narrow ledges as it cuts through the dramatic gorge of the Río Cares. At Sotres, the CA-185 leaves the river route for the high ground, winding up, up, and up to the village of Fuente Dé. This is the highest village in the Picos at about 3,500 feet, and it's popular with hikers. Since getting here inevitably takes some time, it's best to spend the night at the very reasonably priced *parador*—really more like a hunting lodge than the typical historic estate. The dark skies here are awash with stars.

After a good breakfast in the café, it's only a couple of minutes' walk to the base of the Fuente Dé Teleférico, the super-swift gondola system that whisks twenty people at a time up to an observation platform at 5,980 feet on the Áliva ridge. The ride takes just four minutes. From the cable car platform, a wide packed-dirt path leads slightly downhill for about twenty minutes, where it divides into three separate trails. Walking on these heights feels like being at the top of the world. The best way to revel in that feeling without really breaking a sweat is to take the split marked as the Puertos de Áliva route (PR-PNPE 24). About a half hour down this trail, you can stop at the Hotel de Áliva lodge for hikers, have a drink, then return to the *teleférico*. The route actually continues downhill another 8 miles (13 km) or so to Fuente Dé, I've been told. But if your mountain cravings have been fully satisfied, take the gondola back.

✳ www.cantur.com

# 36 The Unsung Star of Vicky Cristina Barcelona

## CELTIC CITY OF OVIEDO

Oviedo, the capital of northern Spain's Principality of Asturias, has been in the spotlight of late, mostly because it's the birthplace of Queen Letizia, wife of Felipe VI. She's only been queen since the June 2014 abdication of Juan Carlos I, but she has already made her mark in the world of fashion. *Harper's Bazaar* has proclaimed the former journalist a "style icon," noting that she "infuses her professional wardrobe with chic statement pieces and a hint of sultry appeal."

But for straight out sultry, you can't beat Oviedo's cameo appearance in the 2008 Woody Allen film *Vicky Cristina Barcelona*. When soulful painter Juan Antonio (Javier Bardem) wants to seduce two young American women spending the summer in Barcelona, he invites them on a weekend jaunt to Oviedo. "The city is romantic, the night is warm and balmy, and we are alive," he purrs as he goes about breaking down the defenses of Vicky (Rebecca Hall), the more reserved of the two women.

Writer and director Allen is equally enamored of the city, though he seems better at putting words in the mouths of his characters. Actually, Allen and Oviedo seem to have a mutual love affair. After awarding him the Premio Principe de Asturias de Las Artes (the Prince's Prize for the Arts) in 2002, the city erected a life-size bronze statue of Allen in full stride on Calle Uria at the corner of Calle Milicias Nacionales. (Perhaps he's in a hurry to do some shopping since the shops are known for good prices on leather goods.) In a plaque at his feet, Allen enthuses over the "delicious, exotic, beautiful, clean, pleasant, tranquil and pedestrianised city. It is as if it did not belong to this world, as if it did not exist. ... Oviedo is like a fairy tale."

✳ www.turismoviedo.es

Fairy tale may be going a bit far, but I see what Allen was getting at. The city does have its own unique sensibility. Men in three-quarter-length breeches and waistcoats and women in puffy white blouses and full skirts flood across the plazas on summer weekends to dance to the piercing skirls of *la gaita* (the Asturian version of bagpipes). It's a reminder of the region's deep Celtic roots.

Waiters put on a show as they pour local hard cider from shoulder height into small glasses without spilling a drop, aerating the barely sparkling drink to wake up the flavor. In a frenzy of civic whimsy, Oviedo has erected more than one hundred sculptures on the pedestrian streets since the early 1990s. And the city's green center, Campo de San Francisco, is home to pea fowl who often wander off the grass and onto the sidewalks. I once saw two peacocks, dragging their tails behind them, dutifully use the crosswalk to strut across the street in front of the Hotel de la Reconquista, now a Eurostars property.

The landmark building opened in 1770 as an orphanage and children's hospital and became a luxury hotel about two centuries later. In the movie, Juan Antonio, Vicky, and Cristina (Scarlett

Johansson) spend their nights here—and end one evening drinking far too much wine sitting on the cushy couches in the grand central lobby where Renaissance columns support the upper arcade.

Juan Antonio was most eager to show the women the austere, weighty pre-Romanesque churches on Monte Naranco, a little more than a mile from the city center. Built as a royal chapel for Ramiro I of Asturias (best known to history for fending off Viking attacks) in the ninth century, the diminutive San Miguel del Lillo nestles on a green lawn backed by forested hillside. The much larger—and surprisingly tall—Santa María del Naranco was originally Ramiro's hunting lodge before being converted to a church in the twelfth century. Although Santa María still boasts some intricate carved hunting scenes and beautifully articulated Visigothic capitals, both churches have been stripped of religious statuary. They stand like sentries above the city, revealing the barebones essence of faith.

Back in town, you can wander the atmospheric stone streets of the old city as lovers would, delighting in the details. The highest point, naturally, is occupied by the Catedral de San Salvador, where the Holy Chamber has magnificent examples of Asturian goldsmithing. The stars of the archeology museum behind the cathedral are the pre-Romanesque sculptures removed from the churches on Monte Naranco and some of the other early chapels in the foothills of the Picos de Europa. Across from the cathedral, the Museo de Bellas Artes de Asturias has a particularly detailed and gory depiction of the third-century life and martyrdom of Santa Marina—including a panel where she emerges from the belly of Satan, who had been disguised as a dragon.

The narrow streets lead downhill from the cathedral. The fresh food market is on Plaza del Fontán and the restaurants surrounding it offer hearty plates of *fabada Asturiana*, the regional stew of beans studded with sausage and pork. Adjacent Plaza Daoíz y Vélarde is a favorite performance space for bagpipers and folk troupes and hosts a lively flea market on Sundays.

# 37 Galicia's Joan of Arc

## THE TALE OF MARÍA PITA OF A CORUÑA

Legend holds that Hercules founded the Galician port city of A Coruña by beheading the monster Geryon and making this Atlantic-facing peninsula safe for settlement. But the most revered defender of A Coruña is not a Greco-Roman demigod, but a flesh and blood woman whose bravery turned the tide during a devastating sixteenth-century British invasion.

A monument to the four-time married and four-time widowed María Pita lies at the heart of this seafront city that launched the 130 ships of the Spanish Armada in 1588. The so-called "invincible" fleet was charged with defeating queen Elizabeth I and bringing England under the control of the Spanish king Felipe II. Although the Armada was foiled more by terrible storms than English cannon, England's Sir Francis Drake claimed the glory for Spain's resounding defeat. In 1589, he led an English fleet across the English Channel to teach A Coruña a lesson and to establish a foothold in Spain.

After days of fighting, all seemed lost as English troops breached the walls of the old city where the outnumbered citizens had taken refuge. Suddenly María Pita mounted the wall, killed a British soldier, and captured the British colors. A Coruñans—men and women alike—rose to fight another day. The sight of an ordinary housewife overwhelming a trained warrior had a disspiriting effect on the British troops. Confronted with an energized resistance and fearing Spanish reinforcements, Drake eventually withdrew.

The electrifying moment is captured in a bronze statue on Plaza de María Pita. In her twenties at the time, María Pita, sometimes called the "Joan of Arc of Galicia," stands defiantly with a lance in her raised right arm and a sword tucked in her belt. At her feet, a British soldier slumps face-up over the barrel of a cannon.

María Pita lived until 1643, and her effigy surveys her city in perpetuity from a granite perch. Her eponymous plaza divides the old town from the newer city and is A Coruña's social and political center. It's dominated by the ornate, three-domed city hall and ringed with residential buildings with the elegant glassed-in upper galleries that earned A Coruña the nickname "City of Glass." Sheltered beneath arcades, bars and restaurants draw people into the square all day and well into the night. Arrive during Las Fiestas de María Pita in August, and on many evenings you'll find concerts in full swing on the plaza.

❊ www.turismocoruna.com

If you want to delve deeper into María Pita's life and times, you can peruse the exhibits in the nearby Casa Museo de María Pita in the home that she shared with her first husband. But I find it more satisfying to simply take in the city that—free from British domination—prospered on its own terms.

There's a lot to be said for A Coruña's peninsular location. The city is almost always suffused in soft ocean light, and with nowhere to sprawl, it has remained compact and eminently walkable. The main gate of Plaza de María Pita leads toward the harbor where you can watch the comings and goings of the fishing fleet of about 50 deep-sea trawlers and 120 in-shore fishing boats that supplies famous Galician seafood to all of Spain and most of Europe. In

1803, the ship *María Pita* sailed from the harbor to deliver smallpox vaccine to European colonies in the Americas, Philippines, Macau, and Canton. Led by physician Francisco Xavier de Balmis, the expedition pioneered vaccination on a global scale.

From the working port, it's easy to connect to the Paseo Marítimo. The city capitalized on its geography by creating this eight-mile beach promenade for walking and bicycling. The promenade officially begins at Castelo de San Antón which was built in the sixteenth century to fortify the harbor after Drake's raid and now houses an archeology museum. The paseo roughly sketches the outline of the peninsula as it leads past pleasure boat moorings, seaside gardens, an aquarium, and hidden coves and rocky cliffs. It follows the sandy sweep of Orzán and Riazor beaches (separated by the Meliá María Pita Hotel) before finally concluding at the fishing port of Portiño with its technicolor sunsets.

At about the midpoint of the promenade, a lone lighthouse stands on a high bluff. Built by the Romans at some point after Julius Caesar pacified the area in the first century B.C., it still guides ships around the dangerous outer rocks of the peninsula. The blocky stone exterior dates from the eighteenth century, but A Coruña's beacon is considered the oldest Roman lighthouse in the world. A climb to the top will reward you with a seagull's eye view of the bay and port. The lighthouse, by the way, is called the Torre de Hercules. María Pita may be first in the hearts of A Coruñans, but the muscular ancient hero still gets his due.

# 38 *Step by Step*

## PILGRIMAGE ON THE CAMINO DE SANTIAGO

"[R]eputation has played a large part in the history of travelling women," wrote Jane Robinson in the introduction to *Unsuitable for Ladies: An Anthology of Women Travellers.* "It is hardly surprising that the first women travellers of all (or at least, those who first wrote about their travels) were pilgrims. While a worthy name in this world may not have been a priority to them, the report they hoped to accompany them to the next most certainly was."

Many of those lady pilgrims probably walked the Camino de Santiago—the most famous and well-beaten pilgrimage path in continental Europe. For nearly twelve centuries, pilgrims have journeyed to the tomb of St. James the Apostle, the patron saint of Spain, in Santiago de Compostela (see Chapter 39). There are many roads to Santiago, but the path most traveled is the French Route, which begins in St. Jean-Pied-du-Port in the foothills of the French Pyrenees and concludes 485 miles (780 km) later. Other routes merge with it along the way, including paths through Bilbao and Oviedo, and across Aragón through Pamplona. Still other pilgrims walk the Camino Portugués from Lisbon through southern Galicia or the Vía Plata from Sevilla through Extremadura.

Whichever route they followed, early pilgrims undertook the journey in the hopes that it would ease their way into heaven. Their modern counterparts have a far more mixed bag of motivations and expectations. Ann Kirkland, who founded Classical Pursuits to offer culturally oriented learning vacations, decided to give herself the gift of time and contemplation for a milestone birthday in 2010.

✳ peregrinossantiago.es

"I did something I had never done before," she says. "I took off six weeks on my own and walked the French Route for five weeks, up and over the Pyrenees and on...."

The experience did not change her in a radical way, Kirkland admits. But "it's there with me all the time. When I find myself getting too busy, it's a reminder that there is a way of being in the world that is different." She came away from the journey with "a kind of awareness—a sense of being in a place that always brings out the best in you and in the people you meet along the way. Everyone is wishing everyone '*buen camino.*' It seems so simple. Why can't the world be like that?"

The route varies from a narrow path through the mountain woods to a spacious carriage road paralleling modern highways as it crosses broad plains planted with grapevines and row crops. It passes through ancient villages and large cities, marked at least every kilometer by a sign with a scallop shell, symbol of St. James. In cities, the shell is usually made of brass and embedded in the pavement. Pilgrims pause at country churches and glorious Gothic cathedrals and rest the night in bare-bones hostels, ancient inns, and—when exhaustion overtakes them too far from town—in open fields beneath the starry sky. Even in town they recognize each other by the scallop shells on their walking sticks or backpacks. A camaraderie of shared purpose takes hold.

By 2012, Kirkland had incorporated a Camino walking tour into the offerings of Classical Pursuits. After three pilgrimages along the French Route, she plans to offer a journey along the Portuguese Route. Grass has never grown over the Camino, but the number of pilgrims has certainly ebbed and flowed, particularly during times of war. Interest is fairly high right now, thanks in part to the 2010 film *The Way*, in which Martin Sheen portrays a father who decides to complete the pilgrimage that his estranged son had started before his untimely death. According to a June 2015 article in *The New York Times*, 237,810 people were certified as having completed the route in 2014—a jump from just 423 in 1984.

Women make up at least half the members of Kirkland's groups of no more than twelve. They tend to walk 9 to 14 miles (15 to 22 km) per day at their individual paces and reunite each evening for food, conversation, and rest. (After the 2015 murder of a woman pilgrim, Kirkland advises single walkers to always keep other pilgrims in sight on the trail.)

❊ www.classicalpursuits.com

Some people walk simply for the challenge of making it to the end of the route, while others share something of the faith that motivated the earliest pilgrims. Kirkland recalls two Filipino sisters who sang and prayed the rosary as they walked, as well as a Mormon doctor from Salt Lake City who was eager to participate in Masses and Vespers. "She wanted to explore a different type of spirituality," Kirkland says. Still others are Catholics who have fallen away from the Church, but find along the Camino a more personal, less rule-bound way to practice their faith.

All pilgrims savor the deep sense of history. "The Camino is so old," says Kirkland. "Just knowing that people have been walking these routes for a thousand years gives you a sense of being part of something bigger than yourself."

## RECOMMENDED READING

*Unsuitable for Ladies: An Anthology of Women Travellers* edited by
   Jane Robinson

*Off the Road: A Modern-Day Walk Down the Pilgrim's Route into Spain* by
   Jack Hitt

*The Road to Santiago* by Kathryn Harrison

# 39 New Jerusalem

## THE END OF THE ROAD AT SANTIAGO DE COMPOSTELA

It is a privilege to stand in the Praza de Obradoiro to watch pilgrims enter the plaza and approach the Catedral de Santiago de Compostela. They may be sunburned or drenched from a sudden downpour (Santiago is Spain's rainiest city), nursing a sore knee or a blistered heel. But all scrapes and discomforts pale in that moment of pure elation and accomplishment. Each pilgrim earned that unrestrained joy step by step on the way to the tomb of St. James the Apostle, patron saint of Spain.

Oral tradition holds that St. James spread the word of Christ in northern Spain before returning to Jerusalem, where he was beheaded in A.D. 44. His disciples brought his remains back to Spain by boat and buried them near the site of his Iberian mission in Galicia. When the saint's burial place was rediscovered by a hermit in the ninth century, Santiago de Compostela was set on the path to becoming one of the three most important Christian pilgrimage sites, along with Rome and Jerusalem. In the twelfth and thirteenth centuries, up to a quarter million pilgrims would undertake the journey to Santiago each year.

Begun in the eleventh century, the cathedral is the fourth Christian house of worship to mark the site of the ancient tomb.

Despite renovations and expansion in ensuing centuries, it remains the greatest and most moving example of Spanish Romanesque architecture. So large and imposing that it is almost impossible to stand back far enough to take it all in, the dramatic and beautiful building offers precisely the ceremonial and inspirational welcome that any pilgrim could desire after weeks on the road.

The Pórtico de la Gloria is, well, the crowning glory. The work of master builder and sculptor, Maestro Mateo (c. 1145-c. 1217), the entrance on the western facade was carved between 1168 and 1188. There are more than 200 carved granite figures in the assemblage, which illustrates the salvation of humankind through the Crucifixion. As theologically complex as it  is masterfully carved, the recently restored portico is easily the finest group of Romanesque stone sculpture in Spain.

Pride of place, of course, goes to St. James, who is seated at the top of the central marble column, safe from pilgrims' hands that have left a soft patina on the Tree of Jesse carved beneath him. Once inside, after weeks or even months on the Camino, pilgrims climb the stairs behind the altar and embrace a polychrome statue of the saint.

There's another tradition associated with the portico carvings. Not only did Maestro Mateo sign and date the sculptures (1188) on a lintel, he also added a small self-portrait sculpture just inside the portico at about waist height. Pilgrims or not, many Galician mothers still adhere to an old superstition that gently bumping their infants' foreheads with Mateo's noggin might cause some of his talent and genius to magically rub off.

The Praza de Obradoiro, once lined with stonemason's workshops, neatly sums up all that is important to the city. The symbol of St. James, the scallop shell, is cut into the stone in front of the cathedral—the final marker on the Camino. Other handsome buildings that enclose the plaza span historic styles from Romanesque to Baroque and house city government, university offices, and the archbishop's palace.

The grandest and most historic building on the plaza—other than the cathedral, of course—is the lodging for pilgrims established in 1492 by Isabel and Fernando. Called Hostal Dos Reis Católicos, it now serves as one of the most historic and atmospheric properties in Spain's *parador* system (see Chapter 46). Even some pilgrims who have walked an abstemious and penitential path to Santiago, sleeping on modest cots and eating the simple fare of the road, sometimes treat themselves to a night or two in this *parador*'s pampering embrace. The monarchs built it for knights and nobles, and even a brief stay provides a very Spanish taste of privilege.

Wherever they decide to bed down for the night, pilgrims shed their packs and change their hiking boots for sandals to wander the ancient streets. A university town, Santiago is also a market town for Galician farmers. Its flagstone streets and noble city palaces lend Santiago a fairy-tale air. Arcaded Rúa do Vilar may date from the tenth century, but its modern shops take credit cards for their ornamented crosses and other souvenirs and pastry shops abound to satisfy a pilgrim's sweet tooth. Pilgrims or not, visitors have been heading to Rúa da Raína and Rúa do Franco since the twelfth century for eating, drinking, and—for pilgrims—sharing tales of the road.

The pilgrims don't need to stop at the Museo des Peregrinacións, or Museum of Pilgrimages. They have learned everything they need to know first-hand. For those who drove or took the train, the museum's dioramas, artifacts, and wall texts address the phenomenon of pilgrimages, as well as the legend and archeology associated with the transfer of the body of St. James here after his death.

Maybe more to the point, the museum explores the important role that pilgrims played in the dissemination of knowledge in the medieval period. If the experience of being in Santiago inspires you to plan your own pilgrimage, this is a good place to start. And everywhere in the city, you will find no shortage of experienced pilgrims eager to offer advice and encouragement.

✳ www.santiagoturismo.com

# 40 *On the Edge*

## THE END OF THE WORLD AT FISTERRA

If I had walked 485 miles (780 km) on a pilgrimage from the foothills of the French Pyrenees to Santiago de Compostela, I'm pretty sure that I would be happy to hang up my walking stick and declare my journey done. But many pilgrims, reluctant to leave the road, lace up their boots once more and set out for Cabo Fisterra, 55 miles (90 km) farther west.

And there, no matter what their feet tell them, they have to stop. Fisterra (Finisterre in Castilian Spanish) literally means "the end of the earth," and the rocky peninsula dangling off the tip of Galicia's west coast is indeed one of the most western points in continental Europe.

By providing a satellite's eye view, Google Earth has taken some of the mystery out of such places. Cabo de Roca in Portugal is about 10 miles (17 km) farther west. But that doesn't make the sunsets at Cabo Fisterra any less brilliant or the rugged landscape and tumultuous sea any less evocative. According to legend, the ancient Celts came here to make sacrifices to their sun god on a rock altar. The Roman soldiers posted here are the ones who dubbed it *finis terrae*. Here their empire sprung from the heart of Middle Earth (*media terrae*, as in "Mediterranean") reached its limits. This broken rock face of extreme western Europe was where knowledge ended—and mystery and imagination began.

Full disclosure, I did not walk to Fisterra. I went by car, following the so-called Costa da Morte, or coast of death, which acquired that name because so many ships were wrecked along these windy, rocky shores. The road is what Europeans euphemistically call a "corniche" road—i.e., narrow ribbons of asphalt cut out of the side of a headland. If you can bear to look, the A445 from the rocky harbor of Sardineiro de Abaixo past the long beach of Escaselas to the fishing village of Fisterra offers one scenic vista after another.

There's even an observation turnout above Fisterra that clearly shows why this village fishes for a living. There is no arable land for miles around, and the harbor at Fisterra is a narrow slot well protected from the sea. The inshore boats seine for sardines and squid; larger offshore boats bring in bigger game like bonito and hake. The catch of the day at the little dockside restaurants is usually squid cooked on a hot griddle or sardines, lightly breaded and grilled whole. They make a fine last supper before heading out to the end of the world, where the lighthouse frantically warns sailors off the rocks.

Lighthouses often occupy dramatic points of land, but Fisterra's light sits on one of the least hospitable crags of rock I have ever visited. The promontory of Monte Facho stands 781 feet above the ocean, and the blocky lighthouse building, constructed in 1853, squats partway down the wind-scoured rocks at 452 feet above sea level. On even the sunniest days, the wild and swirling sea below throws up a shroud of mist that casts the point in a mystical haze.

The point of Cabo de Fisterra is forbidding, but once I arrived, I immediately grasped its attraction. It is the place where, after holding it all together for so long, one can break down in tears of relief and cast off all burdens. A bronze boot on a rock above the ocean symbolizes the end of the journey, and there is a fire pit where many burn some of their clothes—or a note. I imagine that they do it while watching the sun sink into the ocean in a glorious glow, bringing a close not just to the day, but to their pilgrimage. They must then sleep the sleep of the just and rise by dawn's light, the end of one journey becoming the beginning of the next.

# 41 *Making a Splash*

## SPAIN'S TOP SPOTS FOR WATER SPORTS

Spain is one of the sunniest countries in Europe, and nothing tempers the Iberian sun like a splash of cold water on freckled skin. While the country's many beaches are spectacular for soaking up rays and cooling off with a dip, some have far more active wind and waves ideal for water sports. Even a few northern Spanish rivers, where melt from the winter snow cap flows off the Picos de Europa to the sea, make paddle sports an exhilarating option.

### Whitewater Rafting on the Río Miño In Galicia

The Spanish national whitewater rafting championships are held each spring on the stretch of the Río Miño near Arbo. Here, the broad, lazy river surrounded by marshlands suddenly enters a canyon. The constriction speeds up the flow, churning up level I-III rapids for about the next eight miles. The competitions are held during the big water of spring, but if you're traveling with a group of four or more, you can book a private excursion with a guide-instructor from May through October. Most trips begin upriver from the rapids, so you get to paddle with the ducks and herons along a riparian landscape of willows, cork oaks, and eucalyptus with Spain on one bank, Portugal on the other. Remains of ancient Roman eel weirs mark the mouths of some of the Miño's smaller tributaries. But the river idyll ends once you encounter the faster currents and obstacles of white water. The inflatable boats are actually pretty easy to control but the tumble and jounce of the rapids create the intoxicating illusion of danger. By the time you've reached Barcela (about two hours), you'll probably be ready to beach on the Spanish side and haul out in time for a drink. One of the most dependable outfitters is Aventuras en Galicia.

✳ www.aventurasengalicia.com (Spanish only)

## Canoeing on the Río Sella in Asturias

The Río Sella flows down from the Picos de Europa, wrapping around the mountains and wending its way through sheep and goat pastures and thick woods until it meets the Bay of Biscay in Ribadesella. From Arriondas to the coast, the Sella runs deep and fairly slow—making it a perfect river for canoeing. In fact, on the first Saturday in August, you can practically walk from shore to shore on the boats competing in the annual Descent of the Sella. Truth is, most competitors these days make the journey in kayaks because they are much faster and more maneuverable than canoes. But Paddle in Spain offers canoe trips on the Sella from April into November for paddlers who want to enjoy the stroke-and-glide simplicity of canoeing on an easygoing river with picturesque scenery. It's pretty much an all-day adventure, since the introductory paddling and safety lessons are required, even for experienced paddlers. Lunch is included and there are numerous spots along the riverbank where you can haul out to eat and admire the scenery. From Arriondas, Paddle in Spain offers two options or terminus points—in Torano, about four miles downriver, or at Llovio, a little more than nine miles downriver. Time on the water generally ranges from three to five hours. Although it's more fun with a friend, single paddlers can also sign up. For details, contact Paddle in Spain.

✳ www.paddleinspain.com

## Surfing Mundaka's Left-Hand Barrel in Basque Country

If surfers had their way, Mundaka's barrel wave would be declared a world heritage site. When offshore waves reach just the right pitch and prevailing winds strike the mouth of the Río Gernika just right, a left-hand barrel wave stretches nearly a quarter mile on the seaward side of a long sandbar. It is such a spectacular tube of roiling water that many surfers consider it the finest wave in Europe and one of the best surfing wave sets in the world. International surfing competitions often use Mundaka as the European leg of their world tours. Mind you, the Bay of Biscay is cold here, even in the height of summer, making a wetsuit all but mandatory. The best surfing season is from September into January, when the sandbar is fully filled and the barrel runs its length. The barrel is most dependable when the surf is between six and ten feet—anything smaller tends to collapse while bigger waves tend to break offshore. Check the tide tables, too. Because this is a rivermouth break, it's usually shut down for two hours on each side of high tide. Australian expat Craig Sage opened the Mundaka Surf Shop here in 1984. He has rentals—including longboards for old-school surfers—and offers classes. If you're good and the conditions are right, you might get four tube rides from a single wave.

✳ www.mundakasurfshop.com

## Kiteboarding and Windsurfing Off Tarifa

Except to switch from onshore to offshore, the wind truly never stops at Tarifa, the southernmost point of mainland Europe. (It's farther south than the North African cities of Tunis and Algiers.) The picturesque town with its tenth-century castle has been the de facto capital of windsurfing ever since the sport debuted in the late 1960s. Because winds rarely dip below fifteen knots, Tarifa is a good place to hone your skills if you already windsurf, but beginners can find it hard to learn maneuvers in the constant moderate breeze. If you're more into watching than windsurfing, the annual championship races generally take place during Semana Santa (the week before Easter). Since the 1990s, kitesurfing (aka kiteboarding) has threatened to eclipse windsurfing here. In fact, large sections of Los Lances and Valdevaqueros beaches are reserved for kitesurfers so they don't interfere with swimmers and windsurfers. If you're new to kitesurfing, plan to take a three-day course to get certified. It's an unquestionable thrill the first time you leave the surface of the water to jump from one wave to the next—somersaults and other gymnastic moves optional. The Virgin Kitesurf World Championship usually takes place in mid-July. Dragon Kiteschool is one excellent outfitter.

✳ www.dragonkiteschool.com

# III

# La Mancha & Moorish Spain

# 42 Eyes of the Artist

## TOLEDO, AS SEEN BY EL GRECO

An art historian once called El Greco (1541-1614) the first "Homeless Man of Art," but I think that the city of Toledo would beg to differ.

Doménikos Theotokópoulos was born in Crete, where he first studied as a painter of icons. He later traveled to Venice where he possibly worked in the studio of Titian, whose expressive use of color made a lasting impact on the young artist. El Greco, as he came to be known, also worked in Rome and even famously offered to paint over Michelangelo's *Last Judgment* in the Sistine Chapel with a scene better suited to the sensibilities of the Catholic church.

By the 1570s, El Greco was in Spain, a country flush with the riches of the New World and a magnet for artists seeking work. In 1577, he secured two commissions in Toledo, but nevertheless aspired to be a court painter to Felipe II. El Greco's style didn't mesh with the needs of Felipe's ambitious building projects. That left him free to develop his own artistic vision in Toledo, the city the king had turned his back on when he moved the court to Madrid in 1561.

It must have been a blow to the proud city that had enjoyed centuries of power. Toledo sits on a high bluff above the plains of La Mancha. A bend in the Río Tajo wraps around the promontory like a moat, leaving only a single direction to defend. That secure position made it in succession a Roman, Visigothic, and Muslim capital before the kings of Castilla chose Toledo as the capital of Spain in 1085.

Once the temporal powers decamped to Madrid, the Toledo cathedral remained the seat of Spain's primate. Even today it is the country's religious capital. The ecclesiastical city met its match in an artist with a singular vision. Rather than painting for the monarch, El Greco painted for the Church—and for the churches of Toledo. No other city is so closely identified with a single artist.

One of the most medieval of Spain's large cities, Toledo is only a half hour from Madrid by high-speed train. Most of the defensive walls have been removed over the centuries, but some ceremonial gates remain. A good approach to the city is by the regal Puerta de Alfonso VI at the base of the hill. The stone stairs up to Plaza Merced are long and steep, but modern escalators make the ascent an easy one.

✳ www.toledo-turismo.com/en

The history of Toledo's heyday as a multicultural Muslim, Jewish, and Christian city is literally written in stone along the warrens of its narrow streets. But wandering through them is most rewarding if you have a point of departure or an interest to guide you. In Toledo, that's El Greco. By the time you have made your way to his greatest works, you will have seen the city.

The logical place to begin is the Convento de Santo Domingo el Antiguo, where El Greco got his start with a commission for nine paintings. The main panel depicts *La asunción de la Virgen,* or the *Assumption,* and it already demonstrated the powerful S-curve composition that would become a signature of his work. The dynamic beauty of the painting made worshippers and patrons alike take notice of the talented young foreigner. After you've spent time in front of the painting, buy a box of marzipan made by the nuns. The almond paste treat is a Toledo specialty.

If you head to the western edge of the city on Cuesta Santa Leocadia, you'll walk past the gates of the Monasterio de San Juan de los Reyes, built by Isabel and Fernando after their 1476 victory over the Portuguese (see Chapter 15). They had originally planned to be buried at the monastery, but ultimately spurned Toledo for Granada. The monastery sits on the edge of Toledo's Juderia, a thriving medieval community that provided many of the scholars and the administrative talent that helped run the court and the country. In fact, Pedro I gave his former royal treasurer a special dispensation to build the Sinagoga del Tránsito in 1355. One of only two synagogues left in Toledo, it is incorporated into the Museo Sefardi, which traces Jewish history in Toledo and across Spain.

Across the street from the museum, the Mirador Barrio Nuevo is one of the vantage points for long views across the flatlands. El Greco could look out and behold the temporal plain below while staring the heavens square in the eye. That elevated point of view would recur again and again in his paintings.

Less than a hundred yards from the synagogue, the Museo del Greco is the only museum in Spain dedicated exclusively to the artist. Exhibits examine his impact on his adopted city, but El Greco speaks for himself from the canvas. Among the works on display are a series of twelve apostles and portraits of some of his friends and patrons. His masterpiece, *Vista y plano de Toledo*, or *View and Plan of Toledo*, painted 1610–1614, shows the sketchy yet powerful modeling of his last works. In addition to an aerial perspective (complete with a tangle of angels fluttering around the Virgin as she places a garment on San Ildefonso), it includes a young man holding a detailed street map of the city. The Río Tajo is depicted allegorically as a sculpture pouring water (and hence prosperity). El Greco depicts his adopted city as a place doubly blessed by the natural and the divine.

El Greco's own parish church, the little fourteenth-century Iglesia de Santo Tomé, gave him the commission for one of his greatest masterpieces, *El entierro del conde de Orgaz*, or *The Burial of Conde Orgaz*, completed in 1588. The church's patron had died two centuries earlier, but El Greco conjured a persuasive realism for the 16- by 10-foot canvas of the miracle of the count's burial. As the skies open to reveal Jesus, the Virgin Mary, and a group of saints watching from on high, St. Augustine and St. Stephen personally attend to the burial.

One of El Greco's earliest Toledo commissions is inside the cathedral, which dominates the center of the old city. Workers began constructing the church in high Gothic style in 1226 and the structural work was finished in 1463. Some critics consider it one of the finest Gothic cathedrals in Spain—it is certainly one of the largest. Characterized by a masterful modeling of light and shadow and depicting a teeming humanity—saints and soldiers, lords and commoners—surrounding the red-robed Christ, El Greco completed *El Expolio*, or *The Disrobing of Christ*, for the high altar of the Sacristy in 1579.

Some of the greatest El Grecos are hung in the Museo de Santa Cruz, which sits just off Plaza de Zocodover, an old market square now filled with café tables. The museum occupies a former hospital building with beautiful Mudejar architectural details. It displays archeological finds and local crafts and artisanry—along with a wealth of sixteenth- and seventeenth-century paintings consolidated from now-closed churches and convents around the region. They include about a dozen by El Greco. Just look for artists standing at easels to find the museum's greatest treasure, a 1613 version of *La asunción de la Virgen*, or the *Assumption of the Virgin*. Because it is hung at eye level, you can see every dynamic brushstroke that made the oils flow like rivulets on the canvas. You need neither religious faith nor an affinity for fine art to appreciate the aging El Greco's excitement as he threw himself into the act of painting.

✳ en.museodelgreco.mcu.es

El Greco died the next year. His friend, the poet and preacher Hortensio Félix Paravicino (whom El Greco had painted in 1609), summed up the "homeless" artist's journey through life in the sonnet he composed to honor the man: "Crete gave him life and art, Toledo a better home, where through death he attained to eternal life."

### RECOMMENDED READING

*El Greco* by Michael Scholz-Hänsel

# 43 *Written on the Walls*

## THE CERAMICS OF TALAVERA DE LA REINA

After a couple of days in Spain I start planning to transform my tiny home bathroom into a tiled Moorish fantasy. There is so much tile in Spain that it sometimes seems that every surface of the country is glazed and I fall hard for the play of color and pattern. Dazzling geometric tiles festoon every bar and courtyard in Andalucía, while exuberant, even whimsical advertising tiles cover storefronts in Madrid and elsewhere so that anyone can find the egg seller, barbershop, or pharmacy at a glance. They are Spain's architectural tattoos—more decorative than functional but signaling that each place so marked belongs to the Iberian tribe.

Eventually the reality of transporting all those tiles and actually mounting them on my walls sets in. So I opt instead for a serving platter or a pitcher to add verve to my monochromatic mid-century plates and bowls. Tableware is also central to Spain's ceramics tradition and I never leave the country without something—even if it's only a couple of mugs to replace the ones that have broken since my last visit.

Every archeology museum abounds with evidence that people were making pottery long before the Moors brought their tile-making techniques, ovens, and flair for elaborate geometric patterns across the Strait of Gibraltar in the eighth century. After the Reconquest, Spanish ceramicists remade the art form in European terms. Following their own Baroque impulses, they added filigree upon Moorish filigree and expanded the design vocabulary to embrace the intricacies of figurative painting.

The city of Talavera de la Reina, about 47 miles (76 km) west of Toledo, is one of Spain's most famous ceramics centers. Its wares fill the shelves of souvenir shops throughout the country and there's no question that the profusion of olive trays with a separate cup for the pits or deep ashtrays girdled by painted hunting scenes can veer off into kitsch. But Spain's ceramics tradition is much more artful. A short visit to Talavera will train your eye to see the finer points of craftsmanship when the shopping impulse finally becomes too strong to resist.

The area was under Moorish control from 712 until 1083, and finally blossomed as a European ceramics center in the fifteenth and sixteenth centuries. Talavera wares were in demand for the finest castles and estates of Spain and throughout Europe, but the industry fell into decline by the early nineteenth century when Napoleon upended Spain's monarchy and economy. Juan Ruiz de Luna (1863-1905) revived the tradition at the cusp of the twentieth century and although his workshop has closed, a number of small manufacturers remain. There are also plenty of retail shops, many along the main roads into and out of town—Avenida de Portugal on the west, Avenida de Extremadura on the east.

Ruiz de Luna collected historic Talavera pottery and his personal holdings form the basis of the Museo Ruiz de Luna, which occupies an austere seventeenth-century Augustinian convent. There are examples of tenth-century Moorish pottery discovered during the process of converting the building into a museum, but the most striking pieces date from the sixteenth to twentieth centuries. A walk through the galleries traces the rapid evolution of painted motifs from simple sponged designs, to stylized hare and deer caught mid-cavort, to images of saints with generic city scenes behind them. The artisans hardly stopped at single pieces of tableware or single tiles. They also created a tile facade for the Ruiz de Luna factory, an altar-sized scene of the Annunciation, and another of Santiago the Moorslayer on horseback striking down the enemy.

❋ www.patrimoniohistoricoclm.es/museo-ruiz-de-luna
   (Spanish only)

If the museum seems exhaustive in its variety and artistry, it has nothing on the Basilica de Nuestra Señora del Prado. This Renaissance-style church, about a ten-minute stroll from the museum, is so encrusted with painted tiles that it is sometimes called "the ceramic Sistine Chapel." The nave is lined with characters and stories from the Old and New Testaments—teaching moments for religious instruction. But the tiles on the exterior of the church strike the big themes, and despite the erosion of wind and sun, they declare an unquestioning faith and artistry. The artists depict Eden, complete with fig-leaf-modest Adam and Eve. Grandest of all is a frieze of the Adoration, where Spanish soldiers in full armor and weapons line up to pay homage to the Christ Child.

Other less grand but equally lovely surprises await on the streets of Talavera. It takes only a little wandering to discover pharmacies, butcher shops, taverns, and even *churrerías* with tile facades. Los Jardines del Prado, the garden near the basilica, is fitted out with a tiled duck pond, a tiled bandstand, and many tile benches for resting beneath the broad shade of the trees. I usually sit here to decide what I'm going to purchase—and how to fit it in my suitcase.

# 44 *Flights of Fancy*

## ABSTRACT ART IN THE MOUNTAINTOP
## AERIE OF CUENCA

It was inevitable that artists would make their way to Cuenca. But don't expect to find painters with their easels planted on every street corner. Arrested between earth and sky—or, more accurately, planted between the deep, plunging gorges of the Júcar River on one side and the Huécar River on the other—the old mountaintop city is more improbable than picturesque.

These days, Cuenca is a favorite weekend getaway for Madrileños, who can leave their metropolis on a high-speed train and find themselves at the foot of this seemingly timeless hilltop fantasy in less than an hour. But the dry and dusty pinnacle was much less hospitable in 714 when Moorish warriors built a walled fortress town atop the precipitous limestone escarpment. Their defensive instincts were so good that it wasn't until 1177 that Alfonso VIII brought Cuenca into the Christian fold. The Muslim street layout was subsequently filled with convents and monasteries, making Cuenca a place where the life of the spirit jousts constantly with the city's unlikely geography.

That dynamic was irresistible to abstract artists seeking a place of inspiration and contemplation during the intellectually deadening years of the Franco regime. Cuenca, it seemed, was a place where they might defy gravity. Discovered by El Grupo Paso, Cuenca emerged as the epicenter of Spanish abstract art in the 1960s. It's easy to see why the artists felt such an affinity for the decaying old city. Like their art, Cuenca distills space into trajectory and displaces object with symbol. Physically a dry rocky aerie, it is fertile ground for the spirit, where creativity is practically a civic credo.

Cuenca also has bravado. When the old city ran out of terra firma in the fourteenth century, medieval builders simply cantilevered houses over the gorges. Only a few of these Gothic-era engineering marvels remain. The largest of the *casas colgadas* or "hanging houses," became the site of the Museum of Spanish Abstract Art, which was founded by artist and collector Fernando Zóbel (1924–1984) and opened in 1966.

Zóbel knew that placing his bold collection of modern art in the confines of one of the city's iconic buildings would create a certain frisson. He made sure that architectural details such as ornate wooden ceilings were preserved when the space was transformed into galleries. I always notice the windows first, with their stomach-lurching views into the fifteen-story deep Huécar gorge. Once I've convinced myself that the museum is not going to tip over the edge, I can turn to the art that resonates with echoes of the city. The sheer upward sweep of Cuenca's streets translates onto Zobel's own canvases as grand, vigorous vectors. The alleyways of the old medieval quarter are distilled into the broad black snarls painted by Antonio Saura (1930-1998). The flatly painted walls of the old houses metamorphose into patterned blocks of color in the works of José Guerrero (1914-1991).

✳ www.march.es/arte/cuenca

The museum was a springboard for Cuenca's long-awaited renaissance after the depredations of the Spanish Civil War. Painters rehabilitated ruined medieval buildings and created artistic salons in tired old bars. At the same time, they left largely untouched the pastel stucco exteriors that glow softly in the high-altitude light.

The street plan is also little altered. Triangular Plaza Mayor remains the social nerve center and place to linger at a café table over lunch of local specialties of spicy rabbit-partridge pâté called *morteruelo* followed by a plate of chewy *zarajos*, or grilled lamb intestines, usually served coiled around a vine shoot like a ball of yarn. Conquenses (as residents of Cuenca call themselves) like their food rustic to the point of rude, and Cuenca is not the sort of place for a timid eater. So order a carafe of Ribera del Júcar red or rosé. The label will say it's made from Cencibel, but that's just the lusty local clone of the tempranillo grape.

Two streets rise steeply from Plaza Mayor. The left-hand branch leads to Casa Zavala, an eighteenth-century palace that is home to the Antonio Saura Foundation. One of Spain's leading twentieth-century artists, Saura first came to Cuenca as a teenager to convalesce from tuberculosis and the view from his sickbed window became key to his artistic vocabulary. Saura himself commented toward the end of his life that for decades he had been unconsciously painting "the hypnotic mask between the rock—the blackberry eyes. The curve of the mountain looks like the mound where the head of Goya's dog emerges." He spent nearly three decades working in Cuenca and most of the galleries of the foundation museum, which opened in 2008, showcase his mature work. His destruction of more than one hundred of his early paintings in Cuenca in the 1960s is often cited as a watershed in modern Spanish art.

✳ www.fundacionantoniosaura.es

Antonio Pérez (b. 1934), who was Saura's contemporary, had a more quirky point of view. Up the right-hand fork from Plaza Mayor, the Antonio Pérez Foundation, created in 1997, fills the former Barefoot Carmelite convent with his own work and that of other artists that he admired and collected, including Pop Artists like Andy Warhol. Pérez had a weakness for found objects that he would give fresh context. His "Castrati" installation—a trio of antique bells missing their clappers—catches him at perhaps his witty best.

When I leave the Pérez Foundation, I like to follow the road up the hill to the crumbling Bezudo arch at the top that marks the remains of the Moorish fort partially destroyed in 1177 and definitively demolished by Napoleon's soldiers. Just beyond the gate are the loudest and liveliest bars of Cuenca. At sunset, Conquenses gather with glasses in hand at the overlook across the street from the bars. Living in Cuenca has given them a particular eye: No one bothers to look at the colors of the sky—they focus instead on the gathering dark at the bottom of the gorge.

# 45 Learning the Art of the Stripper

## THE SAFFRON ROSE FESTIVAL, CONSUEGRA

There's a moment in making paella when the fish, meat, vegetables, and rice are suddenly transformed into a dish that's so much greater than the sum of its parts. I feel like an alchemist when I stand in my galley kitchen in Cambridge and hold the magic ingredient—a big pinch of saffron threads—gently between my thumb and forefinger. Like Spanish chefs, I crumble the threads in the sign of the cross over a big steel paella pan and watch as the dish blooms the deep yellow-orange that is the very definition of saffron yellow. The assertive, yet subtle, aroma that rises from the pan is almost impossible to describe. If pressed, I'd say it's a bit like toasted tea. Pressed further, I'd say it smells like Spain.

Spanish cooking makes more liberal use of saffron than any other cuisine I've encountered. Sometimes I can't help thinking about the cost of each little thread, but Spanish cooks seem immune to the extravagance. After all, the country produces about two-thirds of the world's culinary saffron, and, if you ask the folks in La Mancha, virtually all of the top grade of the spice. Maybe that's just pride talking, but saffron is one of the most expensive crops in the world and one of the few, it seems, that can flourish in this arid landscape where befuddled knight Don Quijote famously tilted at windmills.

On the last weekend in October, the town of Consuegra, about 90 miles (144 km) south of Madrid, celebrates the saffron harvest with the Fiesta de la Rosa del Azafrán, or Saffron Rose Festival. It's

become a foodie cliché to expatiate on the relation of food and culture, as if we need an excuse to take time out from visiting museums to have a good meal. This low-key festival is largely off the tourist radar, but it's the real thing. The few people who seek it out find a community that has come together to celebrate and confirm its agricultural traditions. Visitors are certainly welcome, but the festival is really for the people who do the hard work.

Consuegra and saffron go way back. The Moors introduced saffron culture to the windswept plains of La Mancha about a millennium ago. Apart from using tractors to turn over the soil in the spring, the techniques for growing, harvesting, and preparing *crocus sativa*, the saffron crocus flower prized for the bright red stigmas hidden among its petals, have barely changed since. Chief among them is early rising. For roughly the last three weeks in October, farmers wait in the fields for the first glimmer of dawn so that they can gather up the blooms just as the sun springs the petals apart.

That's why I found myself rattling in a tiny rental car through the featureless landscape of brown plains before dawn. A feeble autumn sun broke through the overcast horizon just as I reached the outskirts of Consuegra and finally spotted tiny plots of purple flowers checkering the roadside fields. Men and women straddled the muddy rows, bending to pluck the flowers and deposit them into wicker baskets, then shuffling ahead.

As I watched from the side of the road, a couple ran over and pressed big bunches of flowers into my arms. This generous welcome was just the first sign that harvest season is a time of high spirits. Charcoal braziers burn day and night as farmers toast the saffron stigmas, sending the spice's heady scent wafting through the countryside. Traditionally, young girls set aside part of the family's harvest to contribute to their dowry. Nearly everyone in the village wears a corsage of crocus blooms as growers, brokers, and dealers from throughout central Spain congregate on the little Roman town of Consuegra.

Like most harvest festivals, Consuegra's has its share of colorful regional costumes and demonstrations of folk dances. At one point, I followed a long line of villagers as they marched up to one of the ancient windmills topping the ridge above town for a ceremonial grinding together of saffron from each of the seven communities where it is grown. But the main event is the fierce competition among La Mancha's most skilled strippers, whose special talent is the swift separation of the three red stigmas from each purple blossom. The children's competition seemed innocent enough, with an official reminding the crowd that the youngsters "represent the future of La Mancha's red gold."

The adult contest, on the other hand, was a tense battle among representatives of the saffron-growing communities. Throughout a series of elimination rounds, women with swift fingers and laser-like focus dominated. The best could divest 100 flowers of their precious threads in less than three minutes. The field finally narrowed to two women and the crowd was rapt as the pluck-off of 100 blossoms ended in a tie. Finally, a ten-blossom tiebreaker determined the winner of a generous cash prize and serious bragging rights.

I didn't fully appreciate the strippers' skills until later that evening when I dumped my own bag of crocus flowers onto a table in a local tavern and set about clumsily trying to dislodge the stigmas. My saffron pile was barely growing until two local women sat down

at my table and patiently demonstrated the proper technique—
holding the flower just so and flicking a finger and thumb with a
practiced motion. By the end of the night I had a few hundred precious threads that I packed carefully in absorbent paper.

Over the next several days, I toasted my saffron threads over hot
radiators. Not a perfect solution, I know, but when I got home and
incorporated them into a pan of paella, I swear it was the best I've
ever made. And I'll never complain again about the price of saffron.

✳ www.spain.info/en_US/que-quieres/agenda/fiestas/toledo/
   fiesta_de_la_rosa_del_azafran.html

# 46 *Room for the Night*

## SOME GREAT SPANISH *PARADORS*

Alfonso XIII (1886-1941) may not have been Spain's best or strongest king, but he certainly believed in the restorative power of a good night's sleep—and in the symbolic value of excellent hostelries to raise his country's standing on the European stage.

Dismayed at the lack of suitable accommodations for guests at his wedding to Victoria Eugenia of Battenberg in 1906, he ordered the construction of the Ritz and Palace hotels in Madrid. They opened in 1910 and 1912 respectively and remain among the city's more opulent lodgings. In 1928 (just three years before he left the country and opened the doors for the Franco dictatorship), the king set his sights on the whole country with the opening of a hotel in the Sierra de Gredos between Madrid and Ávila. It was the first in what would become Spain's iconic *parador* system.

The chain of hotels now numbers almost one hundred and pretty much covers the country. While some, such as the ocean-front property in Cádiz or the mountain lodge in Fuente De in the Picos de Europa, are of modern construction, most of the *paradors* occupy ancient buildings. These monasteries, convents, fortresses, mills, pilgrim hostelries, prisons, and noble palaces have lived and breathed the history of Spain. It's no exaggeration to say that staying in such storied surroundings offers much more than just a place to rest your head. Here are a few to give you an idea of what to expect.

✳ www.parador.es/en

The first historic property to enter the *parador* system was in the town of Oropesa, about 71 miles (115 km) west of Toledo. Legend holds that the town name refers to the ransom—her weight in gold— demanded by a Moorish soldier for the return of a kidnapped young princess. By the thirteenth century, the area and its fortress were back under Christian control and the Counts of Oropesa built their Renaissance palace here in the fifteenth century. Surrounded for miles by grazing sheep and silver-leafed olive groves, it opened as the Parador de Orepesa in 1930. Famous visitors have included Santa Teresa (see Chapter 16) and Carlos V—as well as Cary Grant, Frank Sinatra, and Sophia Loren, who came to shoot the 1957 film *Pride and Passion*.

Many *paradors* occupy fortresses, but the Parador de Cardona, about 60 miles (97 km) northwest of Barcelona, occupies one of Spain's oldest standing forts. Built in the ninth century to guard a river passage inland from Barcelona, it was part of the strategic ring of fortresses that allowed Wilfred the Hairy to consolidate the lands that would become Catalunya. By the thirteenth century, it had passed to the Dukes of Cardona, vassals of Wilfred's descendants. The fortress is a powerful early medieval structure that looks like it was designed by a Cubist architect using children's blocks. Most of the public areas have rough stone walls, and squat Romanesque arches divide the rooms. The oldest standing portions of the complex date from the eleventh century: the church, and the 33-foot wide, 50-foot-high Minyona tower. Legend holds that in the eleventh century, a young noblewoman was confined to the tower because she would not renounce her Moorish lover. She died in her prison and it's said that a male ghost in medieval dress haunts the castle to this day.

When Isabel I needed to escape the duties of being queen and the distaff half of Europe's first power couple (see Chapter 15), she found rest, reflection, and medical attention in the little Extremaduran town of Guadalupe. It had been a pilgrimage site since cowherd Gil Cordero had a vision of the Virgin Mary in the early fourteenth century and directed area priests where to uncover a statue of the Black Madonna. The Monasterio de Santa María de Guadalupe, built at the behest of Alfonso XI, houses the statue that still attracts tens of thousands of pilgrims. Many of them stay at the monastery's modest lodging, but some prefer the more luxurious Parador de Guadalupe, just across the plaza from the church. It occupies both the 1402 medical hospital where pilgrims came to be treated and royal court physicians trained, and the adjacent grammar school for the children of nobility. When Isabel came to consult the physicians and pray to the Virgin, she was probably a guest of the monastery. But the serene courtyards of the *parador*, which are filled with citrus fruit trees and pots overflowing with geraniums, are every bit as restful as the similarly Mudéjar cloister of the monastery.

The so-called "Renaissance City" of Úbeda, 88 miles (141 km) north of Granada and 92 miles (148 km) east of Córdoba, deserves its nickname. More than any other community in Andalucía, it literally embodies the principles of the Renaissance. When Isabel and Fernando took the city from the Moors, the physical layout was altered to something approaching a rational grid system that excluded the Jewish and Muslim quarters from the new, grand plazas that would follow in the next century. They also installed clocks that sounded the hours for daily prayers. The new city became a showcase for Renaissance style and taste. The Parador de Úbeda opened in 1930 in the grandest of the sixteenth-century palaces that share the plaza with the chapel of San Salvador. The handsome building, which was further renovated in the eighteenth century, is, like the city around it, a model of elegance and grace.

Possibly the most romantic—and by historical claim the most royal—lodging in the system is the Parador de Olite. Located 29 miles (46 km) south of Pamplona, the palace-castle above a high fortified wall was rebuilt at the beginning of the fifteenth century by Carlos III, the king of Navarra, at the high point of that northern Spanish kingdom's wealth and glory. Born in Mantes, north of Paris, to a family with noble titles in Normandy and Champagne, he brought French learning and taste to the Navarrese court—and French architects to redesign the palace-castle at Olite. The result is a beautiful late Gothic structure with graceful archways. His wife, Leonor de Trastámara (a great aunt of Isabel I), made it her main home and functioned as regent here when her husband was away on family business in France. It became the permanent seat of the court of Navarra in 1410. Although the castle was severely damaged by Napoleon, the surviving wing was restored in the early twentieth century. Stained glass windows in the dining room and along the main staircase, and arcades with coffered wooden ceilings, wrought iron lamps, and hand-woven rugs lend it a medieval air. It is among the most popular of the *paradors* for weddings, and beloved by wedding photographers for the atmospheric nooks and stately architectural frames where they can pose the happy couples.

# 47 *Rome Remains*

## THE ANCIENT COLONIAL CITY OF MÉRIDA

When Caesar Augustus founded the city of Emerita Augusta in 25 B.C. (and modestly named it for himself), he didn't build any golf courses, condominium complexes, or assisted living centers. But he did intend the new capital of Lusitania, Rome's westernmost Iberian province, to at least partially serve as a retirement community for veterans of the Roman Legions. It even looked and felt like modern-day retirement capitals—say, Phoenix. It was largely warm and dry, so that old soldiers could rest  their weary bones without the rheumy cold and damp of a seaside Roman city like Tarraco (see Chapter 82).

Augustus looked after his vets. Whether he wanted to keep them happy or just wanted to keep all those experienced warriors as far from Rome as possible, he ensured that the city, now known as Mérida, would have all the comforts of home. It was even known as a Rome in miniature, and today possesses the largest ensemble of Roman ruins in Spain. Some lay buried beneath the accretion of dust and sand, and some simply remained in use as the Roman inhabitants slowly evolved into modern Spaniards.

Mérida is 214 miles (344 km) west of Madrid on the border with Portugal. Coming into town, the first evidence of the Roman past is for the birds these days. On the north side of the city, thirty-eight majestically picturesque arched pillars extend into the distance. Standing eighty-two feet high, they are all that remain of one of three aqueducts built in the first century A.D. to supply clean water. The ruins are called the Acueducto de los Milagros, or aqueduct of the miracles, purportedly because they inspired awe in medieval inhabitants of Mérida. The real miracle happens here each spring when white storks nest atop the pillars, raising their broods on the Roman remains.

✳ www.turismomerida.org/en

South and west of the aqueduct, the Puente Romano, or Roman Bridge, spans the Río Guadiana. Constructed in A.D. 98–117 by Trajan's engineers, it is one of the longest Roman bridges ever built and the longest still in use. The bridge's original sixty-two spans between granite ashlar abutments stretched an estimated 2,477 feet, or nearly half a mile. Only sixty spans remain, with three of them buried in the southern bank, reducing the bridge's span to 2,365 feet. Although it carried auto traffic as recently as 1990, it now serves as a pedestrian approach to the old city.

From the foot of the bridge, it's only a short walk uphill on Calle Santa Eulalia into the very center of old Mérida. The so-called Temple of Diana is along the route. The name is misleading, as the temple might not have been devoted to the goddess at all. But its pillars and the frame of the roof neatly sketch out a sacred space against the blue sky.

About five minutes up the street, clear signage directs you to the most prominent ruins and real treasures of the city. On one side of a plaza stands a massive modern icon, architect Rafael Moneo's stunning Museo Nacional de Arte Romano, or National Museum

of Roman Art. On the other side is the entrance to the two grandest surviving monuments from antiquity, the Teatro y Anfiteatro
Romano, or Roman Theater and Amphitheater. It is hard to know
which site—the modern or the ancient—is more impressive.

✳ museoarteromano.mcu.es

Moneo translated Roman proportions and materials to the
needs of a modern museum, while preserving beneath the structure
part of a Roman road, a necropolis, and a residential neighborhood discovered during excavations for the structure. Panel after
panel of brick arches march through the building, supporting several levels of galleries linked by suspended walkways. The contents
of the museum include many pieces of broken statuary, carved columns and capitals, striking and colorful mosaics, jewelry, ceramics, and stelae inscribed with messages for the ages. The souvenirs
in the gift shop effectively curate the museum's many artifacts by
highlighting the most popular and most significant.

Ultimately, the most impressive Roman remains are not
temples or government buildings but entertainment venues. The
Amphitheater, completed in 8 B.C., seated 15,000-16,000 people
to behold the spectacle of the gladiatorial games. The walls were
constructed of rough local stone, sometimes augmented by bricks,
and about three-quarters of the original structure is still in place.
Small rooms flank the corridors leading to gates into the arena—
some were used by gladiators preparing for battle, some were cages
for wild animals.

Next to the Amphitheater is the smaller Roman Theater, which
sat about six thousand. Artistic pursuits such as theater were far
less popular than the blood sport next door, but it was deemed
essential that any Roman city worthy of the name have a theater
for presentation of the dramatic arts. Until the site was excavated
in 1910, the entire theater was buried except the now quite

deteriorated highest tier of seating. Constructed in 15-16 B.C., the theater was built on a hillside to speed construction. Seating consisted of concrete faced with small cut rock. Bring your own cushion, if you have one, to see one of the performances of Latin and Greek classical theater on warm summer nights in July and August. As darkness steals over the stage and the actors emerge from the shadows, the tales of Euripides, Sophocles, and Seneca come once again to life.

✳ www.festivaldemerida.es (Spanish only)

# 48 *Excess of Splendor*

## SEVILLA'S MASSIVE GOTHIC CATHEDRAL

Of the eighty chapels in the Catedral de Sevilla, young women are most compelled to pause in the baptism chapel before the huge painting of the *Vision of St. Anthony* created in 1656 by Bartolomé Esteban Murillo (1617-1682). Sevilla's great artist is best remembered for his endearing pastel images of the Immaculate Conception (see Chapter 7), but San Antonio de Padua was also among his favorite subjects. Murillo depicts the Lisbon-born friar in his simple brown Franciscan robe kneeling before a table. San Antonio gazes upward as the infant Jesus descends on a golden cloud surrounded by a court of angels.

✳ www.catedraldesevilla.es (Spanish only)

San Antonio is generally considered the patron saint of finding lost objects or people, but he is also venerated in Spain and Portugal for reconciling couples. The women of Sevilla seek out his chapel for assistance in finding a boyfriend. The custom may seem quaint in this age of Match.com and eHarmony, but there's something to be said for the power of faith over the impersonal efficiency of technology.

The painting, by the way, is one of about a dozen that Murillo painted of the saint and at ten feet wide and eighteen feet high, it's also the largest. It seems only fitting that it resides in the Catedral de Sevilla, a place of worship that seems made for superlatives.

When Sevilla returned to Christian rule under Fernando III of Castilla in 1248, the victors immediately claimed the sacred ground. They converted the Almohad mosque into a cathedral and  in 1402 began construction of a new cathedral on the same spot.

The riches of the New World wouldn't reach Sevilla for another century, but the city was already a wealthy trading port. The Castilian clerics were determined to make a statement by building a cathedral "so beautiful and so grand that those who see it will think we are mad." Whether mad or merely prideful, they launched the construction of what would become one of the world's largest Gothic cathedrals.

Built on the footprint of the original mosque, the cathedral began to take shape in 1402 and was largely completed in a little over a century. The central nave soars 138 feet toward heaven, thanks to the beautiful Gothic pointed arches that ingeniously distribute the weight onto supporting columns. Architects wisely retained the Moorish entrance court full of orange trees and the twelfth-century minaret, considered a masterpiece of Almohad style. It was topped with a Renaissance-style belltower in the sixteenth century. Visitors can climb a series of ramps to the top of La Giralda for marvelous views across the rooftops of the old city down to the massive arena of the bullring on the banks of the Río Guadalquivír. The Moorish tower with its Christian herald has become the definitive symbol of Sevilla.

With its elaborately carved wooden choir stalls, centuries-old stained glass windows, ornate iron screens, and gold leaf throughout, the cathedral is a grand dowager weighted down by her jewels.

The chapels are hung with paintings by some of Spain's greatest masters. In 1817, the church commissioned Francisco de Goya (1746-1828) to depict Sevilla's third-century Christian martyrs Santa Justa and Santa Rufina, humble sisters and potters from Triana (see Chapter 55) who endured torture and imprisonment rather than renounce their faith. Rufina was even thrown into a pit of lions, but escaped death when the beasts refused to attack her—leaving it to local leaders to complete her execution. According to legend, the sisters returned from heaven to protect La Giralda from an earthquake and they are usually depicted with a model of the tower that they saved from destruction.

Christopher Columbus (1451-1506), who seemed as restless in death as he had been in life, found his final resting place in the cathedral after several interments in both Spain and the New World. His tomb is lifted skyward by four allegorical figures representing the kingdoms of Castilla, León, Aragón, and Navarra. History and symbolism aside, the tomb is overshadowed by the main chapel of the cathedral, where the carved wood and gilded altarpiece depicting scenes from the life of Christ is one of the largest in the world.

The chapel makes a grand stage where Sevilla's rich and famous marry. The Infanta Elena, older sister of King Felipe VI, married here in 1995. (The marriage ended in divorce in 2009.) People still talk about the wedding of the fabulously flamboyant Duquesa de Alba (see Chapter 54) to her first husband in 1947. *The New York Times* extolled it as the "most expensive wedding in the world" and it was thought to trump the glamour of the nuptials of Queen Elizabeth II and Prince Philip a few weeks later.

Even if San Antonio answers the prayers of the young women of Sevilla, few of them will probably be able to stand before the glorious altar to recite their vows. Somehow I don't think that they will mind.

# 49 *Of Cigars and Arias*

## IN THE FOOTSTEPS OF CARMEN, SEVILLA

The Gypsy free spirit Carmen is one of the most mesmerizing characters in opera. When French composer Georges Bizet (1838–1875) decided to break from operatic tradition to focus on more proletarian characters, he turned to exotic southern Spain for his inspiration. Carmen first came to life in the 1845 novella by Prosper Mérimée, but she found immortality in Bizet's music. Even if you're not an opera buff, you'll instantly recognize "La Habanera," Carmen's flirtatious song in Act I and the "Toréador Song" in Act II sung by the cocky bullfighter Escamillo.

In the libretto by Henri Meilhac and Ludovic Halévy, Carmen and her smuggler friends proved a little too real for the proper Parisians who first saw the opera performed in March 1875. Alas, Bizet died a few months later thinking that the opera was a flop. A year later it did boffo box office in Vienna, and the story of the iconic femme fatale became one of the most performed operas in history. Yet the character of Carmen transcends opera. Modern Spanish women embrace her as one of the earliest symbols of a free woman who lived life on her own terms, whatever the cost.

Even today it doesn't take much imagination to picture Carmen strutting through the streets of Sevilla, her skirts swirling about her ankles. The fictional Gypsy remains such a vivid presence, in part, because the sites of her imagined escapades—and ultimate demise—are embedded into the fabric of the city. You can seek them out on a private tour offered by Sevilla Official Tours (complete with opera singers providing the soundtrack), download a free app for your phone, or simply follow a walking tour map from the city tourist office.

The opera opens at the Royal Tobacco Factory, an imposing Neoclassical building just outside the Puerta de Jerez that is now part of the Universidad de Sevilla. In the early sixteenth century, Spain became the first European country to manufacture tobacco, and this mid-eighteenth-century factory amply demonstrates the importance of tobacco to Spain's economy. When it opened, it was the second largest building in the country.

By the time that Carmen was written, almost all of the four thousand workers were women. Cigars rolled by the *cigarreras* were considered superior to cigars rolled by men. Popular belief held that the women rolled the tobacco on their inner thighs—an image so frankly sexual and evocative that it no doubt sold many a cigar. The factory did nothing to discredit the image, although it's pretty much impossible to roll a good cigar without using both hands.

As the opera opens, *cigarreras* on a break are smoking and flirting with soldiers at the factory gates. As the most vivacious, Carmen is the center of attention. She immediately captures the interest of corporal Don José, who has just promised to marry a sweet peasant girl. When the women return to the factory, a fight erupts between Carmen and another worker. When his superior orders Don José to take Carmen to jail, he lets her escape and is sent to jail himself.

This being opera, the story is quickly complicated by subplots about smuggling plans and mountain hideaways—none of which really detracts from the central narrative of love thwarted and spurned. Much of the drama of Act II takes place in the old Judería, or Jewish Quarter, where Carmen and her smuggler pals could easily hide in the narrow streets and where she and her Gypsy friends could sing and dance and entertain soldiers in the taverns. The opera was fiction, but spots such as Restaurante Corral del Agua on Calle Agua stand in for the tavern where Carmen once again sees Don José and where she meets and enchants the dashing bullfighter Escamillo.

I don't think I need to issue a spoiler alert when I reveal that the love triangle doesn't end well. The final scene takes place outside the Plaza de Toros de la Real Maestranza de Caballería de Sevilla, one of the oldest and most storied bullrings in Spain. Dressed in silk finery, Carmen arrives on Escamillo's arm. As he enters the ring, she is detained by Don José, who implores her to leave with him. She declares her love for Escamillo and—as cheers for the bullfighter rise from the ring—Don José pulls a knife and stabs his beloved.

Although Carmen sprang from the imaginations of a band of Frenchmen, Sevillanas proudly claim her as their own. A bronze statue of the fiery Gypsy stands across from the bullring on the banks of the Río Guadalquivir where her gaze across the Paseo de Colón forever beholds the spot of her violent death.

"Many people think, 'what an end!'" says guide Carmen Izquierdo of Sevilla Official Tours. "But she was a strong personality. She preferred to die rather than lose her freedom."

## TOURS

Private opera tour: www.sevillaofficialtours.com

City of Opera phone apps: www.visitasevilla.es/en/Seville-city-of-opera

City of Opera walking tour map: www.visitasevilla.es/sites/default/files/rutas_sevilla_ciudad_de_opera_0.pdf

## RECOMMENDED READING

*Carmen* by Prosper Mérimée, translated by Lady Mary Loyd

*Project Gutenberg*, tinyurl.com/CarmenGutenberg

# 50 *Spanish Rhythms*

## MUSEO DEL BAILE FLAMENCO, SEVILLA

The Museo del Baile Flamenco was made not for—but by—an artist, and that sensibility and devotion to craft make all the difference. It doesn't hurt, of course, that the artist is Cristina Hoyos, one of the greatest and most expressive flamenco dancers of the twentieth century.

Hoyos was born in 1946 in Sevilla's medieval barrio of Alfalfa and came full circle when she established her museum in the same neighborhood in an eighteenth-century building on the site of a Roman temple. She had danced in the narrow streets and in showy flamenco *tablaos* of the sort that purists often dismiss as too touristy. (In their defense, such spectaculars are often the first introduction to the art—certainly for me—and give performers work and the chance to perfect their skills.)

✳ www.museoflamenco.com

Hoyos was not one to get lost in the supporting cast, and she was invited to join the company of acclaimed dancer and choreographer Antonio Gades. As the lead dancer from 1968 to 1988, she left an indelible mark on Gades's work, including the film adaptations of *Carmen*, *El Amor Brujo* (*Bewitched Love*), and *Bodas de Sangre* (*Blood Wedding*), all directed by Spanish filmmaker Carlos Saura. Watch a

177

video of any one and you will quickly see why Hoyos's seemingly effortless combination of muscular power and feminine grace earned her the title of "Andalucían High Priestess of Flamenco."

After leaving Gades's company, Hoyos founded Ballet Cristina Hoyos, toured extensively, beat breast cancer, and founded her museum in 2006. That same year, the government of Andalucía recognized flamenco as an essential part of Andalucían cultural identity.

Flamenco artists channel sorrow and joy into an art of rhythm and movement, and life experience only imbues them with greater authority and dignity. In his lecture on the "Theory and Play of the Duende," poet and playwright Federico García Lorca (see Chapter 74) describes a flamenco dance contest where an octogenarian triumphs over younger women with "liquid waists." She stood in place, lifted her arms, tossed her head back, and stamped her foot on the floor. Her economy of gesture encapsulated a lifetime of emotion.

Hoyos poured that *duende* into the creation of her museum. As the first—and only—museum of flamenco dance in the world, it traces the evolution of flamenco from its popular but disparaged roots to its acceptance as a uniquely expressive art form. But the museum is not a place to develop an intellectual knowledge of flamenco by reading wall texts and studying objects. It is a place to feel flamenco, to let the music and movement seep into your bones.

In one gallery, a video screen covers a long wall and plays a continuous loop of dancers performing seven major forms, or *palos*, of flamenco. Occasionally a word will flash on the screen—joy, longing, despair—but such clues are hardly necessary. Two *palos* associated most closely with female dancers represent the extremes of emotion: Alegrías, which progress from joy to abandon, and the Soleá, which begins in melancholy contemplation and resolves in quiet harmony.

Dancers may be the most colorful—and feature most prominently on posters and other advertising—but they are only one part of the flamenco ensemble. The museum brings all the elements together in evening performances. Held in a small courtyard with Moorish-style brick arches, a low stage, and about one hundred chairs, they usually feature a guitarist, a singer whose high-pitched guttural chanting expresses the deep pain of the music, and one male and one female dancer. The singer and any dancer on the side also count the meter with *palmas*, a complex form of clapping.

Since my first *tablao* decades ago in a tourist restaurant beneath Madrid's Plaza Mayor, I have seen countless flamenco shows in nightclubs, theaters, small clubs, and even bars. But only at the museum have I seen a woman perform while wearing a dress with a cola—a ruffle-covered long train that can weigh nearly forty pounds. She treated it like a dance partner, alternately hugging it close to her bosom, then flinging it away with centrifugal spins. I love you, I love you not, her movements seemed to say. You give me joy, you give me pain. That is, after all, the spirit of flamenco.

# 51 A Slippery (and Delicious) Slope

## THE OLIVE OIL WORKSHOP, SEVILLA

Alexis Kerner smiled as she poured olive oil into a pretty blue glass cup and handed it to me. "Andalucían oils really stand out," she said. "They are bold. You don't get bored with them."

It's a good thing, I suppose, since the region produces three-quarters of Spain's olive oil and more than any other single nation (Italy included). Olive trees seem to cover every hill in Andalucía, their silvery green leaves shimmering in the dusty heat. It was among those trees and the nearby olive oil mills that Kerner found her calling.

Raised in New Jersey and educated in environmental science at Connecticut College, she came to Spain for love and secured a job in the environmental division of the Andalucían regional government.

The self-professed foodie decided to take a one-week course in tasting olive oil so that she could explore the common ground between the Sephardic cooking of her Jewish heritage and the cuisine of southern Spain. "After the first day, I fell in love with olive oil," she recalls. "Once I learned to really taste the differences in olive oil, I knew it was my thing."

One course led to another and it wasn't long before Kerner had earned her diploma as a professional olive oil taster from the University of Jaen and the International Olive Council. She had never really thought of herself as having an unusually refined palate, but realized that tasting is simply a matter of paying attention, becoming more sensitive to the nuances of flavor, and more discerning about what makes a good (or bad) oil.

In 2014, Kerner launched the Olive Oil Workshop to offer tastings and—for the hard core—visits to orchards and mills. Few casual tasters will develop the subtle skills of a professional, but it's possible to learn the rudiments in a ninety-minute session. With increasing interest in the possible health benefits of olive oil—as well as its versatility in the kitchen—it's time well spent.

❋ theoliveoilworkshop.com

That's how I found myself sitting at a table in the meeting room above Oleo-le, where Kerner sometimes holds her tastings. María and Benito Ángeles opened the shop in Sevilla's Arenal neighborhood about five years ago. María's great-grandfather had an olive oil mill on his property in Jaen, and she shares Kerner's passion for olive oil. She personally selects every item in the shop, including many artisanal small-production oils not otherwise available, and counts most of the producers as her friends. For those not interested in Kerner's full workshop class, the little shop is a good alternative as a place to taste and buy.

❋ www.oleo-le.com

Kerner normally selects three or four oils for her small groups to taste. She poured the oils into blue glasses so that we wouldn't be influenced by the color. She also cautioned that we should not rely solely on the grade when evaluating or purchasing oil. Extra Virgin, the top Spanish grade, has no defects and has been bottled and held properly, but may not taste as good as an ordinary Virgin olive oil. Kerner's goal was to guide us in recognizing and appreciating the subtle differences in olives that give each oil a characteristic flavor. That way, we could make our own informed choices.

We began with an Almería oil pressed from Arbequina olives. It was a delicate and mellow oil that Kerner likes to pour over white fish or even vanilla ice cream. The unassertive oil made a good starting point. Kerner demonstrated how to taste, including sipping the oil with enough air to volatalize the aromatics. She talked about the faint potential flavors often associated with olive oil—banana, artichoke, green almond, fig leaf, apple—and I began to discern the subtle differences. A Hojiblanca oil, made from olives picked very green at a farm in Málaga, had spicy notes, like fresh mown grass, black pepper, and bitter almond. It was the perfect oil for seasoning a gazpacho or a beef carpaccio, and would have been ideal for frying eggplant. The intense oil made from Picual olives from Úbeda, one of the Renaissance cities northeast of Granada, demonstrated the characteristic throat-tightening stringency of one of olive oil's chief antioxidants. To my taste, it was an excellent complement to a tart and juicy tomato with creamy mozzarella. Kerner drizzles it over dark chocolate ice cream.

Our final oil was one that Kerner herself was eager to try—an unfiltered Picudo from the hilly village of Luque in Córdoba province that had been bottled just days before. We sipped and sniffed, sipped and swirled, smacked our lips. The ultra-fresh oil was redolent of ripe banana, artichoke, and green almonds. Kerner closed her eyes and inhaled. She was delighted. "It's orgasmic," she said.

That's an oil any woman could love.

# 52 Our Lady of Hope

## LA MACARENA, SEVILLA

Sevilla's bullring is one of the most majestic in Spain and the Triana neighborhood (see Chapter 55) on the opposite banks of the Río Guadalquivír has produced many of the country's most celebrated bullfighters. But macho heroics in the arena aren't everything. Sevilla is also profoundly feminine—and I don't just mean the swirl of ruffles on a flamenco skirt, the sweep of fringe on a shawl, the flourish of a fan on a sultry evening, or even the sweet scent of the tens of thousands of orange trees that burst into bloom in the early spring.

Sevilla is a *Ciudad Mariana*, or "City of Mary," whose residents are utterly devoted to the Virgin Mary in her many manifestations. Native son Bartolomé Esteban Murillo (1617-1682), one of the great artists of Spain's Golden Age, made a career of painting the Virgin, including more than fifty light-infused and *putti*-filled scenes of the Immaculate Conception. A gigantic image that he painted for the Convento de San Francisco now hangs in the Museo de Bellas Artes, itself a former convent with a stunning tile-encrusted courtyard.

The city's most venerated Virgin is *Nuestra Señora de la Esperanza*, or Our Lady of Hope. Sevillanos affectionately call her "La Macarena," since she presides over the Basilica de la Macarena in the neighborhood of the same name on the north side of the city. Constructed in the 1940s, the basilica is painted mustard and white to match the medieval walls and gates directly across the street. Inside, the church is a vision of pink marble walls and gold leaf embellishment. But the eye goes first to La Macarena, ensconced in a niche above the high altar surrounded by a carved gilt Baroque retablo.

The sculpture of polychromed carved wood predates the church by more than three centuries. The Hermandad, or Brotherhood, of La Macarena first carried the Virgin through the streets of Sevilla during Holy Week observances in 1624. No one knows for sure who carved what is perhaps the city's most iconic image, but many speculate that it may have been Pedro Roldán (1624-1700), the noted sculptor who lived, worked, and taught in Sevilla.

Others are convinced that it is the work of Roldán's daughter Luisa Roldán (1652-1706), the first woman sculptor documented in Spain. Taught by her father, La Roldána created sculptures for the Cádiz cathedral and other churches in that city before moving to Madrid in 1688. She later became court sculptor to both Carlos II and Felipe V, but died in poverty.

"People say that only the hands of a woman could make that beauty," a Sevillana once told me. The Renaissance simplicity of the statue's face and hands stands in stark contrast to her Baroque surroundings (the more ardent the faith it seems, the more elaborate the decoration). She clasps her hands to her breast and five teardrops mark her perfect cheeks. Since her 1963 coronation during the papacy of John XXIII, she has worn a resplendent golden crown in recognition of the deep faith that she inspires.

La Macarena is also adorned with five emerald brooches from the revered bullfighter José Gómez Ortega (1895-1920). When "Joselito" was gored in the ring at age twenty-five, La Macarena was dressed in black for the funeral. It was the first and only time.

The Virgin's message of hope is so powerful that many bullfighters carry her image in the mobile chapels that accompany them from ring to ring. In the 1941 Hollywood melodrama *Blood and Sand*, an aspiring bullfighter played by Tyrone Power asks his childhood sweetheart (played by Linda Darnell) how she copes with the anxiety while he is in the ring. "I pray to La Macarena every second," she replies.

But even those who don't choose to stare down death as a profession take the Virgin's promise of redemption to heart. On Good Friday, the holiest day of the Semana Santa, or Holy Week, processions, the Virgin is enthroned in an elaborate silver float that weighs several tons. Members of the brotherhood heft it onto their shoulders for the arduous march to and from the cathedral, which stands at the opposite end of the old city. Musicians play a solemn dirge as the procession creeps through the narrow streets, the members of the brotherhood shuffling along. Worshippers throng the procession, parting like a human sea to step back on the sidewalk to let La Macarena pass. She seems to weep wet tears in the flickering candlelight on this, the darkest night of the liturgical year.

# 53 The Fringe Effect

## SHOPPING FOR SHAWLS, SEVILLA

Tradition weighs heavily on the shoulders of the women of Sevilla, but they don't really mind. Nothing so perfectly accentuates their femininity as the sultry *mantones de Manila*. Exquisitely crafted and unapologetically colorful, they embody the city's spirit of *alegría*, or joy.

The brightly embroidered silk shawls with macrame borders and heavy, heavy fringe first reached Sevilla in the eighteenth century aboard cargo ships from the Spanish colony of Manila in the Philippines—hence the name. The artful creations quickly became a definitive element in Sevillana style and such a cultural icon that picturesque painters of the nineteenth century invariably placed one on the shoulders of every Andalucían beauty they depicted.

Both practical and pretty, the shawls have never gone entirely out of style. Young girls often get their first *mantones* to wear when they make their First Communion. Adult Sevillanas take theirs out of the drawer or closet to wear to weddings, parties, the theater or a concert, or during the feria in April—the weeklong raucous spring festival that is largely reserved for locals and only remotely accessible for tourists.

If she hasn't inherited a *manton* from her grandmother or mother—they truly are heirlooms—a Sevillana may head to Juan Foronda, the shop that has been the go-to place for shawls for generations. There are several branches of the store in the city, including the flagship at Calle Sierpes 33, which opened in the 1930s. The pedestrian street is a gallery of Sevillana style, where shop windows proffer a riot of shawls, hand-painted fans, glittery jewelry, dangling earrings, and shape-hugging flamenco-inspired dresses with ruffled hems. Every Sevillana, by the way, also has one or two of these dresses in her closet, though they only come out for feria when all of Sevilla dresses up in a flashy style on the razor edge between fashion and costume.

❈ www.juanforonda.com (Spanish only)

Of all the street's enticements, the *manton* is the piece that might actually fit in back home as a show-stopping special-occasion piece. (A woman will know if she can pull it off.) Beneath vintage crystal chandeliers in Juan Foronda, wooden shelves are stacked with carefully folded *mantones*. They are available in a rainbow of colors, though black with bright, multicolored flowers remains the classic. To a Sevillana, buying a *manton* is a weighty matter, for she will wear it for the rest of her life.

The original *mantones de Manila* may have come from China by way of the Philippines, but the most desirable ones today are made by hand by Spanish women who work in their homes, using natural silk fabric and silk thread. Some of the most elaborate designs can take up to a year to complete and cost close to $2,000. Foreigners, who are treated with infinite patience at Foronda, are generally attracted first to the beauty of the embroidery. The colorful flowers are perfect on both sides of the fabric so a woman can toss her shawl with abandon with no loss of effect.

Sevillanas know that the fringe, or *fleco*, is what really makes the shawl. The intricate macrame that edges the silk cloth unfurls into long, soft strands. The weight of the fringe—it is surprisingly heavy—creates the magic. It makes the shawl fall gracefully, glide over the body, sway with every step, and caress the curves of a woman's derriere. Slip one over your shoulders and it is impossible not to feel seductive.

Foronda does offer a few shawls with machine embroidery for the bargain conscious. A large handmade shawl begins around $550, and Sevillanas hold out for the best that they can afford. While the uninitiated may not notice the differences in fabric, design or workmanship, Sevillanas will. Smaller shawls are less expensive (starting around $250) and a little easier to manage.

But Soraya Rodríguez, who assists buyers from behind the wooden counter at Foronda, advises that a larger shawl is more elegant and more versatile. The simplest way to wear a *manton de Manila* is to fold it into a triangle and drape it over the shoulders. Fold it into a rectangle and the fringe cascades over the arms and reaches below the knee. The styles of draping are only limited by the woman's imagination. Catch a wedding party filing into a church—or bursting out after the ceremony—and the *mantones* flash like a flock of butterflies.

"You can wear a simple dress and cover it completely with your *manton*," Rodríguez says.

That's power dressing at its prettiest.

# 54 *Duquesa for the Ages*

## LIVING LARGE IN THE HOUSE OF ALBA, SEVILLA

When the Duquesa de Alba died in 2014 at the age of eighty-eight, obituary writers were quick to point out that she held so many titles—somewhere around fifty—that it was not certain who would have bowed to whom in a hypothetical meeting with Queen Elizabeth of England. I can't shed any light on the subtleties of the royal pecking order, but I can say this: If you've ever dreamed of being a member of a royal family, duchesses have more fun.

At least that was true of the Duquesa de Alba, who was known to friends, family, and the European tabloids as Cayetana, a sobriquet that was much easier to remember than María del Rosario Cayetana Alfonsa Victoria Eugenia Francisca Fitz-James Stuart y de Silva. That's the name bestowed on her at birth in 1926 into the House of Alba, a fifteenth-century Spanish noble family.

The duchess was also the richest woman in Spain, with a fortune estimated between 600 million and 3.5 billion euros and with so much property it was said that she could walk the length of Spain without venturing off her own land. Among her holdings was Sevilla's Palacio de las Dueñas, a fifteenth-century Renaissance-style palace with lovely gardens on Calle Dueñas, embedded tightly in the narrow streets of barrio La Macarena, just steps from Plaza San Marcos.

Although she was born in her family's Liria palace in Madrid and spent much of her youth in London, the duchess was a Sevillana at heart. She loved horses, flamenco, and Gypsies and was often photographed at bullfights. The Palacio de las Dueñas was her pri-

mary residence, and was also where she died. On the anniversary of her death, son Carlos Fitz-James Stuart, the XIX Duke of Alba, began opening the palace to the public a few days a month.

The palace has always been a subject of great speculation. Behind huge wooden doors and a fifteen-foot-high iron gate, the tiled-roof buildings are covered with bougainvillea and obscured by gardens of roses and orange trees. Those fortunate enough to have been invited in for a concert or other event while the duchess was alive returned to the real world with stories of beautiful architecture, sumptuous furnishings, and an amazing art collection.

✳ www.fundacioncasadealba.com (Spanish only)

I haven't yet had a chance to venture inside, but I imagine that the palace is still inhabited by the spirit of a woman who was born into a position of great wealth and restrictive traditions, but who managed nonetheless to remain a true free spirit. A notable beauty who declined to model for Pablo Picasso, the duchess first married naval officer and nobleman Luís Martínez de Irujo y Artacoz in 1947 in a lavish wedding in the Sevilla cathedral. She became the XVIII Duchess of Alba in 1953 on the death of her father. The couple had six children, though there was speculation that one son was fathered by a bullfighter. The duchess won damages in a suit against a newspaper that spread the rumor and the marriage survived until her husband's death in 1972.

In 1978, the duchess shocked society by marrying Jesús Aguirre y Ortiz de Zárate, a defrocked priest. Not only had he once been her confessor, he was also eleven years her junior. The marriage, however, lasted until his death in 2001.

Cayetana dressed flamboyantly, let her once perfectly coiffed hair become a mass of white, frizzy curls, wore a bikini into her eighties, and was always rumored to appreciate the plastic surgeon's art. She was not one to go quietly into old age. In 2011 she married Alfonso Diez Carabantes, a civil servant twenty-four years younger. To prove his true love, he renounced all claims to her family wealth and the duchess appeased her children by divvying up her fortune among them before the marriage. The couple married in the Palacio de las Dueñas and the duchess celebrated by kicking off her shoes before crowds gathered out front and dancing flamenco with her new husband.

The Duquesa de Alba remained her own woman even in death. She chose to be buried in the Iglesia del Valle, a modest stucco church on Calle Veronica a short walk from her home. She had provided the funds to rebuild the Neogothic church in the 1990s to serve as the headquarters of her beloved Hermandad de los Gitanos, or Brotherhood of the Gypsies.

I imagine she threw back her mantilla and stamped her heels all the way to heaven.

# 55 Another Side of Sevilla

## BARRIO DE TRIANA

Flamenco singer Gracia de Triana (1919-1989) loved to praise the neighborhood where she was born. "Triana," she would sing in that high, throaty style, drawing out the syllables, "girlfriend of a river known as the Guadalquivir." That sounds about right to me. I have always thought of Triana, a village unto itself on the west bank, as Sevilla's little sister who is certainly saucy enough to seduce a river. For centuries, the Gypsies, sailors, and fishing families who lived in the barrio would gaze across the water at the towering landmarks of the Torre del Oro, the Plaza de Toros, and the cathedral—and then turn to their daily business of making a living and nurturing an insular, earthy culture. When you need a break from more formal Sevilla, Triana is the neighborhood to wander.

The sensibility is very different on *el otro lado*, or "the other side," even though it's just a few hundred yards over the Puente de Isabel II. When I walk across, I like to pause halfway to glance upriver at the futuristic Puente de Alamillo, the bridge designed by Santiago Calatrava and erected in 1992 to tie Sevilla to the Expo '92 fairgrounds. Then I gaze back at the Plaza de Toros on Sevilla's riverbank. Many of the matadors who made a name for themselves in that ring were born in the Gypsy streets of Triana, where small plaques on the buildings recall their names and the years of their births and deaths.

Just over the bridge sits the Mercado de Triana, a fresh food public market erected in the early nineteenth century adjacent to the crumbling Castillo San Jorge. The fortress was built by the Moors to control passage on the river, then used as the seat of the Spanish Inquisition from 1481 to 1785. A small museum inside the restored fort looks past the more sensational aspects of torture in the name of religious fanaticism to examine broader issues of persecution, prejudice, and intolerance.

But most visitors skip the museum and head straight to the market. It was cleaned up, enlarged, and brightened a few years ago, but it wasn't gentrified. It remains a functional market where a home cook can roam the stalls and pick up everything for the family meals. Sometimes, if I'm lucky, I can catch a lunchtime flamenco performance in the small theater at the market's center. Once the stalls close in late afternoon, a few classy tapas bars remain open, making the market a nice spot to linger for a quick bite and a drink.

✳ www.mercadodetrianasevilla.com (Spanish only)

Triana breeds flamenco musicians and dancers as well as bullfighters, and the barrio takes pride in carrying the torch for *flamenco puro,* the raw and unpolished style that is as much folk song and dance as it is entertainment. If I'm with my husband or a couple of friends, I might return to Triana much later at night in hopes of catching an impromptu performance in one of the bars. The best bet is to arrive after 11 P.M. and listen for boisterous clapping and the eerie nasal incantations of flamenco song coming from the doorways of little bars along Calle Betis.

By day, Triana is tamer. I usually pause at some of the tiny shops where women bent over sewing machines carefully stitch form-fitting dresses for flamenco dancers. The first time I lifted one off the hanger, I was shocked at the sheer weight of the cascade of ruffles.

I've never looked at a performer the same way, now that I know how strong she has to be to move with such sensuality and grace.

One reason that Triana is literally so colorful is that many building facades and entryways are covered with intricately patterned geometric tiles. It is as if everyone in the neighborhood got together and decided to advertise Triana's status as the city's—and one of the country's—centers of decorative ceramics.

The riverbank mud was probably the genesis of the industry. Ceramics were first made in Triana in the Roman era, and the Moors revived the industry, infusing the designs with intricate patterns and intense colors. The *alfarerías*, or pottery makers, cluster on Calle San Jorge and its side streets. Most make all kinds of goods for the table and the garden as well as Triana's signature decorative tiles. The flagship shop of the neighborhood is Cerámica Santa Ana, which opened in 1870. Its tile-encrusted facade features medallions of carefree *putti* and larger-than-life images of the third-century Christian martyrs Santa Justa and Santa Rufina, patron saints of Sevilla who were said to have been potters in Triana (see Chapter 48).

In 2014, the Centro Cerámica Triana opened in an old Santa Ana ceramics factory on Calle Antillano Campos. This museum celebrates the artistry of Triana's potteries with exhibits that outline the process of making ceramics and displays of fine pieces from Moorish times through the mid-twentieth century. The unusual reconfiguration of the building by AF6 architects creates a labyrinth through the space, retaining the historic kilns, and using configurations of short pieces of ceramic pipe, set on end, to create walls between exhibits. The ability to look through the pipes between exhibits emphasizes the continuity of the ceramics tradition, even as each era adopted its own style of decoration and glazes.

A number of artists have also taken up the pottery tradition, and their small shops are found near the more industrial showrooms. My favorite is Ceramica Rocio-Triana, also on Calle Antillano Campos. In the crowded little workshop and gallery, a husband and wife team create graceful vessels and simple platters and plates on which they inscribe excerpts from works by great Spanish-language writers.

If I'm burdened with heavy packages, I might splurge on a cab back to my hotel. But if my load is light, I end my visit by walking the short stretch of riverfront from Puente Isabel II downstream to Puente de San Telmo. Small *tabernas* and *marisquerías* set up outdoor tables along the riverbank in nice weather. Waiters dash across the street with trays of *tinto verano* and bowls of salty Marcona almonds. I settle in and watch the river flow by.

# 56 *Marriage of Styles*

## THE ALCÁZAR OF SEVILLA

Sevilla's ancient Alcázar pops up in several episodes of seasons five and six of HBO's *Game of Thrones,* where it doubled as Dorne Palace and gardens. The choice was obvious. With portions dating from the tenth century, the Alcázar is the oldest royal palace in continuous use in Europe and it practically oozes power, luxury, and elegance. Its synthesis of Moorish and Spanish artisanry embodies the intriguing juncture of East and West.

Although they chose well for atmospherics, the filmmakers might have missed the boat. They didn't need to resort to George R.R. Martin's medieval epics to find tales of adventure, romance, and intrigue. The Alcázar has seen all that and more over the last twelve centuries. Instead of serving as a set for a fictional tale, it could easily host its own series about medieval danger and desire.

✳ www.alcazarsevilla.org (Spanish only)

The palace has been enlarged, redecorated, and renovated more times than a flipped house on HGTV, but it retains some surprisingly evocative hints of even its earliest eras. The Sala de la Justicia (Hall of Justice) and the Patio del Yeso branch off from the left side of the Lion's Gate entrance. Serene and spare—the Almohads were such purists that they rarely built with ornament—they serve as the gateway into the Moorish parts of the palace complex. What survives of the Almohad palace are several open gallery rooms and a series of courtyards designed around fountains. The main palace was replaced in the mid-thirteenth century by the Castilian king Alfonso the Wise, shortly after his father, San Fernando, took Sevilla from the Moors in 1248.

This so-called "Gothic Palace" was completely overhauled when Holy Roman Emperor Carlos V chose it as the site for his marriage to his cousin Isabel in 1526. It was an arranged political marriage, but Carlos made the romantic gesture of decorating one grand hall with tile portraits in profile of himself and his bride. They did not meet until the day of the wedding, and contrary to expectation, they were smitten with each other. A chronicle of the day noted that "although there are many people around, they do not notice anyone else. They talk and they laugh and nothing else distracts them." Carlos and Isabel had five children and she ruled Spain when he was absent for years at a stretch. When she died in childbirth in 1539, Carlos was inconsolable. He dressed in mourning until his death in 1556 and never remarried.

Fortunately, Carlos largely left alone the fourteenth-century Mudéjar palace of Pedro I, also known as Pedro the Cruel. Built largely by Moorish artisans working for the Christian king, it is the architectural and artistic gem of the Alcázar complex. The centerpiece of the palace was the Patio de las Doncellas, or Courtyard of the Maidens, which was until recent years obscured by marble flooring and a Renaissance fountain. It has been restored to its fourteenth-century glory with a long reflecting pool flanked by sunken gardens with orange trees. The intricately carved arches surrounding it display peaked lobes—almost a hybrid between Christian Gothic and Moorish horseshoe arches. The lavishly appointed surrounding rooms are models of Mudéjar decorative carving and tiles.

The most beautiful surroundings do not guarantee domestic bliss. Only a teenager at the time, Pedro had been pushed into an arranged marriage with Blanche de Bourbon of the French royal line. But he loved another, and might have secretly married the Castilian noblewoman María de Padilla before the prospect of Blanche ever arose. In any event, Pedro abandoned Blanche three days after the marriage, claiming infidelity and noting that her dowry never arrived. He went back to living with María de Padilla, with whom he had four children. Since his mother and the main court were in Castilla, they made their home in the Alcázar. Their life was apparently tumultuous. Blanche, still recognized as queen, died at Medina Sidonia (French historians claim that Pedro had her poisoned or executed with a crossbow) in 1361 at age twenty-seven. María died of the plague the same year at age twenty-five in Sevilla. She was interred at a convent she had founded in Castilla, but Pedro had her body returned to Sevilla and buried in the Royal Chapel of the cathedral. Eight years later at the age of thirty-five, he would be slain by his half-brother, Enrique the Bastard, in a struggle over the throne.

When Isabel and Fernando held court in Sevilla, they were all business. Columbus met with Isabel at the Alcázar in early 1494 after his second voyage to report on his success in establishing the first Spanish colonies. Less than a decade later in 1503, the Catholic Kings built the third major group of buildings at the palace, the Casa de Contratación, or House of Trade, to oversee all the legal aspects of Spanish exploration and colonization. The Chapel of the Navigators evokes that era of go-for-broke exploration with paintings of Columbus and some of his officers on his first voyage, a painting representing Magellan's circumnavigation of the globe that left from Sevilla in 1519, and a resplendent version of Nuestra Señora de Buen Aire, Our Lady of Good Winds, the patron saint of navigators. By tradition, explorers and conquistadors came here to pray before they sailed out to expand the reaches of the known world.

# 57

## Park of the Princess

### PARQUE DE MARÍA LUISA, SEVILLA

With its gorgeous gardens, towering pines and palms, fragrant orange trees, horse-drawn carriages, and fanciful buildings, the Parque de María Luisa almost seems like something out of a fairytale. But the story of its benefactress, Infanta María Luisa Fernanda, Duchess of Montpensier (1832-1897), is hardly what little girls dream of. Thanks to her generous gift of land to the city, María Luisa is probably better loved by Sevillanos than she was by her power-hungry, scheming husband.

María Luisa was only a year old when her father Fernando VII died and her sister—herself just a toddler—ascended the throne as Isabel II (1830-1904). In 1846, the infanta and the queen were both married in a joint wedding ceremony. What sounds romantic— even if the girls were awfully young—was less about love than power. María Luisa's groom, Antoine, Duke of Montpensier and the youngest son of Louis Philippe, the king of France, hoped to marry Isabel and become king. María Luisa, alas, was his Plan B. Isabel's groom, her first cousin Francisco, Duque de Cádiz was rumored to be homosexual. Taking the long view, the French hoped that the royal marriage would be barren and that the throne would eventually pass to María Luisa or her heirs.

Much to Antoine's disappointment, Isabel gave birth to twelve children, although the paternity of some was always a matter of speculation. María Luisa and Antoine had nine children. Antoine's naked political ambition made him unwelcome at court, so the family spent much of their time in the Palacio de San Telmo in Sevilla. By an odd twist of fate, Antoine's strategy seemed to pay off in 1878 when María Luisa's daughter, Infanta María de las Mercedes (1860–1878), married Isabel's son, Alfonso XII. He had become king just a few years earlier when the queen abdicated in his favor. But Antoine's elevated status as royal father-in-law and María de las Mercedes's turn as queen were brief. About six months after the royal marriage, the teenage queen died from typhoid fever.

María Luisa outlasted her husband and spent her last years in the Palacio de San Telmo. It's a lovely spot and I hope she found peace. She and Antoine bought the late seventeenth-century palace in 1849 and it's now the seat of Andalucía's regional government. The former naval training center is easily identifiable by carvings of allegorical female figures representing the nautical arts and sciences on its facade.

In 1893, several years before her death, María Luisa donated the gardens and grounds of the palace to the city. French architect Jean-Claude Nicolas Forestier, designer of the Bois de Boulogne in Paris, was engaged to design the park. María Luisa's gift received its mature, if somewhat eccentric, appearance when the city began to redevelop this area for the 1929 Exposicion Ibero-Americano with the park as the centerpiece.

Alas, the start of the Great Depression dimmed the spotlight during Spain's turn on the international stage. But the city did gain a great green space with broad avenues, exotic trees, verdant pools and ponds, and tiled fountains and benches. The buildings seem like flights of imagination and the fantastical sculptures make the Baroque encrustation of Sevilla churches appear streamlined and modest. The park is well suited for all levels of activity, from stretching out on the grass with a good book to jogging to morning tai chi. It's also great to explore by bicycle, a mode of transportation the city encourages. (Sevilla's public bike share program, SEVICI, was one of Spain's first. Bicycles are available to residents and visitors alike, though the latter must make a fairly large deposit.)

At the northeast gates to the park, Plaza de España was the architectural magnum opus of Expo '29. A gigantic semi-circle of golden brick with inlaid panels of blue-and-white tiles, it is a unique blend of Renaissance forms with Mudejár and Art Deco decorations. The relief formations of the brick also make it look part Lego. (The building has stood in for exotic locales in a number of films, including *Lawrence of Arabia*.) Since any impressive building in Andalucía screams for a water feature, a canal crossed by four bridges forms a sort of moat to the front entrances. Families, in fact, often rent rowboats to glide around the canal. Landmark towers punctuate either end of the building, and the facade features niches of colorful tiled scenes that represent each Spanish province—and highlight the skill of Sevilla's Triana tile-makers (see Chapter 55). Spanish visitors usually pose for photos in front of their province.

There is just as much camera snapping a block east at Plaza de América, more often known as Plaza de las Palomas. The whole park is a haven for birds, but white doves have taken over the plaza, waiting for folks to buy some cracked corn and stretch out their hands to feed them. The fanciful buildings that surround the plaza house the city's Museo Arqueológico and the Museo de Artes y Costumbres Populares.

Pedaling along the pathways is like wheeling through a whimsical wonderland of nineteenth-century gardens, exotic trees from former Spanish colonies, swans gliding about on small ponds, water flowing from the mouths of lions into stone and tile fountains, a red-and-white-striped miniature castle, and several other garden follies and caprices. Of all the pieces of public sculpture, I think María Luisa might have best related to the over-the-top homage to Sevilla-born poet Gustavo Adolfo Bécquer (1836-1870), the lyric poet whose love poems often ended in dark disillusionment.

The "glorieta" consists of a white marble bench wrapping around the thick trunk of a tree with drooping branches. Carved marble images of three women represent hopeful love, possessed love, and lost love. A marble bust of the author stands behind them and two bronze cupids hover about. Young, hopeful Cupid shoots arrows at the women, no doubt inspiring love. Adult Cupid knows better; he has been stabbed and is dying. I can imagine María Luisa passing by, sagely nodding in agreement.

✳ www.sevilla.org (Spanish only)

# 58

## The Most Evil Man Who Ever Lived

### DON JUAN IN SEVILLA

Every woman alive has suffered the attentions of some guy who imagined himself as Don Juan, and I suspect every man alive has at least once fantasized about being the irresistible womanizer. No doubt the type would have existed anyway, but it was Madrid's playwright monk Tirso de Molina who gave him a name. Placing him within a minor noble family from Sevilla, he made Don Juan Tenorio his central villain in the 1630 play *El Burlador de Sevilla*, or *The Trickster of Seville*. He has proved an enduring character who represents the darkest side of Spanish machismo. Seeing Don Juan in his natural element of Sevilla is a way, I like to think, or getting to know one's enemy.

The monk's Don Juan was a seducer, murderer, and more than once he is identified as the incarnation of Satan. In the end, he unsuccessfully repents his errant life and is condemned to burn in hell for all eternity. That de Molina placed his wicked character in Sevilla was no accident, and authors who appropriated Don Juan over the years saw no need to change his zipcode. In the imagination of other Europeans (including Mozart's librettist for *Don Giovanni*, Lorenzo de Ponte), Sevilla was an exotic and mysterious city where passions ran high and moral aberrations were no doubt rampant.

The Mozart opera is possibly the most famous version of the story in the rest of the world, but Spaniards—especially Sevillanos—are more partial to the version written in 1844 by José Zorrilla (1817-1893), in which Don Juan's immortal soul is redeemed by the love of a good woman. Zorrilla at least had the decency to write his play in Sevilla, providing it with a genuine sense of place. He stayed at the Hostería del Laurel, an ancient inn located in the Barrio Santa Cruz near the Cathedral and the Alcázar. Ask a local, and chances are that she knows the opening lines by heart: *"¿La hosteria del Laurel? / En ella estáis, caballero."* In the play, Don Juan and his friend, Don Luis, meet at the inn to see which of them has won the bet made a year before that he could seduce more women and kill more men than the other.

✳ www.visitasevilla.es/en/Seville-city-of-opera

More than one hundred and seventy years later, La Hostería del Laurel is still there. It's a modest little hotel with twenty-one simple rooms, and the bar is a fine place to have a drink and admire the carved wooden panels with scenes of the Don Juan tale. It's just a couple of blocks from Plaza de los Refinadores, where a statue of Don Juan stands, and a block in the other direction from the house of Don Luis's fiancée, Doña Ana Patoja, whom Don Juan woos and seduces in Zorrilla's version of the story. (The "City of Opera" walking tour map of the city pinpoints all the relevant spots.)

Leading men from John Barrymore to Johnny Depp have portrayed Don Juan in film, and many men no doubt imagine themselves as the hand-kissing womanizer. But one Sevillano, Don Miguel de Mañara (1627-1679), apparently took the fiction to heart. When he was just thirteen he saw a production of Tirso de Molina's *El Burlador* and announced his intention to grow up to be Don Juan. Whether he ever really lived up to the character is hotly disputed. His deathbed confession certainly makes it sound that way. He calls himself the most evil man who ever lived and confesses that he "served the devil, the prince of darkness, with a thousand abominations, pride, adultery, oaths, scandals and thefts." He asks to be buried where everyone will step on his grave. It was such juicy copy that at least two other operas were written about "Don Juan de Mañara."

Toward the end of his life, the real-life Mañara tried to atone for his sins, real or imagined, by building Sevilla's Hospital de Caridad, or Charity Hospital, that still stands right behind the stunning new opera house, the Teatro de La Maestranza. If you visit the hospital's church of San Jorge with its stunning Baroque altar, you can also see the tomb of Mañara. The Catholic Church has begun his slow rehabilitation. In 1680, the archbishop submitted his candidacy for sainthood, and 305 years later, Mañara was declared "Venerated," the first step to becoming Saint Don Juan.

In Zorrilla's version, the woman Don Juan has most wronged takes matters into her own hands. She makes a bargain with God in the afterlife to have her soul and Don Juan's bound together for all eternity. As Don Juan dies in the final graveyard scene, he chooses to be with the saintly Doña Ines in heaven rather than plunge them both into hell. Every Sevillano knows the story, as it is performed every year on All Saints Day. As one Sevillana once told me, "We don't have Halloween, but we do have Don Juan."

# 59

## *The Intimacy of Women*

### BATHS OF ANDALUCÍA

No one prizes water more than desert people. In Spain, the Moors left a legacy of shady courtyards with burbling fountains and gently flowing channels of water. Architects as much of delight and illusion as of space, they knew that even the sight and sound of running water would evoke a sensation of cool refreshment.

But the body craves more. The Moors also built on the tradition of the Roman thermal bath, introduced to the Iberian peninsula centuries earlier, to create facilities that merged aesthetic beauty and engineering ingenuity. The goal may have been to keep the populace clean and healthy, but even in those practical times, people knew that a good soak could also be restorative to the mind and spirit. Pools of water of different temperatures are the essential feature of the bath. The Romans generally started in the cool pool and worked up to the hot, while the Moors preferred to end in the cool.

In Andalucía, remains of ancient baths in Córdoba, Granada, and Ronda offer good opportunities to appreciate the lovely but functional architecture—with the signature star-shaped openings in the ceiling to let in light. But admiring the baths in the abstract is no substitute for a sybaritic soak. Fortunately, the tradition of the *hammam*, or bath, has enjoyed a revival in the past twenty years. Modern versions have popped up in Granada, Córdoba, Málaga, Jerez, Almería, and Sevilla, where Aire de Sevilla—a hybrid of Roman and Moorish traditions with modern plumbing—is a good example. It opened around the turn of the millennium in a sixteenth-century palace in the heart of the old city. Like most of its kind, it offers optional massages and even a vigorous scrub, but concentrates on the pleasures of the pools.

Truth is, these days we have easier and more efficient ways to simply get clean in the privacy of our homes. But there is an elemental appeal to the ritual of the bath, an intimate experience shared with like-minded souls. The Arabic word *hammam* translates as "spreader of warmth," but its meaning, I think, goes well beyond the physical experience of immersing yourself inch by inch in a pool of water that at first seems so hot you want to jump out of your skin. It's about the warmth of belonging in a safe, comfortable, soothing place. For women, who were historically isolated in their homes, the bath was a treasured opportunity to relax in the company and comfort of other women.

In our day, many baths no longer maintain the tradition of keeping genders apart in either separate facilities or during separate hours. While I'm usually all for gender equality, I think this is a misstep. The last time I visited Aire de Sevilla, a few men had accompanied the women in their lives, but their demeanor suggested that it was more a duty than a joy. For one thing, they were learning firsthand that the image of the bath as a place where women primped for seduction was more a fantasy promulgated by Romantic writers and painters than a reality.

That's not to say that the experience isn't sensual. But a woman should relish it as a special, personal pleasure. So visit with a few close female friends—or almost better, by yourself. In ancient times, taking a soak was one of the best ways to catch up on gossip.

Today we have an onslaught of information and the bath is much better used as a place to unplug from everything, even idle chat.

By herself, a woman can find her own rhythm, following candle-lit lanterns from space to space. The ritual usually starts in a steam room where the moist heat loosens your body and the aroma of eucalyptus opens your breath. After that, a cool shower brings the body back to attention.

Five chambers of water await, and the order of experiencing them is entirely up to you. I could spend all my alloted time in the salt pool, where it is impossible not to float like a cork. The feeling of weightlessness is pure joy, and when I lie back in the water until my ears are submerged, I can hear the blood thrum in my temples. This, I imagine, is what the womb must have felt like had I been conscious enough to enjoy it.

Aire de Sevilla's sequence of warm (96.8°F), hot (104°F), and icy cold (61°F) pools all link up together. For me, which order I take them is a matter of listening to my body's dictates. Does it want to be coddled or challenged? Cooked or chilled? Like most people at the bath, I end in the final warm pool with hydromassage jets. The gentle bubbles seem to complete the process of bringing mind and body into harmony.

*Medicam mens sana in corpore mundum*, as the Romans might have said: Soothed mind in a clean body.

✳ www.beaire.com

✳ www.hammamalandalus.com

✳ www.hammamandalusi.com

# 60 *Fino and Finesse*

## SHERRY CULTURE, JEREZ DE LA FRONTERA

Once dismissed as a libation sipped by British dowagers or the prissy Crane brothers on the television sitcom *Frasier,* sherry has made a comeback, ironically enough through the explosion of cocktail culture. A new generation has seized on the complexity of flavors in traditional sherry. Talia Baiocchi, the Brooklyn-based editor-in-chief of the drinks magazine *PUNCH,* was so captivated with sherry when she first started tasting the good stuff—as opposed to the sticky-sweet "cream sherries" that had given the wine a bad name—that she recently wrote the book *Sherry: A Modern Guide to the Wine World's Best-Kept Secret.*

According to Baiocchi, the most popular American cocktail in the mid-nineteenth century was the Sherry Cobbler, which combines sherry with citrus and simple syrup. Bartenders who are resurrecting classic cocktails have rediscovered the versatility of the Spanish wine. But the sherry resurgence is also part of a larger shift in the American palate, theorizes Baiocchi. She hails the declining interest in sweet, fruity food and drink and the simultaneous "embrace of bitter and intensely savory flavors." She also believes that in the search for authenticity, many drinkers are learning to prize sherry for its singularity.

There are thousands of wines in the world, but there is only one sherry, and it is integral to the landscape, history, and lifestyle of its homeland in Andalucía's Cádiz province. "It's a unique part of the world," says Baiocchi. "The lifestyle is very specific. It's quite slow and people really enjoy themselves."

Jerez de la Frontera is the largest of the communities in the Sherry Triangle, the strictly defined area that received the first Spanish wine denomination in 1933. The white Palomino grapes for sherry are grown primarily in a hardpan chalky soil called *albariza* and the wine is produced in often centuries-old *bodegas*. The other points on the triangle are seaside Sanlúcar de la Barrameda (see Chapter 62) and El Puerto de Santa María, a small community as well-known for its shellfish restaurants and bullring as for its *bodegas*.

Winemaking in the Sherry Triangle is more than three thousand years old. The Phoenicians were likely the first to make wine here, and the process flourished under the Romans. Jerez came under Moorish rule in the early eighth century and remained a frontier between Christian and Islamic powers for the next 500 years. (Its Alcázar, which began to take shape in the eleventh century, is worth visiting for its gardens, traces of the mosque, and for its intact Arabic baths with their striking boiler room.) Despite the Islamic prohibition on alcohol consumption, wine production continued under Moorish rule—ostensibly for trade—and really picked up after Alfonso X of Castilla reconquered Jerez in 1264.

Trade with England began in the fourteenth century and the English soon developed an insatiable thirst for sherry. By the mid- to late-eighteenth century, both the English and Spanish-speaking Americas had followed suit. Looking at the hulking sherry *bodegas* that dominate so much of the city of Jerez, it's hard to believe that demand ever flagged.

One of the largest modern *bodegas*, González Byass, was founded in 1835 and remains in family hands. Its flagship is Tío Pepe, a bright and lightly oxidized sherry that is as well known for its logo—a bottle with red hat and bolero jacket and a flamenco guitar—as for its delicate flavor. The *bodega*, which makes more than thirty different sherries, has one of the city's busiest tour schedules.

✳ www.bodegastiopepe.com/en/visit/sherry-wine-and-brandy-tour

Sherry is a fortified wine. That means that after the newly harvested grapes ferment for a few months, the young wine is fortified with a mix of brandy and old sherry (called *mitad y mitad*) to stop the fermentation. The wine is then racked into barrels of porous North American oak to age, where it becomes more concentrated and develops the characteristic oxidized flavor of sherry. For most of the wines, a little air space is left at the tops of the barrels so that a crust of yeast, called *flor*, will develop and modulate the amount of oxygen that the wine absorbs.

Sherry is aged in a *solera*—a stack of barrels—where wine for bottling is drawn off from the lowest tier. Wine is transferred down from the next highest level to top up the barrels, with new wine going into the uppermost barrels. Each *solera* produces a blended wine that is consistent from year to year, and a very old *solera* (like some at González Byass) produces sherry where some tiny fraction of the wine can be more than 100 years old. Managing these barrels is the fine art—and alchemy—of making sherry. The real artist of the sherry world is the *capataz*, or cellar master.

The proof of the *capataz's* skill lies on the tongue. Most *bodegas* end tours with tastings where visitors sip and compare the three main styles of sherry. Baiocchi finds that first-time sherry drinkers gravitate toward oloroso, which is aged longer and is therefore richer. Since it is more oxidized, it can be nearly as dark as molasses and often tastes raisin-y. At the other end of the spectrum, fino, the driest and palest style, tends to be light, refreshing, and taste faintly of toasted almonds. Between the two is amontillado, which begins life as a fino and receives additional aging and oxidation to concentrate its flavors.

One of the finest small artisanal sherry makers in Jerez is El Maestro Sierra, which is one of the few *bodegas* run by women. Send an email ahead if you would like to visit and tour (in Spanish only). Founded in 1832 by a cooper whose barrels are still in use, El Maestro Sierra has some of the oldest stocks and oldest *soleras* in the sherry world. It has been in the hands of Doña Pilar Plá Pechovierto since her husband's death in 1976. Now in her nineties, Plá Pechovierto has been joined by her daughter Carmen Borrega Plá and by *capataz* Ana Cabestrero. They have succeeded in making El Maestro Sierra one of the "most sought after and beloved boutique *bodegas* in Jerez," says Baiocchi.

✳ www.maestrosierra.com/nuevaweb/el-maestro-sierra

There is still room for newcomers in this tradition-bound region. In 1998, wealthy entrepreneur Joaquín Rivero established Bodegas Tradición. Aiming to catapult sherry back into its place among the world's greatest wines, Rivero jump-started the process by purchasing old, high-quality barrels of winery stock. Many were available in tiny lots, but through skillful blending, Tradición creates masterful wines with an average age of twenty or thirty years. Tours include Rivero's private art collection of about three hundred paintings by Spanish masters. The elegant, restored *bodega* with whitewashed walls, arched doorways, and a tranquil central patio is one of the best places to imagine the lifestyle of a wealthy sherry baron.

✳ www.bodegastradicion.es

Sherry itself, though, is more democratic. The lifestyle of a sherry-drinking Jerezana is open to all—and is the key to appreciating this corner of Spain.

"Go to sherry bars," advises Baiocchi. " Hop around and go to different restaurants to have a couple of bites of whatever that place's specialty is. Then continue on to another place and then another. That's the way to really get the feel for Jerez."

## RECOMMENDED READING

*Sherry: A Modern Guide to the Wine World's Best-Kept Secret* by Talia Baiocchi

# 61 *Practice Makes Perfect*

## REAL ESCUELA ANDALUZA DEL ARTE ECUESTRE, JEREZ DE LA FRONTERA

Spanish women have been rocking short-heeled knee-high boots since long before the style caught on in the United States. Even in Spain nobody can carry off the look of tight jeans or a short black skirt with boots better than the women of Jerez de la Frontera. I suppose that they come by their confident strut and sense of style naturally. Riders or not, Jerezanas are surrounded by horse culture. The region is as famous for its horses as it is for its sherry (see Chapter 60).

And these aren't just any ponies. In the fifteenth century, breeders at the Carthusian monastery in the Jerez countryside began to establish the top bloodlines of the Andalucían horse, also known as the Spanish horse or *pura raza espanola*. With the blessing of the Spanish crown, the monks nurtured and improved the line until they had created the most regal breed of European horses. The Andalucían was highly prized in battle and became a favorite mount for kings posing for equestrian portraits. When Napoleon's armies invaded France, mares and stallions were secreted out of the monastery and hidden from the enemy.

These days, the noble horses are turned to artistry rather than warfare. In 1973, the Fundación Real Escuela Andaluza del Arte

Ecuestre was created to train horses and riders and to operate one of several breeding farms in the area. With their natural rhythm and balance and showy high-stepping trot, the pale gray steeds soon earned the nickname "dancing horses." They star in a grand spectacle or "equestrian ballet" in which horses and riders in eighteenth-century-style costumes perform some of the most difficult classical dressage movements. In what are called "school jumps," the horses exhibit the muscular grace of dancers by rearing back and tiptoeing through the air.

✳ www.realescuela.org/en

Such artistry doesn't come easily, even to these equine athletes. I prefer to skip the pageantry of performance days and visit instead to watch the workouts and practices. The grounds are less crowded and I can wander through the gardens, visit the museum that traces the evolution of the bond between humans and horses, and watch as harness-makers craft elaborate examples of their art in the saddlery. Finally, I stand by the fence of the outside exercise rings to watch the horses as they revel in the sheer joy of movement.

That unbounded outdoor joy is channeled into choreography in the indoor arena, or *picadero*, an oval surrounded by stands that can hold up to sixteen hundred people for a performance. The rest of the time it's put to use as a practice ring. The Royal School lets visitors sit in the stands to appreciate the hard work that takes place behind the scenes. Those hours outside the spotlight make the showtime artistry seem effortless.

Even without fancy costumes, the horses and riders are generally a polished team. But there are exceptions and I always remember a nervous horse that balked at performing the signature chorus-line *courbettes*, dancing with its forelegs raised off the ground. Every few minutes, trainers paused to entice the horse into performing, speaking to it softly, rubbing its nose, and patting its flanks. They never raised their voices or showed the slightest impatience. It was an ultimate collaboration, as the trainer coaxed the horse's natural grace and beauty into the open, and the horse let go of its fears and reserve to shine in the ring.

# 62 *Easter on the Beach*

## SALT ON THE TONGUE, SANLÚCAR DE LA BARRAMEDA

One of the boons of spending time among Spaniards is that their considerable capacity for enjoying life tends to be infectious. That became abundantly clear when I spent a long Easter weekend in Sanlúcar de la Barrameda, where my goal-oriented approach to R&R was thrown into stark contrast with the lighter, more improvisational Spanish style.

Many Spanish businesses shut down during Holy Week and Spanish families were taking advantage of the break to enjoy a few days in the sunny south. Located on the Bay of Cádiz at the mouth of the Río Guadalquivir, Sanlúcar is an undemanding kind of place with bright plazas, sandy beaches, and an abundance of fresh seafood.

It's also one of the points on Andalucía's Sherry Triangle. The *bodegas* focus on manzanilla, a dry and delicate fino-style sherry that captures the essence of the salt wind off the bay. More than a dozen companies make manzanilla in Sanlúcar, and several have named their sherries after alluring female figures, including La Gitana, or the gypsy, and La Sirenita, the mythical half-woman and half-bird Siren whose song seduces sailors to their deaths.

✳ www.sanlucarturismo.com

Not nearly as colorfully christened, Bodegas Barbadillo is one of the very few sherry houses with a woman cellar master, or *capataz*. Now one of the region's largest producers, Barbadillo got into the sherry business in 1821 and remains in the hands of the founding family. But it is *capataz* Montse Molino whose fine-tuned palate dictates the flavor, balance, and character of each of the firm's sherries. The tour of Barbadillo's centuries-old warehouse facility includes a visit to a small museum of the sherry trade and a tasting. Tours, however, were suspended for the holiday and I would have no chance to delve into the details of Sanlúcar's signature drink.

✳ barbadillo.com/enoturismo-y-espacios/visitas-barbadillo

The Spaniards, however, were unperturbed. In lieu of a history lesson, they proceeded directly to the tasting. By late morning, the outdoor café tables in Sanlúcar's main square, Plaza del Cabildo, were filled with vacationers who had settled in for conversation, a sip of sherry, a bowl of olives, a plate of peel-and-eat shrimp, and some more sherry. I did the same. It was much easier to appreciate the slightly bitter almond tang of the manzanilla when I sipped it with olives from nearby groves and shellfish harvested just off the beach.

As a gateway to Andalucía's arterial river, once navigable all the way to Sevilla and Córdoba, Sanlúcar flourished as a trading center for the better part of three millennia. In 1498, Columbus outfitted his third voyage at Sanlúcar and in 1519 Magellan began his circumnavigation of the globe here. He is said, by the way, to have spent more on manzanilla than on armaments. (When he was killed in the Philippines, he might have wished it was the other way around.) The river and the harbor have grown ever shallower with centuries of accumulated silt, and since the late nineteenth century, most trade on this coast has passed through nearby Cádiz. Sanlúcar has put its figurative feet up and settled into a comfortable retirement.

The grand buildings in the upper town recall the city's heyday and I roused myself to climb the steep streets to the limestone cliffs where Sanlúcar's noble houses stand. This time, I was not as surprised (or honestly, disappointed) to find that no tours were being offered of the 1517 palace of one of Spain's most powerful families, the dukes of Medina Sidonia. (Part of the palace has been transformed into a nine-room lodging.) Instead, I wandered the streets full of crumbling Baroque buildings, bright flower gardens, and dark, ponderous churches.

The Spaniards, on the other hand, followed the sun, strolling through a strip of parkland down to the sea and the concrete walkway that borders the contours of the beaches. Children played in the sand and riders trotted their horses along the water. At Baja de Guía, weekenders share the beach with Sanlúcar's fishing fleet. Most fishermen set nets at night and land their catch near dawn, so during the day their small boats sit overturned on the beach and their slightly larger ones bob offshore. The shallow harbor and sandbars are part of one of the richest crustacean fisheries in Europe: plump red and pink shrimp, brawny king prawns, spiny cigalas (also known as "Norway lobster" or "Dublin Bay prawns"), and even true Atlantic lobster.

The working docks are also Sanlúcar's main restaurant district, so it's a short carry from the net to the kitchen to the plate. By early afternoon, waiters along the Bajo de Guía were scurrying to push tables together and drape them in white linens for extended families intent on enjoying a long, lazy feast. As kids darted from table to beach and back, parents and grandparents slurped clams, peeled shrimp, nibbled fried pieces of the small shark called *cazón*, and tucked into big bowls of rice with whole cigalas perched on top.

I selected a sunny outdoor table and ordered an omelet stuffed with crunchy whole tiny shrimp. As a complement, I treated myself to a glass of Pasada's Bota Punta manzanilla so I could savor the silky saltiness. A taste and a sip told me all I needed to know about Sanlúcar.

✳ www.ruralduquesmedinasidonia.com/ofertas.html
　　(Spanish only)

# 63

## By the Sea, By the Beautiful Sea

### CÁDIZ, THE FIRST CITY OF WESTERN EUROPE

If you're a fan of James Bond films, you've probably caught a glimpse of Cádiz. In the most indelible scene of 2002's *Die Another Day*, Halle Berry emerges from the waves off Playa La Caleta in an orange bikini with a knife tucked into a wide white belt.

Admittedly, Berry upstaged the city and the waterfront, but Cádiz was an inspired choice to stand in for Havana. Both cities have a worldly, weather-worn sensuality. Nor was it a stretch for Cádiz to assume yet another identity. Since it was founded by the Phoenicians as the trading port of Gadir in 1100 B.C. (residents still call themselves Gaditanos), the city has been Carthaginian, Roman, Visigoth, and Moorish by turn. The Christian kings took it back in the thirteenth century,  and by the 1550s, it was the main port of the Spanish fleet sailing to and from the New World.

Like women, cities only get more interesting with age. As the oldest continuously inhabited city in Western Europe, Cádiz harbors a wealth of stories. It has been tested by various conquerors, and has withstood pirate attacks, a 1587 raid by Sir Francis Drake, a siege by Napoleon's army, and the 1755 Lisbon earthquake. When the earthquake obliterated most of the historic city, Cádiz rebuilt with harbor forts to protect the shipping trade, a rational grid-style street plan, and a surprising number of tall buildings with watchtowers so merchants could keep an eye on the comings and goings of their ships.

The spot was simply too good to abandon. Located on a finger-shaped peninsula between the open Atlantic and the serene Bay of Cádiz, the city basks in seaside light that illuminates even the narrowest streets. Andalucían poet Manuel Machado (1874-1947) once described Cádiz as "*salada claridad*" or "salt-laden brilliance."

It's impossible not to feel good basking in that broad, diffuse light. After your own swim in Playa La Caleta, the small city is made for strolling. Almost the entire perimeter is lined with a shoreline promenade, so it is hard to get lost for long if you trace your way along the headlands, through the old city, and back to the shore. If you're disoriented, remember that the big waves lap the Atlantic shore, the little ones wash the harbor on the bay.

Playa La Caleta sits between two of the city's remaining fortifications. Built in 1598, the Castillo de Santa Catalina was the port's main protection for many decades, and the view from its ramparts emphasizes its strategic position. No ship can reach the port from the Atlantic without passing by.

A short walk along the seaside promenade past fishermen surf-casting from the rocks leads to the manicured Parque Genovés, a tribute to Spain's lost empire planted with trees and plants from around the globe. A defensive battery at the northwest corner of the city marks the transition to the broad boulevard, Alameda Marqués de Comillas, with resolutely Andalucían tile-covered fountains and benches and the heady scent of Seville oranges hanging in the air.

This is where I like to leave the breezy peripheral promenade, and head down one of the cool, narrow streets into the city proper.

In a heavily modernized palace on Plaza de Mina, the Museo de Cádiz combines the collections of the fine arts museum and the archeological museum. When the crown expropriated the property of the Catholic church in the nineteenth century, the art museum became the safe haven for a soulful series of Zurbarán portraits of saints that had hung in a Carthusian monastery in Jerez.

✳ www.museosdeandalucia.es

The archeological museum was founded in 1887 after a fifth century B.C. carved sarcophagus of a man was unearthed at the Cádiz shipyards. To the unending delight of romantics, his female counterpart was discovered a century later. Solid and serene, they now lie side by side, stars in one of the finest collections of Phoenician artifacts in the Mediterranean. Another display high-lights more than three thousand gorgeous pieces of Carthaginian gold jewelry excavated in 2012. Stunning in their design and the sheer virtuosity of the goldsmith's technique, the pieces are evidence that the urge to adornment is as old as humankind.

In a region with such deep history, it's hard to imagine what else might be literally underfoot—or even what treasures hide behind closed doors. It is easy to walk right past the Oratorio de Santa Cueva on the main street of Calle Rosario because this fine Neoclassical structure is sandwiched tightly between other less distinguished buildings. Inside, a trio of frescoes by Francisco de Goya (1746-1828) includes an unusual *Last Supper* where Christ and his disciples sit eastern-style on the floor.

Not the least bit hidden, 148-foot Torre Tavira was the high-est of the 160 watchtowers that dominated the Cádiz skyline in the eighteenth and nineteenth centuries. From its dominant position in the center of town it still offers commanding views of Cádiz, a tethered bauble on the sea. Even better than the unaided view with the naked eye, a chamber at the top functions as a *camera obscura*, projecting an inverted image of Cádiz rooftops on the wall opposite a narrow slit.

❈ www.torretavira.com

All temporal power in Cádiz concentrates on the Plaza de San Juan de Dios, which also happens to be a good place to enjoy a plate of the region's signature *pescaito frito*, or mixed fried fish. The Ayuntamiento, or city hall, presides over the plaza. Its clocktower chimes the melody of "Amor Brujo" ("Bewitched Love"), composed in 1914-15 by native son Manuel de Falla (1876-1946).

One of Spain's greatest twentieth-century composers, Falla rests in the crypt at the Catedral Nueva, practically back at the waterfront on the bay side. This voluptuous Baroque church was Spain's last cathedral financed by its overseas riches. Begun in 1772, construction paused in 1796 and was effectively abandoned during the Napoleonic invasion. What began as a show of ecclesiastical wealth became a symbol of civic pride when Gaditanos finished the cathedral in 1838 with volunteer labor. It fits the city perfectly—the marble-clad walls seem to glow from within, and the great golden dome glistens in the moonlight.

❈ www.cadizturismo.com

# 64 The Thrill of the Drive

## CROSSING THE MOUNTAINS OF ANDALUCÍA'S WHITE TOWNS

A glance at a topographic map shows that, apart from the central plateau, Spain is crinkled around the edges. Mountain range piles upon mountain range, the result of the bump and grind of European and African tectonic plates. Driving a twisting mountain road is a quintessential Spanish experience and few drives offer the breathtaking natural beauty and village charms of Andalucía's Ruta de los Pueblos Blancos or "route of the white towns." Along the 75-mile (121-km) drive between Ronda (see Chapter 65) and Arcos de la Frontera, Spain's famous white-washed villages cling to the rough security of their peaks or nestle in the green valleys. The drive is an exhilarating up, down, and up again route through the territory of warlords and highwaymen to "the city of poets."

For 2,000 years these mountains sheltered guerrilla warriors, from the Celts resisting Roman rule to the Moors and Christians engaged in their epic 800-year struggle over southern Spain. The *serrania de Ronda* and adjoining *serrania de Grazalema* were even a rare stronghold of the Republicans during the Spanish Civil War. The most colorful inhabitants were the brigands who roamed the hills from late Roman times into the early twentieth century. Spain's national police force, the Guardia Civil, was created in 1844 to clean up the mountains.

The countryside is far less lawless now, but Spain's daredevil drivers still seem to channel the reckless spirit of the bandits along the mountain roads. On a "highway" as twisting as a heap of twine, my husband and I found ourselves tailgated by a BMW whose driver held a cellphone in one hand and a cigarette in the other. He finally passed on a blind curve. Fortunately, one of the buzzing motorcyclists leaning almost horizontally into a turn wasn't coming the other way.

Even for those of us with a greater inclination toward self-preservation, the drive is a rush of sensation. It's tempting to take it in one long sweep, but that's like eating the entire box of chocolates at one sitting.

Taking the route one bite at a time, tiny Algodonales, with its Roman ruins and whitewashed, tile-roofed houses, is a good introduction to the Moorish architecture that fits so harmoniously into the landscape. Only about 20 miles (32 km) from Ronda, Algodonales was discovered at the turn of the millennium by a new breed of daredevils who made it Spain's capital of paragliding. The town sits in the foothills and the thermals at the beginning and end of the day lift colorful, kite-like paragliders to dizzying heights.

It's a wonder that the gliders don't try launching from the fort at the top of Zahara de la Sierra. At 1,985 feet above sea level, the stone tower is the highest man-made object around. From Algodonales, Zahara is only 16 miles (26 km) south along a switchback highway that follows the ridges before circling up the massif to reach the town's eagle-nest perch above the plain. Its "castle" is one of the best preserved frontier forts of the thirteenth century, and it repeatedly changed hands between Muslim and Spanish rulers. A graded track ascends the hill from the village to the fort past cacti, wildflowers, and almond trees. The massive iron door is usually closed but not locked, and a climb up stone stairs to the ramparts explains instantly why the fort was built: Approaching enemies were visible for miles in every direction.

The 10-mile (16-km) drive south from Zahara to Grazalema is the most dramatic stretch in these mountains. The road climbs for 5 miles (8 km) from the artificial lake-reservoir at the base of parched Zahara to the Puerta de las Palomas, or "Pass of the Doves," as the 4,450-foot-high mountain pass is called. There's an observation point where drivers can turn off, relax their grip on the steering wheel, and take in the views across the forested mountains to the hills of Africa shimmering in the distance. Then it's an exhilarating downhill spiral to Grazalema, which nestles in a valley at an altitude of 2,660 feet. The town is Spain's wettest, receiving about 85 inches of rainfall a year.

While Zahara was built around A.D. 800 as a military site, Grazalema was settled about the same time by peace-loving Berber farmers from northern Morocco. They never fortified their town, so warring armies simply bypassed it and the Grazalemans went about their business of growing crops and tending flocks, flourishing while other towns were besieged and pillaged. Now a town of weavers, potters, painters, and jewelers, Grazalema has never shed that laidback attitude. It's a chief staging ground for mountain hikers heading into Grazalema Mountains Natural Park. In the center of town, bars and restaurants with outdoor tables are perfect for kicking back after a gnarly day on the trails.

The first 10 miles (16 km) west of Grazalema snake through deep forests of the national park. Then the road suddenly breaks into the sunshine for a straight 20-mile (32-km) sprint to Arcos de la Frontera, whose name recalls that it was once the borderland between Christian and Muslim Spain. Like other white towns, Arcos looks from a distance as though a giant bucket of whitewash were sloshed over a mountaintop, and like the others, narrow streets ascend to the old quarter around the summit.

What invaders could never destroy, nature did. In 1765 the Lisbon earthquake toppled most of the city, leaving the Arcos cork and wine merchants to rebuild with stately Neoclassical palaces crammed onto a street plan of medieval donkey alleys. Incautious drivers often discover the hard way just how tight the passages are. Shopkeepers rush out to help motorists negotiate corners without leaving a swath of automotive paint on the building.

For all of that, Arcos is a city of respite for travelers, a place to partake of interior patios cool with shade and bright with flowers. It is a place to watch swallows skim along the mountain wall at dusk, a place to marvel over the coats of arms over every doorway (Alfonso X knighted all the inhabitants when they sided with him against the Moors in 1264), a place called "the city of poets" for its sheer lyrical beauty. At day's end, westward across the fertile plains, the sun sinks like a red ball into the distant Bay of Cádiz.

✳ www.cadizturismo.com

# 65

## *Living on the Edge*

### THE DARING CITY OF RONDA

Ronda is a city for women who were always attracted to the bad boys in high school. It's seen more than its share of revolutionaries, bullfighters, and bandits—and men who hope to bolster their own machismo by association. There is something improbably romantic about Ronda. It's a city that lives on the edge and always seems to flirt with danger. If you were one of those girls in high school, you know what I mean.

It's hard to believe that Ronda could even exist. The city clings to the top of a 394-foot limestone escarpment that rises practically straight up from the plain below. If that weren't enough, it's cleaved in two by a deep gorge cut by the Río Guadelevín. Ronda is essentially two settlements with a big, vertigo-inducing hole between them. La Ciudad, as Rondeños call it, is the older of the two, an Iberian settlement urbanized by the Romans and elaborated into a spiral staircase of a city by the Moors. Across the gorge, El Mercadillo, which began to take shape in the sixteenth century, counters the narrow twisting streets of La Ciudad with a more modern and orderly grid layout.

✳ www.turismoderonda.es/indexeng.htm

Spain's oldest bullring, La Plaza de Toros de Ronda, was built in El Mercadillo and inaugurated in 1785. The white-and-mustard building with a statue of a big bronze bull out front is one of the most storied in the history of the sport. Even if you disapprove of bullfighting, it's hard to ignore the fearlessness and grace that bullfighters exude. That seductive combination may have taken root in this ring when fabled matador Pedro Romero (1754-1839) revolutionized the contest between man and bull by taking the bullfighter off horseback and placing him eye to eye with his opponent. Romero is said to have killed more than 5,000 bulls in a six-decade career. He died of natural causes in 1839, but not before serving as the inspiration for Francisco de Goya's series of bullfighting prints *Tauromaquia*. Every September, Romero is honored with the Feria Goyesca that culminates in a bullfight in nineteenth-century costume.

For the 2009 event, fashion designer Giorgio Armani designed the suit of lights for smolderingly handsome bullfighter Cayetano Rivera Ordóñez, who has also posed with Penelope Cruz for a *Vogue* cover shot by Annie Leibovitz. Armani is not the only tastemaker to get caught up in the allure of the bullring. None other than Pablo Picasso designed the suit of lights for Antonio Ordóñez, Cayetano's grandfather, when he inaugurated the Feria Goyesca in the 1950s. Antonio was a friend of Orson Welles (who is buried on his property) and Ernest Hemingway. Both men spent many summers in Ronda and were fascinated by what the museum at the Plaza de Toros calls the "oscillation between luck and death" that plays out in the ring.

In 2015, the city of Ronda erected plaques outside the bullring to honor the two old friends who burnished Ronda's rakish image and presented it to the world. Each also has a section of the scenic walkway along the edge of the gorge named for him. The Paseo Ernest Hemingway starts behind the bullring and continues toward the city's green park, the Alameda del Tajo, while the Paseo Orson Welles leads the opposite direction toward the Puente Nuevo.

Spanning the gorge at its vertiginous top, the Puente Nuevo crosses between the new and old cities, but creating that connection was no simple feat. A bridge originally opened in 1739, but collapsed two years later, carrying fifty people to their deaths. The "new" bridge was begun in 1759 and inaugurated in 1793. An interpretation center in the bridge explains the challenges caused by the tough geography of the area. But you'll probably get the point if you peek over the edge of the low wall and look straight down. Those unfortunate people crossing the first bridge were not the only ones to lose their lives here. During the Spanish Civil War, Republicans executed a group of Nationalist sympathizers on the edge of the gorge. Hemingway based the haunting scene in *For Whom the Bell Tolls* on that event.

Hemingway and Welles based themselves in the old town where they soaked up the atmosphere, hung out in the bars, and ventured across the bridge to attend corridas. It's easy to imagine them relishing the sense of mystery of the old streets and passageways.

They were, alas, too young to have met the storied bandits of the eighteenth and nineteenth centuries. The remote area was a haven for thieves who preyed equally on trade caravans and travelers. Many of them rose to folk-hero status and more adventurous travelers came to view a hold-up as a thrilling part of their journey. The Museo del Bandolero has a selection of the newspaper stories, comic books, and pulp novels that celebrated their exploits. José Maria Hinojosa Cabacho (1805-833), known as "El Tempranillo," or "The Early One," was one of the most charismatic. He was said to be a real charmer, who once sweet-talked a woman by telling her that she didn't need the ring on her finger because her hand was already so beautiful. Once he had relieved her of the ring, he kissed her hand and wished her a safe journey.

That's one way to a woman's heart.

# 66 *Jet Set Playground*

## RICHES OF MARBELLA

Visiting Marbella is a guilty pleasure on the order of following Kim Kardashian's Twitter feed or binge-watching Real Housewives. It's where the merely rich like to be taken for famous, and the truly famous hide behind Ray-Bans.

A convincing case can be made that the Costa del Sol's swankiest resort derives its name from its one-time Moorish rulers who called it Marbil-la. But I prefer the story that Isabel II (1830-1904) inadvertently christened the town when, on a visit, she exclaimed "¡*Que mar tan bello!*" or "What a beautiful sea!"

After all, Marbella is much better known for its association with the rich, famous, and royal than it is for its typically Andalucían history of successive settlements by the Phoenicians, Romans, Visigoths, and Moors. It came under control of the Catholic monarchs Isabel and Fernando in 1485.

Until the twentieth century, Marbella was just another farming and fishing community—albeit one with a particularly enviable position along 17 miles (27 kilometers) of coastline backed by the foothills of the Sierra Blanca. Tourism began to take root when a couple of hotels opened early in the century. During the Spanish Civil War, Marbella quickly fell under Nationalist control and became a sunshine getaway for Franco's cronies and assorted Nazis from all over Europe.

A better class of clientele discovered Marbella after World War II. The catalyst for transforming a sleepy village into a jet set destination was the Spanish-German Prince Alfonso of Hohenlohe-Langenburg, one of Europe's last great playboys and bon vivants. Visiting Marbella at age twenty-three in 1947 in his father's charcoal-powered Rolls Royce, he was so smitten that he returned the next year to snatch up a huge vineyard estate on the ocean for a pittance. It became the family compound and the prince, ever attuned to a moneymaking opportunity, decided to convert his family *finca* into a luxury hotel. In 1954, it opened as the posh but discreet Marbella Club, putting Marbella on the map as Spain's answer to the French and Italian Rivieras.

When the Puerto Banús luxury yacht harbor opened west of town in 1970, the crowd of well-wishers included Prince Alfonso, future Spanish king Juan Carlos, Prince Rainier and Princess Grace of Monaco, Aga Khan IV, Hugh Hefner, Roman Polanski, and heart transplant pioneer Dr. Christiaan Barnard. Julio Iglesias performed while waiters passed beluga caviar.

King Fahd of Saudi Arabia began visiting Marbella in 1974, a year before he was even crowned prince, and spent considerable time and money here until his death in 2005. In 1981, the Saudi government erected the King Abdul Aziz Mosque in honor of King Fahd. Just west of the town center, the restrained white building with a serrated roofline was the first mosque built in Spain since the ouster of the last Moorish rulers in 1492. The call to prayer from the minaret echoes over beachgoers and shoppers, a reminder of the historic and enduring links between Andalucía and North Africa.

My rental car of choice (a SEAT Altea) is way out of its league among the Bentleys, Rolls Royces, Ferraris, and Lamborghinis typically parked in Puerto Banús. I usually start a visit here, admiring the yachts, checking out the upscale boutiques, and then treating myself to an ice cream—one of the few things I actually can afford.

Then I drive into Marbella center along the so-called Golden Mile, actually a 4-mile (6.4-kilometer) stretch between the city and the yacht harbor. It's lined with the grandest estates and villas (including King Fahd's White House-like palace), five golf courses, and such exclusive resorts as the Marbella Club and Hotel Puente Romano, the latter named for a first-century Roman bridge on its grounds.

In Marbella proper, the Golden Mile turns into Avenida Ricardo Soriano, where the broad sidewalks are flanked by glam boutiques full of designer clothing and over-stated jewelry. To be honest, whether I'm looking at diamond necklaces or tacky souvenirs, the overdevelopment of the Costa del Sol can become tiresome and even overwhelming. But long ago I learned the secret of extracting the best of the Costa del Sol, and it works as well in mass-market Torremolinos as it does in tony Marbella, where the overbuilding has been done with a lot more money and quite a bit more taste.

The antidote to all that concrete and plate glass is simple: the turquoise ocean that stretches to the southern horizon.

Marbella has twenty-four sandy beaches, and a swim and a stroll always restore my equilibrium. Venus and La Fontanilla, the beaches closest to the town center, sit right on the beachfront promenade and have a good choice of *chiringuitos,* or beach bars. Protected from development because of its famous sand dunes, Playa Artola is just 8.4 miles (13.4 km) east from town. There are lifeguards and services on the east end, but the secluded west end is a favorite with naturists.

Even sprawling Costa del Sol resort towns still have an intact historic city center. That's certainly true of Marbella, and once refreshed from a dip in the ocean, that's where I like to end the day. I feel like I'm in a grainy European color film with lots of vibra-phone in the soundtrack when I leave the beachfront promenade and walk inland up a set of marble stairs past several Salvador Dalí bronze statues, then cross the leafy green Alameda, a park with classic Andalucían tiled benches.

The cobbled streets of the Casco Antiguo begin just behind Avenida Ricardo Soriano. I shed the synthetic overlay of monied Marbella as I walk into the old town, with its remnants of a Moorish wall embedded with Roman columns. The streets keep climbing slightly until I reach the broad Plaza de los Naranjos, the heart of the Casco Antiguo. A medieval well at the center attests to the age of the plaza, though it was redesigned during the Renaissance as the seat of church and state alike. As the sun gets lower, I like to find a table on the east side to catch the last golden rays glinting beneath the shade of the Seville orange trees that yield a bitter fruit yet smell so sweet. I sip a chilled glass of wine and listen to the rising chorus of twitters in the branches as the sparrows and finches settle in for the night.

# 67 New Act for an Ancient City

## REINVENTION KEEPS MÁLAGA FRESH

Whether we're adopting a new hairstyle, wardrobe, or career, we women are the masters of reinvention. That's how we keep ourselves fresh and vital over the course of what we hope will be long and interesting lives. Personally, I find myself admiring a city that has managed to do the same thing—and has done it with what seems like simple grace and elegance.

The Spanish language recognizes the inherent womanliness of cities. The word "*ciudad*" is feminine, and Málaga, with its gurgling liquid syllables and feminine ending, seems to me like a beachside siren that has been luring sailors since antiquity. Even when I just want to laze around on a Costa del Sol beach, I stay in Málaga and take the twenty-minute light rail connection to the strand. That way I can wash off the sand and salt and return for the evening to Andalucía's second largest city rather than a beachfront development. Honestly, it's hard not to like a place where Calle Larios, the pedestrian shopping zone, is paved in marble.

✳ www.malagaturismo.com/en

But Málaga has also been a working port since Phoenician cargo vessels docked in the deep harbor 3,000 years ago. It's true that there was a certain dignified grunginess to the working port. But it cut Málaga off from the sea—which is, after all, one of its best features. The city movers and shakers apparently agreed and several years ago began to relocate the giant container ships and oil barges west of the central harbor to make room for new development.

A new cruise port is part of the mix, but the best thing about new Málaga is the Palmeral de las Sorpresas, or Palm Garden of Surprises, which was completed in March 2011. It certainly sur-prised me when I returned to Málaga after a four-year absence. The broad walkway along the water is lined with hundreds of palm trees. It is a joy to walk during the day when the futuristic metal arcade along its length casts undulating shadows on the marble pavement (yes, more marble) shared by walkers, bicy-

clists, and skateboarders. But it's even better in the evening, when strollers can gaze at the illuminated ramparts of the Gibralfaro, Málaga's eleventh-century Moorish palace, zigzagging up the hill-side. The Palmeral has put a graceful, modern spin on the fine old Spanish tradition of the evening promenade—a leisurely stroll with nothing better to do than see and be seen and enjoy the view.

That interplay between old and new has given Málaga a shot in the arm. The city wears the mantle of history more lightly than nearby Sevilla and Córdoba and thus has felt more free to reinvent itself. And it's not just the waterfront that benefits from the new energy and outlook. Also in 2011, Baroness Carmen Thyssen-Bornemisza opened a museum in a Renaissance-era palace to display her collection of nineteenth- and early twentieth-century Spanish painting (see Chapter 69). The Barcelona-born Thyssen placed her bets on Málaga.

✳ www.coleccionmuseoruso.es (Spanish only)

She's not the only one. In March 2015, the first western European outpost of the State Russian Museum in St. Petersburg opened in a renovated 1920s Mudéjar Revival tobacco factory. Plans call for one permanent and two temporary exhibitions from its extraordinary collection every year. Located about a mile southwest of the main train station, the Russian Museum is a bit out of the way but shares the property with a car museum.

When Paris's Centre Pompidou placed its first satellite museum outside France in Málaga, it chose a prime location at one end of the Palmeral—right at the heart of the waterfront. The museum is situated in El Cubo, an all-glass block of a building that looks a bit like a big Rubik's cube. Temporary exhibitions address the same contemporary art interests as the Parisian original, including photography, video, design, and architecture.

✳ centrepompidou-malaga.eu (Spanish only)

From the Cubo, the new wharf of Muelle Uno doglegs off the Palmeral and brings new shops and restaurants to the waterfront. Muelle Uno stretches out into the harbor to La Farola, the 1816 lighthouse that still guides sailors into the port city. Some classics just don't need to be improved.

# 68 Cradle of Genius

## PICASSO IN MÁLAGA

Biographers often give short shrift to Málaga, where Pablo Ruiz Picasso was born and lived for the first decade of his life. Some even suggest that the artist was ill-disposed to the Andalucían port city, considering it backward and provincial. But it's not really so easy to dismiss the community where baby Pablito first apprehended the world around him, and where young Pablo first grasped a pencil and a brush and began to define himself as an artist.

He came into the world in a rented apartment at 15 Plaza de la Merced on October 25, 1881, the first child of painter and art teacher José Ruiz Blasco and his much younger wife María Picasso Lopez. Thought to be stillborn until a doctor uncle breathed cigar smoke into his nostrils, Pablo began life in the cozy embrace of women. María doted on her little son, as did her mother and two unmarried sisters who lived with the family for at least part of Picasso's youth.

The artist's birthplace is now the Museo Casa Natal, where one room recreates the sort of bourgeoisie parlor, with red walls and heavy wooden furniture, where Pablo would have spent much of his time. His father's painting studio, which occupies one end of the room, is set up with one of the many paintings of the pigeons that so fascinated the senior artist. Fortunately, someone in the family was a pack rat. The most affecting objects in the museum are baby Picasso's christening gown, umbilical cord cloth, and tiny t-shirt—touchstones of the genius as an infant.

The four-story corner building has big windows that overlook Plaza de la Merced, which was, in effect, Pablo's front yard. In his later years, Picasso would recall making drawings in the dust of the plaza while other children played. As lively today as in his day, the plaza is lined with shops, bars, and cafés. Life-size cutouts of the mature artist are often put into service to hold menu boards. Much more dignified is the bronze statue of Picasso as elder artistic statesmen seated on a bench. It's a favorite with kids who climb on it and sometimes stare the artist in the eye.

Blue and white tile markers identify other spots that bask in the glow of Picasso associations. Picasso was baptized in the same parish church where his parents were married, the Iglesia de Santiago on Calle Granada 62, just off the plaza. Originally the site of a mosque, the church's simple facade retains the Moorish horseshoe doorway, while the interior is encrusted with baroque flourishes. I often wonder if young Pablo stared around as the Mass droned on, mentally editing the details down to the church's handsome bones.

Nearby, the back room of the apothecary at Calle Granada 75 was one of José Ruiz Blasco's hangouts where he and friends would discuss art and literature in the grand Spanish tradition of the *tertulia* or literary gathering. It's a habit that Picasso took with him to France—and hardly the only aspect of Andalucían culture that he never left behind. The artist had a lifelong love of the bullfight and drew on its imagery throughout his career. He was equally enamored of the *cante jondo*, the most heart-wrenching vocal style of flamenco. Moreover, he defined himself as a man in distinctly Andalucían terms, embracing the swagger of *machismo*. At its best, *machismo* lends a rough nobility to the masculine role in the world.

At its worst, it becomes a weak justification for a variety of inexcusable sins, such as what John Richardson, Picasso biographer and friend for the artist's last twenty years, describes as Picasso's "disconcerting oscillations between tenderness and cruelty" toward the women in his life.

In his later years, Picasso made peace with Málaga, or at least developed an old man's fondness for the place of his youth. Thirty years after the artist's death in 1973, the Museo Picasso Málaga opened in the Renaissance-style Buenavista Palace to fulfill his wish that some of his work be displayed in his birthplace. The bulk of the collection of almost 250 works was donated by Christine Ruiz-Picasso, widow of the artist's eldest son Paulo Ruiz-Picasso, and their son Bernard Ruiz-Picasso. As  in most of Picasso's art, public and private intersect, particularly in his images of women. Portraits of three of the most significant women in his life are represented in the collection.

✳ www.museopicassomalaga.org

Paulo Ruiz-Picasso was the only child of Picasso and his first wife Olga Khokhlova. Painted in 1917 before the couple married, *Olga Khokhlova in a Mantilla* is a fairly naturalistic image of her transition from Russian ballerina to Spanish maiden. By 1921, Olga has been transformed from maiden to mother. In *Mother and Child* from that year Picasso depicts her in a typical pose of seated Madonna and Child, but imbues her with the weight and solidity of classical sculpture. She holds baby Paulo in gigantic hands.

Olga's grip was not so firm on her husband, whose stylistic innovations seemed to parallel his romantic infatuations. In 1936,

Picasso was most enthralled by photographer Dora Maar, though he was still married to Olga and had recently had a daughter with Marie-Thérèse Walter. Dora Maar is the subject of *Woman with Raised Arms*, painted that year. Its exuberance signals Picasso's joy at having a new love in his life; Marr is identifiable by the dramatic gestures of her hands and her signature long pointed fingernails.

Picasso was outlived by his last wife, Jacqueline Roque, whom he met in 1952 and began painting in 1954, the year of the museum's *Jacqueline Seated*. As Picasso always seemed to do, he sought to show her personality quirks in the portrait. Her oversized head displays tightly pursed lips, and she holds herself in a defensive pose, arms wrapped around her legs. The broad bands of color behind the figure, some art critics believe, is a reference to the artist's dying friend and rival Matisse, who typically painted women backed by flat patches of color.

Picasso never stepped foot in Málaga after age nineteen. But in death, he came home again, and the city has celebrated his life as one begun on Andalucían terms. Walking the museum galleries filled with images of bulls and pigeons and women, it could be argued that in his heart he never left.

✳ fundacionpicasso.malaga.eu

## RECOMMENDED READING

*Picasso: Creator and Destroyer* by Arianna Stassinopoulos Huffington
*A Life of Picasso, Volume I 1881-1906* by John Richardson

# 69

## A Museum of Her Own

### MUSEO CARMEN THYSSEN, MÁLAGA

*"¡Muy Andalucía!"* That's the phrase my high school Spanish teacher would exclaim whenever he was talking about something that was bright and vibrant and full of life. I expect that the Baroness Carmen Thyssen-Bornemisza uttered the phrase frequently when she assembled her collection of nineteenth-century Spanish art, with an emphasis on Andalucía—the region that means Spain for many people.

Born in Barcelona in 1943, the baroness took a circuitous route to becoming a major art collector. She won the title of Miss Spain in 1961 and several years later married the American Lex Barker, best known in the U.S. as the tenth athletic actor to portray Tarzan. Thyssen appeared in a few films herself, including *Night of the Howling Beast* (1975) and *The Perfect Killer* (1977).

She eventually found her soul mate in Baron Hans Heinrich Thyssen-Bornemisza (1921-2002). The couple married in 1985 and the baron encouraged her to pursue the family passion for collecting art. She clearly found her calling and selections from Carmen's collection of European and American art over the centuries are displayed in the Museo Thyssen-Bornemisza in Madrid (see Chapter 2).

✳ www.carmenthyssenmalaga.org/en

But the baroness's self-assured taste is most evident in her epony-mous museum in Málaga. Working with a narrow focus, she was able to assemble a cohesive collection that includes many works previously in private hands. Dominated by Spanish genre paintings, it captures the idealized and romanticized Spain of song, legend, and story.

The museum opened in 2011 in a sixteenth-century palace in Málaga's old city. The renovation preserved the intricate carved wooden ceilings and other Renaissance-style details. About two hundred works from the baroness's collection are displayed in several floors of galleries surrounding an arcaded courtyard. It is a lovely place to spend a couple of hours.

Works on the ground floor include a number of landscapes, such as harborside images of Cádiz and Málaga. But the most engaging canvases were created by artists intent on capitalizing on the European fascination with the romance and passion of Spain. Joaquín Domínguez Becquer (1817-1883), for example, was one of the most successful and respected of the Romantic-style painters in Sevilla. His *Maja and Bullfighter* (1838) captures two of the most familiar Andalucían types—the bullfighter in his suit of lights and his coquettish admirer—in a moment of light flirtation.

Spain's exoticism was also a lure for artists from throughout Europe. French artist Alfred Dehodencq (1822-1886) painted a number of works for the Duke and Duchess of Montpensier to display in the San Telmo palace in Sevilla. (The duchess was the sister of Isabella II. See Chapter 57.) One of the most striking large canvases, *A Confraternity in Procession along Calle Génova* (1851), depicts black-hooded members of the brotherhood carrying torches as they make their solemn Holy Week march through the crowds lining the streets of Sevilla.

Works on the first floor reveal the trend toward greater real-ism in the second half of the nineteenth century. Málaga-based painter Emilio Ocón y Rivas (1845-1908) is represented by several seascapes, including *Preparing for the Catch* (1897), which carefully depicts a Phoenician-style boat still used by local fishermen against the misty, atmospheric light of dawn. One of the masterpieces of the collection is *Bullfight, Wounded Picador* (c. 1867) by Catalan painter Marià Fortuny i Marsal (1838-1874), who had a fascination with the pageantry and ever-present danger of the bullfight. His quick, loose brush strokes and hurried applications of patches of color conveyed a sense of urgency and chaos in the ring.

By the end of the nineteenth century, Spanish painters were increasingly influenced by the artistic trends emanating from Paris. Galleries on the museum's second floor present a good overview of Spanish subjects treated with a French accent. In *The Concha, Nighttime* (c. 1906), Darío de Regoyos y Valdés (1857-1913) created a lovely Impressionist scene of people chatting along the promenade at the Playa de la Concha in San Sebastián in the dusky evening light.

Around 1915, Ramon Casas Carbó (1866-1936) depicted his favorite model (and later wife), *Julia*, in stereotypical Spanish attire of a red toreador jacket heavy with black embroidery and an elaborate comb holding flowers in her hair. The painting draws on the *espagnolade* tradition of crowd-pleasing works in late nineteenth-century Paris, but Casas rescues her from the genre with a forthrightness that is thoroughly modern. Her direct gaze, red lipstick, and confident placement of her hands on her hips depict a woman who knows her own mind, while her bare neck and décolletage hint at an eroticism that she owns without apology.

Don't leave the museum without seeing one final portrait: the benefactress herself painted by her friend, artist Mercedes Lasarte. *Carmen en Málaga* dates from 2011, the year that the museum opened. Blond-haired Carmen is dressed in pink, and poses against a pink background. The canvas hangs beneath the arcade on the second floor, so that the baroness can survey all that she has created.

# 70 *Traces of the Wind*

## EL PARAJE NATURAL TORCAL DE ANTEQUERA

Spain has no shortage of mountains and badlands, but none is quite as startling as El Paraje Natural Torcal de Antequera. The parched hills of water-etched and wind-blown limestone are so strange that they seem to belong to another planet, yet not so long ago in geological time, they were at the bottom of the ocean.

⁂ torcaldeantequera.com (Spanish only)

Located 19 miles (31 km) north of Málaga, the 6.5-square-mile nature reserve was established in 1978, but the eerily beautiful landscape has been protected since 1929. It's a place where the processes of nature are writ large, from the dramatic upheavals of colliding tectonic plates to the slow and steady erosion by wind, rain, snow, and blistering sun.

After lashing back and forth across the switchbacks to climb through the strange terrain to the topmost ridge, it's almost a shock to suddenly encounter a flat parking lot and a modern visitors center with a small café and interactive displays that elucidate the forces that conjured up this magical place. Admittedly, the earth science lesson can be a little geeky, but it does help explain the transformation of ancient oceans and sea creatures into the stratified rocks and fossils that await outside. And a little knowledge hardly detracts from the mystery of the place.

El Torcal is best appreciated on foot, and the center offers guided tours that can be reserved in advance. I prefer to go it alone, or with someone who appreciates companionable silence. Just stick to the hard-packed dirt paths that range in difficulty from a flat walking circuit of about a mile (1.6 km) to a fairly daunting 2.8-mile (4.5-km) trail with some rock scrambling required. At the highest overlook, the whole park unfolds below and the shores of Africa shimmer in the far distance. Even the shortest route quickly leaves behind the world of air-conditioned automobiles and buildings. Once I've turned the first bend, I feel as if I've stepped out of time and into a world of stone.

Oddly, Spanish poets have not sung the praises of El Torcal nor have Spanish painters attempted to render its strange beauty on canvas. It is a landscape that eludes description, and for that very reason seems forever fresh. In the winter, snow softens the rough edges of the harsh rock, and in the spring and fall rainy seasons, wildflowers spring into bloom in every crevice and cranny. I've seen golden eagles and griffon vultures soar overhead and spotted mountain goats seeking cool shade beneath the rocky outcrops. I've startled lizards sunning themselves on the rocks, but I've yet to see an ibex bounding from boulder to boulder. I don't look too hard. The fauna are merely distractions from the fantastical rocks that seem to assume forms just beyond the edge of recognition. They are like clouds scudding across the sky, but literally more grounded and taking eons to shift their shapes.

Some of the rock formations with analogs elsewhere have been given common names—Needles, Camel, Sphinx, and Screw among them. But that very act of naming is a misguided attempt to tame this otherworldly place. El Torcal is better left to the imagination.

# Private Lives

## FIESTA DE LOS PATIOS DE CÓRDOBA

You won't be disappointed whenever you visit this northernmost city on Andalucía's "golden triangle" of UNESCO World Heritage sites. A thousand years vanishes in an instant when you behold the medieval mosque's forest of red marble pillars and receding horseshoe arches, then walk through the Judería's labyrinth of narrow streets lined with whitewashed walls. But if you're curious about the private lives of the inhabitants of this ancient and abiding city, schedule your visit during the two weeks in early May when the doors to the city's domestic sanctuaries are thrown open during the Fiesta de los Patios de Córdoba, or Córdoba Courtyard Festival.

The city began to take shape in the second century B.C. when Romans settled on the banks of the Río Guadalquivir. To cope with the hot climate they built houses around a central patio with a well. Soon the provincial Roman capital had become the "garden spot of Hispania." A Muslim army took control in the eighth century and when Roman architecture met Arab landscaping, the patio garden was born.

The Moors were hardly just avid horticulturists, intent on softening the desert landscape with cool greenery and a riot of color. They made Córdoba the capital of an Islamic caliphate that ruled from Gibraltar to the Pyrenees. By the eleventh century, Córdoba was the richest and most learned city in Europe, a place where Jews, Christians, and Muslims lived and worked in harmony.

Córdoba returned to Christian rule in the thirteenth century and a more recent city now surrounds the old Judería. But that five-square-mile district remains the place where Córdoba was at its best. It's also the largest medieval quarter still standing in Spain and if you're willing to ignore the raspy whine of motor scooters zooming along the twisting streets, you can let the modern world slip away. Put the shops selling kitschy souvenirs behind you and plunge deeper into the neighborhood and you'll encounter home-owners tending their flowerpots or putting fresh coats of whitewash on the ancient walls of their dwellings. Peek through the wrought iron gates that face the street and you'll glimpse the central patios where daily life in Córdoba unfolds.

Those cool patios—with their pots of gera-niums, ancient bougainvillea vines, orange and lemon trees, burbling fountains, and hand-dug medieval wells—are the emotional and aesthetic heart of the city. If you're not satisfied with a glimpse, then the Courtyard Festival is for you. The city launched it in 1921, long before television and social media blurred the boundaries between public and private lives. A number of awards for architecture and horticulture entice homeowners to open their patios to judges and visitors. More than sixty households usually participate and they are marked on a map available on the web site and at tourist information centers.

✳ english.turismodecordoba.org/patios-de-cordoba.cfm

It's best to consider the map as a general guideline, accept the fact that you will get lost, and embrace the serendipity. One wrong turn could lead you to a neighborhood bakery with bread fresh from the oven, an old tavern with cold beer and sizzling casseroles of roasted sausage, or a dusty park where children kick soccer balls willy-nilly. Several routes lead through the Judería, others along the riverbank, and still others into the later neighborhoods northeast of the Judería, where seventeenth- and eighteenth-century homes conform to the tried-and-true patio style so suited to the climate and to Córdoban sensibilities. Most of the people you'll encounter poring over their maps are locals or other Spaniards. Homeowners might display their patio awards proudly, but their main motivation for opening their homes is to enjoy a couple of weeks of intense socializing.

People exchange gardening tips, trade plant cuttings, share gossip, and brag about their children and grandchildren. Some hosts offer visitors small glasses of sherry or entertain with a few verses of a popular song. But the homeowners mostly just go about their business, watering the plants, sweeping the tile floors, eating meals, reading the newspaper, or just relaxing in their shady, fragrant sanctuaries.

The sheer dailiness of it all is immensely reassuring. The last time I visited, I almost overlooked a mother cat and her kittens nestled in a wicker basket in one corner of a beautiful patio. I was admiring the bright red geraniums—Spain's *gitanillas* or "little gypsies"—spilling out of blue pots against a blindingly white wall. A visitor pointed to the basket with a smile. "Last year," he said, "the mother cat was a kitten in that same basket."

In this most ancient of cities, life goes on.

# 72

## Morning Prayers

### LA MEZQUITA, CÓRDOBA

In my ecumenically minded hometown of Cambridge, Massachusetts, the mosque and the synagogue share the same parking lot—and make it available to the nearby Lutherans for overflow parking on Christmas and Easter. I think of the arrangement as almost Córdoban. It's a distant echo of that Spanish city's golden age, when the peaceful coexistence of three religions made it a bright spot during Europe's Dark Ages.

That's not to say that Islam didn't claim the largest sacred space in the secular city. Córdoba's main mosque was begun in 756 on the site of a Visigoth church built over a Roman temple. Modeled on the Great Mosque of Damascus, La Mezquita was designed to announce Córdoba as the political and religious capital of western Islam. Enlarged over the centuries as Córdoba's power grew, it became one of the largest mosques in the world.

Nearly thirteen centuries after construction began, the building remains a holy place. It's common to overhear a Roman Catholic bride-to-be tell her friends, "Oh, I'm getting married in the mosque." There's nothing prettier than a spring wedding where the bride enters through blooming orange trees in the patio where Muslims once conducted their ritual ablutions. The building's official name may now be Santa Iglesia Catedral de Córdoba, but I wouldn't be surprised if even the bishop still calls it La Mezquita. Everyone else does.

Immediately after the reconquest of Córdoba in 1236, Christians began to use the mosque as a church, but even with the transformation of religion, they left in place the stunning Mecca-facing mihrab of Byzantine mosaics against a gold background. In 1523, Holy Roman Emperor Carlos V authorized the construction of an incongruous Renaissance cathedral inside the mosque. The impressive wooden choir wasn't carved until 1746-47 and the cathedral was finally completed at the end of that century.

❋ www.catedraldecordoba.es

In all, the cathedral only occupies about 20 percent of the interior and the direct and simple horizontal plan of the mosque trumps all the cathedral's filigreed attempts to ascend to the heavens. Even Carlos V seems to have had second thoughts. He is said to have declared in 1526, "You have built here what you or anyone might have built anywhere else, but have destroyed what was unique in the world."

Yet the building has now been a Christian church longer than it was a Muslim mosque. Mass is said here every day, even though La Mezquita is Córdoba's major tourist attraction—and one of the most important sites in Spain. Throughout the day, the vast interior teems with tour groups and guides explaining in a Babel of languages the history of the building and how more than 800 columns—some salvaged from Roman structures—support the building's signature striped horseshoe arches of red brick and white stone.

The building of La Mezquita has a spirituality that transcends the ritual of the daily Mass said beneath its roof, so the powers-that-be have wisely set aside one hour on Monday through Saturday mornings (8:30-9:30 A.M.) for prayer and quiet contemplation. No groups are allowed and those who enter agree to the rule of silence.

I'd be disingenuous if I didn't acknowledge that the spirit of silence is somewhat violated by people walking around snapping photos or making cellphone videos. (Admission during this time is free.) But La Mezquita is a vast space, and it's a simple matter to walk away from the shutterbugs and find a quiet spot to stare into the cavernous distance, letting your eyes follow the receding forms of hundreds of horseshoe arches. The repetition is a kind of visual ecstasy, as if the structure of the building itself were offering a glimpse into the infinite.

# 73

## Last Stronghold of a Lost Empire

### LA ALHAMBRA AND EL GENERALIFE, GRANADA

I was resting on a shady bench in Almería, the most North African of Spanish port cities, when a bus tour group of Spanish pensioners began the long uphill trek to the imposing Moorish fortress. They were dutifully touching the bases of Andalucían history, but their hearts weren't in it. One woman grasped her husband's arm and sighed, as if to remind them both that a better day was coming, *"Mañana, la Alhambra."*

She had her sights set on Granada's "Red Castle," the palace-fortress that crowns the rocky hilltop between the Río Darro and the Sierra Nevada mountains. Even Spaniards feel the need to see, if only once, Granada's Alhambra, the epitome of Moorish artistry and the last stronghold of their power.

When the Christian monarchs raised their flags and cross from the tallest tower in 1492, Moorish rule in Spain came to an end. On his way into exile, the sultan Boabdil wept when he took a last look at his vanquished kingdom. "You weep like a woman for what you could not defend like a man," his mother Aixa reputedly declared, thereby securing her place on history's roll call of least sympathetic mothers. But to cut Aixa some slack, she is believed to have lived in one of the most beautiful towers of the Palacio Nazaries and it's easy to understand why she was so bitter about leaving.

Built primarily during the rule of Muhammad V in the mid-fourteenth century, the Nasrid Palace is the masterpiece of the complex. Virtually every surface is adorned with carved plaster in lacy and delicate abstract patterns and Arabic inscriptions. Floors and many walls are covered with exquisite mosaic tiles, and most ceilings are either ornate plaster or carved wood. Water was the ultimate luxury in this desert climate and the palace is oriented around courtyards with central fountains and pools that bring the cooling and soothing sight and sound of water to virtually every chamber.

❋ www.alhambra-patronato.es

The visitors' itinerary through the Nasrid Palace is strictly pre-scribed. I usually chafe at such rigidity, but, intentional or not, the progression from public to private works as an artful reveal. It first celebrates the grandeur of the seat of power before it goes behind the scenes to the intimacy of the domestic quarters. In a sense, it also slides from history into myth as it tells of the exploits of the Nasrid rulers followed by the imagined tales of their lesser-known wives and daughters.

The first rooms are all about ceremony. In the Patio del Mexuar, the only section of the palace that was open to the public during Moorish times, rulers met with subjects and dispensed justice. At the far end, a richly ornamented horseshoe arch leads to a small oratory with a *mihrab* niche oriented toward Mecca. The nearby throne room is the largest room of the palace. Called the Salón de los Embajadores, it was designed to wow visiting ambassadors and to place the sultan directly under the ceiling dome that evokes the seven heavens of the Muslim cosmos.

If there was ever a place where I wish that walls could talk it's in the Harem, or private apartments, where the wives and children passed their days apart from the world, yet surrounded by beauty. The stunning fountain in the Patio de los Leones rests on the backs of a dozen carved stone lions thought to represent the hours of the day, the months of the year, and the signs of the zodiac. Legend claims that water flowed from the mouth of a different lion each hour of the day.

The juiciest story of longing, intrigue, betrayal, and revenge is linked to the extraordinary Sala de los Abencerrajes. The carved ceiling mimics stalactites, but most eyes gravitate to the fountain in the center. Legend has it that the fate of the kingdom turned here. Suspecting his favorite wife Zorayda of dallying with the head of the noble Abencerrajes clan, the penultimate sultan of Granada invited sixteen members of that family for a banquet—and beheaded them in the fountain. Passion was surely at play, but the family had also conspired to replace the sultan with his son Boabdil. Many believe that the beheading set in motion the internal strife that led to the Moorish downfall. (Boabdil's mother, Aixa, by the way, was said to have lived in the nearby Sala de las Dos Hermanas, or Hall of the Two Sisters. As noted above, it is often cited as one of the best examples of Islamic architecture in Spain.)

By the time writer Washington Irving rented rooms in the Alhambra in the 1820s, it had been ravaged by Napoleon's armies and was occupied by squatters. Irving saw past the decline to evoke the mythic years of Moorish rule in his *Tales of the Alhambra*. The book helped romanticize the decaying palace, which was declared a national monument in 1870 and has been heavily restored.

One of Irving's best-known tales, "The Legend of the Three Beautiful Princesses," revolves around triplets born to a sultan and a Christian captive who converts to Islam and becomes his favorite wife. As young women, the pampered princesses fall in love with captive Christian soldiers that they can spy from their windows. The two boldest escape via a rope ladder and make their way through tunnels cut into the rocky hilltop. In a scene worthy of a Disney movie, they climb on horseback behind their beaus and gallop off to lives as good Christian wives. The third sister stays behind in the Alhambra and, of course, dies young.

Ponder their fates (and the influence of the Catholic church) as you stroll the lovely El Partal gardens, where paths at the end lead either to El Generalife or to the Palacio de Carlos V. The Holy Roman Emperor and grandson of Isabel and Fernando, Carlos demolished a large section of the Nasrid Palace to build his own palace, begun in 1526 and never finished. The architect Pedro Machuca was a pupil of Michelangelo, and this Renaissance palace (which houses a museum of Nasrid art) has elegant symmetry. But it is an alien building for life in Granada's swelter.

The Generalife, the summer place of the Moorish rulers, on the other hand, belongs to the land and climate. Sitting on the slopes of the Cerro del Sol facing the Nasrid Palace, the buildings seem an afterthought to the beautifully laid-out courtyards filled with pools and fountains. Crisply trimmed hedges turn the gardens into outdoor rooms. Trysts between Zorayda and her Abencerrajes lover in one of these cool, hidden spaces led to the bloodbath in the lower palace. Such strife seems far removed from this tranquil setting—but it sure makes a good story.

## RECOMMENDED READING

*Tales of the Alhambra* by Washington Irving

# 74 Lorca and the Dark Heart of Duende

## HUERTA DE SAN VICENTE, GRANADA

Translators and linguists often identify *duende* as the most difficult Spanish word to translate into English. No single word or phrase suffices. *Duende* lies at the heart of the Andalucían sensibility—a primal force more than an emotion or attitude. It is the fire that glints in a flamenco dancer's eye when she stamps her foot, throws back her hair, and casts a defiant pose. It lurks in the faint smile at the corners of the mouth of a matador when the bull brushes past and clips a few sequins from his suit of lights. It is a force to grapple with and to try to comprehend if you wish to understand this part of Spain.

Toward the end of his short life, the great poet and playwright Federico García Lorca (1898-1936) devoted an entire lecture to the subject, "Theory and Play of *Duende*." Delivered in Argentina in 1933, it stands as the best explanation of a force that resists explication. Lorca struggled for *duende* in his work, and he came to be its most compelling symbol when he was murdered by Nationalist forces in the early days of the Spanish Civil War.

Snuffed out at the height of his powers, Lorca left a behind a body of work for the ages, including the operatic tragedy *Blood Wedding*, the romantic and lyrical *Gypsy Ballads*, and the strange and wonderful *Poet in New York*. Without even a stone to mark his grave, the main touchstone of the poet's life is the Huerta de San Vicente on the southern edge of Granada.

Although Lorca studied in Madrid and traveled in Europe and the Americas, he was always drawn back to Andalucía like Antaeus to the earth to gather his strength. Lorca shared the house and its extensive grounds with his parents and siblings during the summers from 1926 to 1936. Representing the landscape of his origins, the property was a retreat where he could create, a safe place within the embrace of his family. The estate was surrounded by farmland then; today it lies within the city's sprawl. It was the home where Lorca spent the last days of his life.

The poet certainly gave Franco's thugs plenty of reasons to kill him. He was unapologetic about his public homosexuality, outspoken in his disdain for the Nationalist cause, and passionate in his defense of the Gypsies against persecution. In the end, though, they may have killed him because they were afraid. He was a poet and playright in whom *duende* raged; next to him, the Falangists with all their boasts were no more than anonymous petty bullies.

Once Franco was dead and Spain could come back to life, Granadinos reclaimed Lorca as their cultural lion. The Huerta de San Vicente was sold to the city in 1985, and opened as a museum a decade later. The rooms are airy, elegant, and spare in their furnishings. Some pieces have come down from the family, and others resemble those visible in period photographs. The museum has a few personal items: Lorca's desk, a gramophone, and a baby grand piano. (With encouragement from his friend, the composer Manuel de Falla, Lorca also composed music.) Lorca's own letters show a man alternately at ease and at loose ends here. Friends would visit, and he would have brief amorous flings ("There is a little bullfighter," he wrote in a 1930 letter). According to accounts by his younger sister, Isabel García Lorca, Federico would often sit on his balcony at night, closing the shutters and writing until the morning light came shining in. He composed *Blood Wedding* (1932) and the tragedy *Yerma* (1934) at the *huerta*.

✳ www.huertadesanvicente.com

In his famous essay, Lorca held that "all the arts are capable of *duende*, but where it naturally creates most space, as in music, dance, and spoken poetry, the living flesh is needed to interpret them." As a performer of his own work and creator of plays where others spoke his ideas, he was eminently dangerous to the falangists. They came for him in the sultry heat of mid-August in 1936. Lorca fled from the *huerta* to the home of friends in the center of the city, but his evasion was shortlived. On August 16, he was taken into custody. Friends tried and failed to get him released. On August 19, he was taken with a few other prisoners to the village of Viznar, in the high country north of Granada, where he was executed.

Lorca's grave has never been conclusively found. But his work survives, while his murderers are forgotten. As he said prophetically in his speech on *duende*, "A dead man in Spain is more alive when dead than anywhere else on earth."

## RECOMMENDED READING

*Federico García Lorca* by Ian Gibson

*Gypsy Ballads* by Federico García Lorca

# The Art of the Deal

## SHOPPING IN GRANADA

It's not just the glories of the Alhambra that confer a North African accent on Granada. Far more plebian, the two little alleyways of Calderería Vieja and Calderería Nueva give the city a little taste of a traditional souk. Pocket-size stalls line both streets, with merchandise spilling out onto the sidewalks. Not nearly as all enveloping as the maze of the souk in Marrakech, this tiny area off Plaza Nueva has many of the same goods that evoke the exotic trade of the North African caravan.

I always set aside a couple of hours for poking around. Little of the merchandise is of particularly high quality, but it doesn't take much effort to find an item or two that will bring some flair to my surroundings back home. I'm a sucker for embroidered and mirrored throws that look great at the foot of a bed, wooden boxes inlaid with mother of pearl, brass-framed mirrors, and tiny colored glass teacups that are so delicate that I always need to replace broken ones. I also count on finding woven tote bags for the beach and cheap, colorful scarves that are fun to wear but not worth worrying about if they get lost in the shuffle of travel.

I would probably make a purchase even if I didn't find something that I wanted. Truth is, I love the art of the deal. While the merchandise is pretty similar from stall to stall, some of the merchants can be quite funny and engaging. After all, they have to make an effort so that you will linger in their shop. They are also savvy and start sizing up potential buyers the moment they walk in the door. I make a point of acting nonchalant when I find something I like and restrain myself from immediately asking the price. When I finally do inquire casually, I know that the merchant hopes that I'll accept the first price offered. But I also know that most shopkeepers expect—and even enjoy—a bit of haggling. And that's where the fun comes in.

I've found that it works best to keep it light. I never buy anything that's very expensive and I figure that the shopkeeper probably needs an extra euro or two more than I do. So I usually act sad (oh so sad!) and disappointed in the price and counter with an offer that is a bit lower than I am ultimately willing to pay. Sometimes I will put the item down and head toward the door. The shopkeeper almost always stops me with a lower price. And there are times that I have walked away from a deal that just didn't feel right. But nine times out of ten, I'll be able to reach a happy accord with the merchant. I figure that my new scarf or mirror will have good karma if I remember the whole interaction fondly when I get back home.

With my purchases in hand, I head into the Albaicín, the hillside neighborhood facing the Alhambra's hill across the Río Darro. During the glory days of the Nasrid empire, this was where the other half lived. After Granada was returned to the Christian fold in 1492, the Albaicín became the home of Gypsies and of the Muslims who chose to stay behind. After centuries of decline, the medieval neighborhood has recaptured its old allure. Whitewashed houses, blooming gardens, patios, ancient cisterns, and fountains framing the narrow streets make the neighborhood both fresh and timeless.

It's a place made for wandering, but I head in the direction of the Mirador San Nicolás and plan to arrive shortly before sunset. The scenic overlook near the top of the hill has the best view of the Alhambra perched on the opposite hill and backed in the distance by the Sierra Nevada mountains. The scene is best in winter and spring when the mountains are tipped with snow. The few café tables in the little plaza are usually filled and the crowd spills over to stand by the wall where a guitarist typically plays a Granadino Gypsy *zambra*. When the sun finally gets low enough in the west, the Alhambra glows golden in the reflected light. The apparition lasts but a few minutes—and then the talking and laughing resume as the music plays on into the night.

# 76 *Song and Dance of the Gypsy Zambra*

## CUEVA DE MARÍA LA CANASTERA, GRANADA

Devotees sometimes place a single rose atop the head of María la Canastera's bronze statue on Granada's Bulevar de la Avenida de la Constitución. Popular vote chose the mesmerizing flamenco artist as one of the most important figures of the twentieth century in Granada. The only Gypsy in the group, she won fame and admiration through her masterful performances of the *zambra* flamenco style native to the cave dwellings in the mountain above the city.

It's hard to capture a force of nature and movement in metal. Sculptor Jose A. Castro Vilchez depicts La Canastera poised in anticipation. She stands with her left hand on a chair back, her right hand clutching her skirt at her hip, and an outsize bronze rose balanced on the top of her head. It's as if she is waiting to hear the first arpeggio of the guitar that launches the swirl of sound and color that defined her life. With respect to the city that placed her image among such notables as poet and playwright Federico García Lorca, composer Manuel de Falla, and bullfighter Salvador Sánchez Povedano, the best memorial to La Canastera is the cave where she lived and performed and where the rhythms and shouts of *zambra* still float out into the night air.

María Cortes de Heredia was born in 1913 and grew up on the Sacromonte hillside east of the Albaicín, where first Moriscos (Moors forcibly converted to Christianity) and then Gypsies lived in caves carved from the hard-packed lime soil. She took her name "La Canastera" from her father's skill as a basket weaver, then changed her family's destiny with her instinctive feel for the *zambra,* a blend of Moorish and Gypsy music and dance traditions. She so made it her own that by age sixteen she was invited to perform at the Universal Exhibition in Barcelona. King Alfonso XIII was in the audience and Carmen Amaya joined her on the stage.

Born in Barcelona to Gypsy parents, Carmen Amaya went on to an international career, touring the world. María, on the other hand, brought the world to her. In 1953 she founded Cueva de María La Canastera in the main room of her cave dwelling. The kings and queens of Spain and Belgium and King Hussein of Jordan made their way into the hills to watch her perform. Ernest Hemingway and such Hollywood stars as Anthony Quinn, Ingrid Bergman, and Henry Fonda were intoxicated with the ecstatic abandon of the *zambras* that lasted into the early hours of the morning.

María died in 1966 and her son, Enrique el Canastero, now retired from performing, maintains the cave more or less as a shrine. The tiny kitchen and two bedrooms are a museum of María's life, and the main living area continues to function as an intimate performance space for *zambra.* Family memorabilia—photos, Gypsy pottery, hammered copperware—cover the rounded, whitewashed walls, and about sixty stiff little chairs with cane seats and straight wooden backs stand in a single row around the walls. At one end, the singers, dancers, and guitarists—including some of María's descendents—sit together. The guitarist strikes a chord and soon everyone is clapping, keeping time and punctuating the rhythm off the beat. One of the dancers stands and makes a pass down the narrow length of the room, stamping her feet on the tiled floor and swinging her skirts so close that they brush the knees of some of the spectators.

Like most flamenco, *zambra* begins slowly and builds, then builds some more, reaching several climaxes, each more frenetic than the last. The heat radiates from all the bodies in the low-ceilinged cave and the music becomes more and more intense. Unlike other flamenco *palos* (or forms), *zambra* follows a narrative structure based on the three stages of a Gypsy wedding. Unlike the wedding, it compresses the entire cathartic, emotionally draining experience into a single night instead of lasting three days. One mesmerizing night is enough.

Visiting La Canastera's cave is also a glimpse of a vanishing lifestyle. Most cave dwellers were forced from their homes when Sacromonte endured a catastrophic flood in the 1960s. A few residents held on, and other caves have been converted to bars, restaurants, and performance venues. Far up the single hillside road, the ethnographic Museo Cuevas del Sacromonte seeks to explain and demonstrate the historic cave-dwelling lifestyle of the sacred mountain. But the true spirit of Sacromonte abides not in earnest recreations of the workshops of weavers or blacksmiths but in the impassioned dance, music, and full-throated cries of *zambra*.

✳ www.sacromontegranada.com

## TOURS

For bookings, visit www.marialacanastera.com/en. Given the distance from central Granada and limited public transportation options at night, I recommend reserving van transport to and from Sacromonte when you buy tickets.

# 77

## Village to Village in the Berber Foothills

### WALKING IN THE ALPUJARRA DE GRANADA

The great monuments of Moorish Spain, culminating in the Alhambra, represent some of the finest art and architecture of their kind in Europe or even in North Africa. But few Moors lived in such splendor. The first time I drove ninety minutes from Granada to the rustic Moorish farming villages of La Alpujarra, I found that I could get a glimpse of how the other half lived.

Long insulated from the rest of Spain by daunting mountain passes and dirt donkey paths that washed out in every spring rain, this unique area of terraced highlands and green valleys sits on the south side of the 10,000-foot range of the Sierra Nevada, south and east of Granada. When Isabel and Fernando sent the Moors  packing in 1492, thousands of them fled to these green hills where the snow melt on the peaks irrigated their agricultural terraces all year long. In the early seventeenth century, Felipe II cleared out the last of their descendants and resettled the region with transplants from northern Spain. But culture is at least partially a product of environment, and the villages have retained their Berber appearance all the way into the twenty-first century.

Crossing the bridge over the ravine of the Poqueira Gorge, it is easy to be seduced by the rugged beauty of the Berber villages ahead. They seem to cling to the east bank of the ravine like large, white birds' nests. The first one along the road is Pampaneira. At an elevation of only 3,281 feet, it is the lowest of three villages linked directly by a hiking path that crosses the ravine wall, and indirectly by a highway full of switchbacks. As I got closer, I could see that Pampaneira retained all the attributes of a Berber mountain farming village. It still had its terraced vineyards, olive groves, and a profusion of wild mulberry trees descended from those the Moors had planted in the tenth century to feed their silkworms.

But it was the houses that I found so arresting. From a distance, one Spanish White Town looks pretty much like another, but Pampaneira introduced me to an indigenous architecture that I had only read about before visiting. The style of house is common in Berber communities in the Rif and Atlas mountains of Morocco, but is found in Europe only in these hills. Broad and squat, the houses are thick slabs of stone, traditionally left their natural gray color but nowadays swathed in whitewash. The flat roofs are timbered with whole chestnut logs covered by sheets of slate that are sealed with *launa*—the crumbly gray mica clay of the region that is watertight when it's firmly tamped down. By tradition, *launa* is only laid on the waning of the moon, the theory being that it will swell on the next waxing of the moon and stick tight. Because they're built into a steep slope, one building's roof provides the entrance patio to the next house up the hill.

Pampaneira has a resident community of weavers, and wandering around feels a bit like revisiting old-time hippie communes. Its other business is outdoor sports. The Nevadensis office on Plaza de la Libertad has guides for everything from canyoning and 4x4 excursions to rock climbing and serious mountaineering into the Parque de Sierra Nevada. But I was more than satisfied to hike the path that had connected the three villages for more than a millennium before a road was built, and in addition to selling guide services, the Nevadenis staff also provided a wealth of information about trail conditions.

Right at the edge of Pampaneira, a hardpacked stony path about three feet wide cuts straight across the hillside to the next village up the slope, Bubión. It is less than a mile (1.6 km) away, although it is also 1,150 feet higher above sea level, and the third village of the string, Capileira, is 280 feet higher yet. Fortunately, the steady uphill grade requires no real climbing. I slathered myself in sunblock, drank some water, and set out at a slow, steady pace that let me smell the resinous scents of wild rosemary and broom and look for the allegedly ubiquitous mountain goats said to pose on the rocky ledges. For the last 0.3 mile (0.5 km) into Capileira, I had to follow the asphalt highway, since the historic trail was washed out. There is not much village center to Bubión except for some houses and a few crafts shops, but larger Capileira has a sturdy Mudéjar church (Nuestra Señora de la Cabeza) said to be built on the site of the earlier mosque. The roundtrip walk is just about four miles (6.4 km), and it took me a little over three hours.

Since I had left Granada early in the morning, I still had time to keep driving on the G411 to reach the region's famous *secaderos*—huge warehouses where hams are hung to age in the dry mountain air. At 4,840 feet, Trevélez claims to be the highest village in Europe. It's really not that charming, but its mountain hams, made from white-footed pigs, are said to be second only to the *pata negra* hams of Jabugo. The village is built on three terraces, with the *secaderos* at the highest level. I found an outdoor table at Mesón Joachin Restaurante on Calle Puente. I ordered a salad, a plate of *jamón de Trevélez,* and a glass of crisp white wine to enjoy in the mountain sunshine.

✳ www.nevadensis.com (Spanish only)

IV

*North By
Northeast:
Catalan Spain*

# 78

## First Love Lives On

### "LOS AMANTES DE TERUEL"

The delicious memory of falling in love for the first time never gets old. That's probably why it's so hard to resist stories of star-crossed young lovers—even when we know that they will end badly. One of Spain's most enduring tales is set in the town of Teruel, perched in the mountains of Aragón about 90 miles (145 km) northwest of Valencia. More than three centuries before William Shakespeare introduced the world to Romeo and Juliet, Teruel's legendary thirteenth-century couple Isabel and Diego were separated by family and by fate, but achieved immortality as "*Los Amantes de Teruel*."

Not surprisingly, the details have changed over the centuries as the story of "the lovers of Teruel" has been told and retold. (Some versions even give Diego's name as Juan.) But the thrust of the narrative remains the same. Although they played together as children, their differences in social status seemed destined to keep Isabel and Diego apart when they grew up and fell in love. Pressed by his daughter, Isabel's father agreed to bless the couple's union—but only if Diego would leave Teruel for five years to seek a fortune that would make him a proper match for the only daughter of one of the wealthiest men in town. Diego promptly joined the Christian armies fighting the Moors for land and glory. For five lonely years, Isabel waited in vain for news of her beloved.

❉ amantesdeteruel.es

Finally, she had no choice but to obey her father's orders and accept the hand of one of her other suitors. As fate (of course) would have it, Diego returned to Teruel on the night of the wedding party. A newly wealthy man and unaware that Isabel was a few hours married, he professed his love and asked her for a kiss. The most dramatic versions of the tale place the climactic scene in Isabel's bedroom, with her new husband beside her in bed. In every version of the story, the chaste Isabel tearfully followed her proper upbringing and accepted the gravity of her new marital status. She refused Diego's plea and beseeched him to leave immediately and find another to love. Heartbroken, Diego collapsed and died at her feet. Distraught at the death of her true love, Isabel attended Diego's funeral the following day and kissed his lifeless body. In a twist worthy of opera, she immediately joined him in death.

True or not, the saga of thwarted love—and bad timing—was too good to be forgotten. It gained new power in the mid-sixteenth century when what many wanted to believe were the mummified remains of the couple were discovered. Los Amantes even captured the imagination of some of Spain's greatest storytellers. Tirso de Molina (c.1579-1648) based a play on the couple's sad fate in 1635 and conductor and composer Tomás Bretón (1850-1923) premiered his opera *Los Amantes de Teruel* at the Teatro Real in Madrid in 1889. But it's the romantics who keep the story alive. Many Spaniards are drawn to the couple's tombs in the Iglesia de San Pedro (and take home an Amantes mug or magnet as a souvenir of their journey).

Teruel is just far enough off the beaten path to make it a perfect pilgrimage to love. If you decide to pay your respects to Los Amantes, you'll find that the 800-year-old tale of doomed love isn't all that the town has going for it. Like many communities on the frontier between Christian and Muslim Spain, Teruel had a complicated political history. Here it played out in some of Spain's most striking late medieval architecture. The style known as Mudéjar—mostly Christian buildings designed and constructed by Muslim architects and artisans—reached its apogee in Teruel and eastern Aragón in the fourteenth century. At its best, the Mudéjar style embues the Romanesque and Gothic structures borrowed from France and Italy with the decorative motifs of Islam. Much of the city was destroyed during some of the heaviest fighting of the Spanish Civil War, but it has been recognized by UNESCO as part of the Mudejár Architecture of Áragon World Heritage Site.

The church of San Pedro is one of the town's most stunning landmarks. The interior walls are encrusted with polychrome abstract patterns that rival in paint the intricate carved plaster of Granada's Alhambra. The soaring ribbed vault above the altar shines with golden stars on a background of midnight blue. The decorative, patterned brickwork and terra cotta roof tiles of the cloisters dazzle the eye.

The adjoining mausoleum where Isabel and Diego lie exposed for all the world to witness brings a more modern vision to the medieval story. Completed in 2005, it separates Los Amantes from the church in a structure where sound and light shows attempt to illuminate the legend with a little high-tech flash. But the young lovers still steal the show. They lie atop their respective marble sarcophagi, imagined in the voluptuous bloom of youth by sculptor Juan de Ávalos (1911-2006). Diego and Isabel each extend an arm to bridge the gap between them. Look closely and you'll see that their hands do not quite touch. Their longing for each other carries into eternity.

When James Michener described his visit to Teruel in his book *Iberia*, he noted that schoolchildren mocked the pair with the jingle

"*Los Amantes de Teruel/Tonta ella y tonto el,*" which translates roughly as "The Lovers of Teruel/She was a fool and he as well."

Of course children can laugh at the tale. They have yet to be stricken by love.

## RECOMMENDED READING

*Iberia* by James Michener

# 79 From the Beach to the Palm Forest

## ALICANTE AND ELCHE

I have always envied one of my former London editors. Whenever she needed a few days in the sun to decompress, she'd hop a budget airline from Stansted or Gatwick and jet off to Alicante for the weekend. The capital of the Costa Blanca is a favorite with Brits and northern Europeans who crave the kiss of sun on their pale skin and the grown-up pleasures of a real city instead of the juvenile antics of a rowdy beach resort. Alicante has good food and wine, atmospheric remnants of a Moorish past, and one of the most elegant seaside walks in eastern Spain.

The odds for good weather are favorable. With few rainy days and balmy temperatures all year round, the city basks in Mediterranean light. Perhaps that's why the Moors named it Alicante or "city of lights" when they fortified Monte Benacantil, the nearly vertical bluff that rises 545 feet behind the town. On top of the hill is the Castell de Santa Bárbara, which was originally built by the Moors and grew into one Spain's largest medieval fortresses under Jaume the Conquerer. It has sweeping hilltop views of the yacht harbor and the Mediterranean shore.

Jaume evicted the Moors, but they live on in local legend. Alicantinos claim that the profile of a Moor—"La Cara del Moro"—can be seen in the rocks and crevasses of Monte Benacantil. The best spot to discern the fanciful visage is, conveniently enough, from El Postiguet, the beach at the foot of the mountain. Many sun seekers find this sandy strand is all they need on a short break, but for those who want a broader, nearly 2-mile (2.9-km) stretch of golden sand, the tram for Playa de San Juan departs just across the road from El Postiguet.

The protective wall that the Moors built around the city survived until the nineteenth century. When Isabel II visited the city in 1858 to inaugurate train service from Madrid, she granted permission to tear the wall down so that the cramped city could grow. Fortunately, Alicante didn't overdo the urban renewal. The old city, Barrio Santa Cruz, remains as colorful as ever with geraniums spilling from its painted flowerpots, staircase streets, and wrought iron window grills.

The best part of the enlarged city was built on the very stones of the old walls, which were used to level and fill the land around the harborfront to create the Explanada d'Espanya. This wide walkway was laid with stones that create a mesmerizing mosaic of undulating waves underfoot. It is one of the great promenades in Spain, a country that loves dramatic places to stroll. It's hard not to imitate the sway of the palm trees with your hips as a cooling breeze wafts off the harbor.

✳ www.alicanteturismo.com

One street into Barrio Santa Cruz from the esplanade, María José San Román, one of Spain's top chefs and proprietor of Alicante's Michelin-starred Monastrell, joined forces with her daughter Geni Perramón to create La Taberna del Gourmet. The gastrobar offers a more casual and affordable introduction to San Román's simple magic with local ingredients. The tapas tasting menu, for example, gives a sampling of nine small plates that can range from sea-salted bread grilled in Alicante olive oil to tempura hake or grilled asparagus with romesco.

✳ latabernadelgourmet.com

The dining scene in Alicante is bolstered by the cruise ships that dock here. During those shore excursions, the city can get pretty crowded. But Elche makes a peaceful getaway only 17 miles (28 km) south. It's one of the important sites of the Celtic Iberian civilization that predated the arrival of Greek and Phoenician colonizers. The 2,500-year-old, shockingly sophisticated ceramic figure of *La Dama de Elche* was discovered here in 1897. It's now in Madrid's archeology museum (see Chapter 13), but Elche's Museo Arqueológico y de Historia has a replica and does a nice job of tracing the history of human habitation in the area.

Elche's other claim to fame is La Palmera, the largest palm oasis in Europe. Date palms have been cultivated here since at least the Iberian era, but the Moors created an orderly irrigation system for full-scale agricultural production. A millennium later, that irrigation network keeps the forest of more than 200,000 trees green and lush. Essentially a North African agricultural oasis, the palm forest features a 1.5-mile (2.5-km) bicycle and walking path beneath the rustling fronds.

✳ www.visitelche.com

Away from that oasis, Elche is a manufacturing center known for shoes and clothing. The industrial park at the east edge of town has more than twenty factory outlets that sell the overstock, last year's styles, and this year's prototypes and samples. The best of the bunch is Pikolinos Tienda Museo where the super-stylish footwear maker's prices can be reduced as much as 50 percent off retail— and that includes boots, or as Bob Dylan put it all those years ago, Spanish boots of Spanish leather.

# 80

## The Perfect Plate of Rice

### BIKING TO L'ALBUFERA AND
### EATING PAELLA IN VALENCIA

The first time I ate at La Pepica, I entered through the back street doors, rather than from the main entrance facing Malvarrosa beach. Once inside, I found myself skirting the edges of a busy kitchen where a forest of paella pans hung overhead. The shallow steel pans

with two handles ranged from the size of a dinner plate to the width of my outstretched arms. I knew I had come to the right place.

You can order paella almost anywhere in Spain and I swear that every tourist restaurant uses the same photograph to advertise the dish on the menu board posted out front. But paella is best eaten in Valencia, where the dish evolved and where its signature rice flourishes. And in Valencia, paella is best eaten at La Pepica.

Founded in 1898 and still in family hands, La Pepica has grown from a seasonal beach shack to a year-round dining hall that spans the stretch between street and beach. But success and fame—it's been popular with celebrities for decades—have made neither the cooks nor the waiters complacent. They prepare each pan with sure hands and serve it with the ceremony that such an iconic dish deserves.

✳ www.lapepica.com/en

Valencianos agree that the rice—a round, stubby, very white grain—is the star of the dish. Other ingredients are secondary and aficionados often have heated opinions about which are appropriate. Most first-time diners at La Pepica are surprised to learn that traditional Valencian paella is made with ingredients from the garden: snails, green beans, and usually rabbit or chicken. La Pepica does offer a version with chicken and rabbit, but the restaurant's own special is made with peeled shrimp and prawns—just as the painter Joaquin Sorolla first requested it. With all deference to Sorolla, for me, the mixed seafood paella (mostly shrimp, cockles, and mussels) is the most exuberant and elevates a meal to a celebration.

Each pan is prepared to order and takes at least half an hour. If you order a bottle of local *garnaxta* rosé to sip while you watch the scene in the 400-seat dining room, the time will pass quickly. Soon the waiter in striped vest and bowtie will approach your table with your perfect pan of paella balanced on a wooden platter. He'll almost bow as he presents it with a flourish—and poses for a photo. Then he will retire to a serving table to scoop the steaming rice onto individual plates. La Pepica never forgets that paella is first and foremost about the rice. Every grain is swollen with the wine, broth, and vegetable or seafood juices of the dish. The bottom layer next to the shallow pan has a decidedly toothy crunch. Never, never, never is it soupy or gummy. It is the Spanish apotheosis of rice.

Valencianos take food seriously. They have a temperate Mediterranean climate, lots of small vegetable farms and orchards around the city, a large fleet of coastal and deep-sea fishing boats, and the rice-growing wetlands. All those makings for great meals come together at the Mercat Central, one of Spain's most impressive fresh food markets. An outdoor marketplace opened on the downtown spot across from the old silk exchange in 1839. The current market building, an elegant Modernista-style masterpiece of iron, glass, and tiles, opened in 1928.

✳ www.mercadocentralvalencia.es

After eating my first plate of real paella in Valencia, I headed to the market to buy a paella pan. The vendor was prepared with a rudimentary recipe roughly translated into five or six different languages for everyone who wanted to try to recreate the dish at home. Whenever I return to Valencia, I still head to the Mercat Central for delicious, green-mottled Valencia oranges to snack on. I also stock up on saffron, sweet and smoked paprika, and Bomba rice. You can buy saffron and paprika throughout Spain, but it's hard to find Bomba rice outside Valencia. No other rice makes quite as good a paella as Bomba, which absorbs more liquid than other strains of Spanish pearl rice.

The Moors brought rice to the region in the eighth century and ensured its success by improving the irrigation system of canals and dikes left by the Romans. Much of Valencia's Bomba rice is grown in those medieval rice paddies in the wetlands around L'Albufera lake about 8 miles (13 km) south of the city. In 1986, the Spanish government designated the entire region as a natural reserve, the Parque Natural de L'Albufera. The lake is a freshwater lagoon of nine square miles located just inland from the barrier beach on the Mediterranean. It's an easy bicycle ride from Valencia to the park, since the N-322 has a parallel bike path most of the distance. I usually make a stop in the little town of El Saler with its white sand beach and rolling dunes that separate it from the wetlands.

✳ www.agricultura.gva.es/web/pn-l-albufera (Spanish only)

L'Albufera is fed by several small freshwater sources, including the Rio Júcar, and the surrounding wetlands are a magical mix of natural habitat for migratory waterfowl and songbirds and a dense network of rice paddies with sluice gates to allow alternate flooding and draining of the fields. You might see farmers preparing the fields in February, flooding the paddies in April before planting the rice seedlings, tending the fields all summer, and harvesting the grain heads in September.

One of the prettiest sights on the lake itself are fishermen in their small, flat-bottomed skiffs as they pole across the water like the gondoliers of Venice. They move silently as they angle for red mullet or haul American crayfish from baited traps. The crayfish were introduced to Spain in the 1970s, and have proven easier to cultivate than shrimp and much easier to catch than their ocean-going cousins, the *cigala* (the mini-lobster that the Italians call *scampi*). Even hardcore traditionalists agree that crayfish tails are perfect in a seafood paella. I'll second that.

## RECOMMENDED READING

*The Foods and Wines of Spain* by Penelope Casas
*The New Spanish Table* by Anya von Bremzen

# Light My Fire

## THE FALLAS FESTIVAL, VALENCIA

If you have a few demons to banish, get yourself to Valencia in mid-March for the practically nonstop whirl of the Fallas Festival. Even in a country known for its over-the-top celebrations (human pyramids, tomato-throwing battles...), Fallas stands alone. Translating roughly as "the Fires," the festival seems to be an excuse to revel in all things that snap, crackle, pop—and burn.

The most widely accepted origin story holds that Fallas started in the eighteenth century when carpenters would celebrate the coming of spring by burning the wooden lampposts they used for light over the winter. Once the fires got going, they threw in other scraps of wood or trash collected in the neighborhood for good measure. All I can say is that Valencianos must have a pyromaniacal streak. They took the idea of spring cleanup and ran with it, eventually replacing the lampposts with towering satirical sculptures that they painstakingly erect—and then burn to the ground—in practically every plaza and intersection in the city. The fires consume all manner of sins, obsessions, vanities, and scandals. Even youngsters get in the action, tossing little *petardos* or firecrackers that are sold in every corner shop. Fallas is not for the nervous.

❋ www.fallasfromvalencia.com/en

Fallas season begins in early March and all the *falla* sculptures must be completed by March 16. On March 19, the feast day of Saint Joseph, the Bible's most famous carpenter, they are all burned to the ground. You'll want a day or two to immerse yourself—and prepare for the finale. The surreal juxtaposition of events makes sense only to a Valenciano, but here's what to expect.

The *falla* figures are the faces of the festival. Originally of wood and papier-mâché, they are now constructed with foam core and polyester films stretched over wooden frames. These modern materials allow for bigger and more elaborate tableaus usually composed of several figures and scenes. Some can be up to 65 feet tall and may cost close to $1 million. They are a sight to behold and during the day, crowds roam from plaza to plaza.

The *fallas* for youngsters are invariably sweet, often composed of figures of animals and cartoon characters. One of my favorites from my last visit featured a chubby little boy drinking a cup of hot chocolate and clutching a *buñuelo*—a lump of pumpkin-flavored fried dough that is the unofficial street food of the festival. The show-stopping *fallas* for adults are unapologetically bawdy and never shy away from political scandals. If sex is involved, all the better. For maximum enjoyment, follow European politics and gossip closely in the months before your trip. No subject is too sacred for Fallas satire.

By early afternoon, throngs fill Plaza del Ayuntamiento (city hall plaza) for the *mascletà*. Bring heavy-duty earplugs. Valencianos describe the *mascletà* as sound fireworks. Approximately a million firecrackers are set off in a synchronized explosion that you feel in every fiber of your body. It's more visceral than even the loudest rock concert. Don't ask why. Just experience it for yourself—and don't forget the more traditional fireworks late at night.

It's all a little pagan, but Valencianos stage a lovely, religious counterpoint on March 17 and 18. Amid the festival-goers are clusters of men, women, and children in eighteenth-century dress. The women and girls really get into it. Decked out in full-skirted dresses of rich brocade, lacy aprons, hair combs, and mantillas they look as if they have just stepped from a Goya painting. They make their way to the Plaza de la Virgen clutching bouquets of pink, white, or red carnations for the patron saint of the erstwhile kingdom of Valencia, the Virgen de los Desamparados. Mothers and daughters weep as they leave their flower offerings for Our Lady of the Forsaken. Then they linger to watch as men on the ground toss the bouquets to others on ladders who cover a 46-foot wooden framework of the Virgin's statue with the colorful blooms. The serene Virgin is one of the few things in the city that won't feel the lick of flames.

On March 19, the city waits for dusk so that *La Cabalagata del Fuego*, or Fire Parade, can wind through the streets. Devils, grim reapers, and jesters whirl to the rhythms of drum corps as they swing scythes or carry hoses that spew streams of sparks into the sky overhead. It's just a taste of what's to come.

By 10 P.M., everyone has gathered at their favorite plaza and the *Cremà* gets underway. First the children's *fallas* are put to the torch and a smoky glow spreads over the city. At midnight, the satirical *fallas* are the final sacrifice. The last to go is the one at the Plaza del Ayuntamiento. National television broadcasts the scene as flames slowly spread upward, devouring leering politicians, preening celebrities, and all manner of pop culture characters. In a matter of minutes, all are reduced to ash.

When the smoke clears, Valencia is ready for a fresh start. I can't promise that Fallas will banish all your psychic pains as well. But it would take a mighty strong demon to come through the fires.

# 82 Jewel of the Gold Coast

## THE ROMAN CITY OF TARRAGONA

The oldest known Latin inscription on the Iberian peninsula is a dedication to the Roman goddess Minerva carved into a stone in the third-century B.C. wall around the city of Tarraco. It's hardly surprising that Roman soldiers would seek the blessing of the goddess of war as they established their military base and prepared to conquer the Iberian peninsula. But they didn't rely solely on divine intervention. They built their walls strong. Nearly twenty-four centuries later, sections of those walls are the oldest Roman remains in Europe outside Italy. For more than seven hundred years, Tarraco was the eastern capital of the Iberian peninsula. Now called Tarragona, the city still has some of the best and most evocative Roman ruins in Spain.

It also has something that even Rome lacks: a beautiful location on a rocky 269-foot bluff above the Mediterranean. Minerva, you see, is not only the goddess of war. She is also the goddess of wisdom and I'll bet that those Roman legions thought it was a great idea to settle in an easily defended spot washed with seaside light and blessed with a 180-degree view of the Mediterranean all the way to the horizon. At its height, Tarraco had a population of about one million people and was the powerhouse of Spain's northern Mediterranean coast. Now eclipsed by much larger and more cosmopolitan Barcelona, Tarragona remains one of the most fascinating historic cities in Spain, yet one of the least visited.

The Roman ruins and the lovely setting are reason enough to visit Tarragona, the largest city on the Costa Daurada, or Gold

Coast, as the region south of Barcelona down to the Río Ebro is now called. It's also a great place to get a sense of the progression of history in Iberia, where the layers of civilizations so often lie buried. The cathedral erected on the site of the mosque built on the remains of a Roman temple is the familiar story of cultural succession in Spain. But in Tarragona, much of the past lingers at the surface, unvanquished by everything that came later. In less than half a square mile, you can explore landmarks of two millennia of Spanish life, including fragments of the Via Augusta (the most famous of the Roman roads in Iberia) that are embedded in some of the city's plazas.

Of the sites that the Romans left behind, the Amfiteatre Ròma is easily one of grandest, most dramatic amphitheaters of the ancient world. Shaped like an oval, it was cut into the limestone cliff above the rocks where waves would crash against the shore. Although it stands in ruins, the tiered seats and the tunnels that open into the arena conjure up a bloody past. As many as fourteen thousand spectators would gather here to watch the blood sports of gladiators or the execution of heretics, criminals, and Christians.

The Romans certainly loved their spectacles, and the first century A.D. Circ Ròma, or circus, is even larger than the amphitheater. One of the best preserved in Western Europe, it could hold up to thirty thousand spectators for horse and chariot races. Victors would make their jubilant exit through the Porta Triumphalis. Not all the Roman remains were such bold architectural statements.

About a block from the circus, the Museu Nacional Arqueològic de Tarragona, Catalunya's first archeology museum, is worth a quick stop to examine the modest household goods—cooking utensils, toys, jewelry—that speak of private lives in ancient Tarraco.

✱ www.tarragona.cat/patrimoni/museu-historia

From the museum, it's a three-minute stroll to the city's medieval quarter centered around the massive fourteenth-century Gothic arcade along Calle Merceria. The thick stone arches once sheltered the city's market stalls. These days, an antiques market sets up on Sunday mornings and spills into the narrow streets.

The streets lead gently uphill to the Catedral on the highest spot of land in the city. The fortress-like structure, begun in the mid-twelfth century and consecrated in 1331, blends the squat arches of Romanesque with sky-reaching spires of Gothic architecture. A mid-fifteenth century altarpiece is dedicated to Santa Tecla, the city's patron saint. She is said to have endured numerous punishments for her embrace of Christianity and for her rejection of several suitors in favor of a life of chastity. In one panel of the altarpiece, artist Père Joan masterfully depicts the saint tied to a stake as flames lick about her garments. She escaped death when an unexpected storm extinguished the fire.

Even more striking is the tomb of Jaume I of Aragón (1208-1276), the dynamic conqueror and lawgiver who drove the Moors from eastern Spain and united the political fates of Aragón and Catalunya. The medieval king is Catalunya's equivalent of El Cid—a symbol of fierce independence for the region. He had, however, been dead for more than six centuries before the Tarragona Monuments Commission got around to ordering the tomb in 1906. As a result, Jaume rests in a Modernista masterpiece designed by Lluís Domènech i Montaner. The red porphyry tomb is topped with a ship carved of white stone. An angel at the stern and a female figure with uplifted arms at the prow help to guide the king over the waves from his earthly dominance to his eternal rest. The tomb was finally installed in 1992 in the Ayuntamiento, or city hall, on Plaça de la Font. The plaza has Tarragona's most lively café scene, so stop for coffee or a sparkling glass of cava as you contemplate that old Roman dictum, *sic transit gloria mundi*.

Other hints of Modernisme pop up around the city, including the wrought iron railing along the Balcó del Mediterrani, the walkway above the harbor, with the best views of the timeless ocean. You'll probably notice Tarragonans reaching out and laying hands on the iron railing as they take their evening promenades. Legend holds that *tocar ferro,* or "to touch iron," brings good luck.

✳ www.tarragonaturisme.cat/en

# 83

## *Wine, Women, and Song*

### CATALAN PALACES OF CAVA AND MUSIC

One mark of a great building is that it makes everything that happens inside or around it seem that much better. Catalunya in general, and Barcelona in particular, are blessed with a wealth of these magical structures—most of them exemplars of the Modernista architecture of the late nineteenth and early twentieth centuries.

The last time I visited the Palau de la Música Catalana, for example, I saw flamenco guitarist Pepe Habichuela in a fusion concert with Indian musicians. The unlikely combination of flamenco guitars and soaring sitars was a huge success, revealing the distant kinship of the two musical traditions. In all honesty, even first graders practicing on plastic Tonettes would have seemed inspired in the Palau, one of the most beautiful and original concert halls in Europe.

✳ www.palaumusica.cat/en

Architect Lluís Domènech i Montaner (1849-1923) designed Palau de la Musica Catalana for the Orfeó Català choral society and it rose in La Ribera neighborhood about a five-minute walk north of the cathedral between 1905 and 1908. Guided tours of the building are available, but it's more satisfying to take a seat in the concert hall and enjoy the space as it was intended.

Even approaching the red brick building is an experience because excess trumps restraint at every turn. With its Moorish arches, exposed ironwork, glazed tiles in floral patterns, portrait busts of composers, and sculptural ensemble celebrating choral music, the exterior makes the surrealism of Salvador Dalí (see Chapter 95), who knew the concert hall in his student days, seem inevitable.

And that's just the outside. Arrive early for your spot in the 2,200-seat concert hall. You'll need lots of gazing-around time to absorb the over-the-top embellishments that both exalt the female form and strike womanly themes. A stained-glass skylight in blue and gold tones evokes the sun and sky, with the rays of the sun delineating two circles of women's heads—perhaps a chorus. The back wall of the stage explodes with a semi-circular group of eighteen young women—often referred to as "the muses." Their lower bodies are depicted in colorful mosaic inlays while their upper torsos emerge as fully formed three-dimensional sculpture. Each wears a different outfit and plays a different musical instrument.

The frame for the stage may be the most dramatic of all the interior decoration. On the left, a bust of Catalan folk music champion Anselm Clavé rises above a sculptural group of young women singing the Catalan song "*Les Flors de Maig*," or "The Flowers of May." In contrast to all that sweetness and light, the right hand side is framed by a larger-than-life high-relief sculpture depicting the "Ride of the Valkyries," a reference to the Teutonic handmaidens who carry fallen warriors to Valhalla in Richard Wagner's opera *Die Walküre*.

The Palau de la Música Catalana is indeed a place of women and song. But Modernista architecture also has a special spot for wine—or more specifically for cava, Catalunya's answer to champagne.

Only 32 miles (51 km) west of Barcelona, Sant Sadurní d'Anoia is the center of the cava-producing region. It's about a forty-five-minute train ride from Barcelona and for most of the year, a special bus also carries visitors from the city directly to the Codorníu winery. The Codorníu winemaking family traces its roots back to 1551, but its signature achievement took place in 1872 when Josep Raventós Fatjó made the region's first cava in the winery's underground aging cellars. He applied the traditional *methode champenoise* of making the second fermentation in the bottle, but used the indigenous grape varieties of the Penedés region: macabeo for body, parellada for structure, and xarel-lo for its floral aromas. Cava's effervescence resembles champagne, but it is a lighter wine—bubbles without the hauteur.

Shortly after that milestone, the family commissioned Modernista architect Josep Puig i Cadafalch (1867-1956) to expand the winery. Work began in 1895 and was completed in 1915. Displaying his characteristic wit, he unified the buildings of the complex by basing them on parabolic arches that suggest the trajectory of a popping cork.

With arched windows outlined in brick, a tile floor, and undulating banquette seating, the Sala Puig Cava Bar summarizes the design elements—materials from the earth combined with lines that suggest the rows of grapes hugging the contours of the hills. The bar is open to walk-in visitors for cava tastings and tapas. You cannot help but feel elegant and sophisticated in the building often called the "Cathedral of Cava."

It's better to book ahead for a fuller tour, since Puig i Cadafalch designed the production facilities and warehouses as well as the public areas. Walk even a portion of the 20 miles (32 km) of limestone cellars (Cordoníu is the second largest producer of sparkling wine in Spain) to grasp the sense of history in the place—and how well it is rooted in the most Catalan of wines.

Tours (naturally) end with a tasting. Look for the labels with a profile drawing of Anna de Codorníu, the heiress to the family vineyards whose 1659 marriage to winemaker Miquel Raventós created the union of the Codorníu and Raventós families. She kept her family name and ran the operation, which remains in family hands more than two hundred and fifty years later. In the late 1970s, Cordoníu successfully lobbied the board that governs the rules for cava to permit the use of chardonnay and pinot noir grapes, the principal grapes in Champagne. The first cava to be made with chardonnay was Anna de Cordoniu brut, and it remains the company's flagship with a soft and persistent bead of bubbles on the surface and delicate aromas of lime, grapefuit, and pineapple. Take a sip and toast the matriarch.

✳ www.visitascodorniu.com/en

# 84 *Living in a Masterpiece*

## MODERNISTA HOMES IN BARCELONA

The architects of Barcelona's Modernisme movement may have had a penchant for fantastical shapes and elaborate ornamentation, but they were committed to creating "designs for living." Even today you can worship, shop for fresh food, or attend a concert in a Modernista landmark. You can also tour the site of a former hospital complex, now the Sant Pau Recinte Modernista, perhaps one of the most uplifting places ever to go to see a doctor.

But private life is another thing, and if you're curious about what it would be like to actually live in a Modernista masterpiece, a few such homes and apartments are now museums. They offer a tidied-up glimpse of how the movement's major architects turned their visions to daily life.

One of Antoni Gaudí's (1852-1926) earliest commissions was Palau Güell, constructed from 1886 to 1890 to enlarge the family home of industrialist and politician Eusebi Güell. Also a patron of the arts, Güell was quite simpatico with the architect's imagination. Yet the main floors of the house—"a normal Venetian palace" a guide once said dismissively—remained in the heavy style of Isabelline Spain with almost reflexive use of marble for columns, floors, and walls, and a lot of carved dark wood paneling. It provides a précis of the aesthetic that Gaudí and his fellow Modernistas were rejecting.

✳ palauguell.cat/en

Gaudí did manage to change the décor throughout, often clad-
ding columns with articulated panels and introducing a skylight
dome to illuminate the central hall. Soaring Gothic supports sur-

round a new bay window in the smoking
room, and leaded glass windows and mirrors
are found throughout the private rooms. But
Gaudí fomented his stylistic revolution above
and below ground. In the underground
chambers, great brick vaults and columns
reprise the supreme achievements of Catalan
Gothic architecture in the honeycomb of
stables. In an early example of his obsession
with skyline, he crowned the building with
chimneys wrapped in broken tile mosaics. It made a fitting opening
salvo of Modernisme's assault on the merely prosaic.

The greatest concentration of Modernista dwellings is within
L'Eixample, the orderly city expansion that took place 1890-1910,
during the height of the Modernisme movement. Two of the greatest examples stand side by side on Passeig de Gracia. Casa Amatller
was designed in 1900 by Josep Puig i Cadafalch (1867-1956) for the
chocolate manufacturer Antoni Amatller. A 2009-2014 restoration returned the principal floor to the era of the first residents,
complete with original furniture. The architect radically altered
the facade of the existing Neoclassical building by adding orna-
mental ironwork and balconies and creating a Dutch-style stepped
roof peak. But the exterior alterations were minimal compared to
the medievalist castle that Puig i Cadalfach created inside. Great
hoop-like arches link the passages between rooms, hardly a piece
of dark wooden furniture is left uncarved, and colorful ceramic
tiles and stained glass abound. A dramatic marble staircase rises

from the central courtyard. Amatller might have been a captain of industry, but he lived like a medieval prince.

✳ www.amatller.org (Catalan only)

If Casa Amatller evokes a kind of northern European epic melancholy, Casa Battló next door is suffused with a Mediterranean warmth. The original conventional structure had been designed by Gaudí in 1877. When textile industrialist Josep Batlló i Casanovas bought the house in 1904, he wanted a more flamboyant showcase and Gaudí was just the person to deliver it. Battló set the architect free to indulge his imagination and Gaudí took as his inspiration no less a subject than the ocean. The facade has hardly a single straight line—everything is as curved as the trough of a wave or as pointed as its crest.

✳ www.casabatllo.es/en

Restored and opened to the public in 2002, the main living quarters (the "Noble Floor") show exactly how Gaudí expected the family to live. Swirls in the ceiling represent waves on the ocean, and curvilinear window casings and trim continue the oceanic theme. Even the furniture was designed by the architect, and its placement offers palpable hints of the inhabitants—right down to the courting bench beside a mushroom-shaped fireplace in one small room. Gaudí imbued the house with a distinctly Catalan identity, tiling the roof in a scale pattern and creating chimneys that made it look like the spine of the dragon slain by Catalan patron San Jordi, or St. George.

Four blocks farther up Passeig de Gracia, the Casa Milà apartment house was Gaudí's final domestic commission, finished in 1912. The neighbors did not take kindly to the facade that looked like rough, weathered rock and they immediately called it "the stone quarry." More than a century later it is still best known by

that nickname, La Pedrera. Some of the apartments in the landmark structure are occupied, but visitors can view a circa-1912
apartment and the Espai Gaudí, an exhibition space that addresses
Gaudí's unusual approaches to design. The apartment is less
monumental than the freestanding mansions open to the public,
and for that reason, it is the easiest to imagine inhabiting. The
Gaudí-designed furniture makes extensive use of marquetry and
inlay (as do the floors), and the shapes draw from nature in classic
Art Nouveau style. (A bed with butterfly head- and footboards is
particularly delightful.)

✳ www.lapedrera.com/en/home

Anytime residents needed a fix of Gaudí at his most fantastic,
all they had to do was visit the roof, where the swirling, sculpted
chimneys form an army of hooded knights in full armor against
the sky. Gaudí was not above a little self-promotion. Even though
construction of the basilica was barely underway, one arch neatly
frames a view toward the site of La Sagrada Familia.

# Walking Barcelona

## THREE PROMENADES TO REMEMBER

The Catalan language often sounds a lot like Castellano, but I've never encountered a cognate in Spanish for the colloquial verb *badar*, which translates roughly as "to walk around with your mouth wide open in amazement." Perhaps there is no word like it in Castellano because there is no other city in Spain quite like Barcelona.

Barcelonans have elevated the stroll to an art form. As art critic Robert Hughes wrote in his 1992 book *Barcelona*, "One of the things that strikes the foreigner there—behind the smog, the din, and the traffic—is the social importance assigned to strolling and the reality of its pedestrian etiquette.... It is a city in which one still sees things from eye level, on foot; where there is always a collective instinct to browse."

Perhaps Barcelonans are predisposed to walking because centuries of urban development have created three completely different promenades. The first is Les Rambles, a three-quarter mile (1.2 km) boulevard laid out in 1766. With a wide pedestrian walkway flanked by narrow roads, it hugs the contours of the thirteenth century walls and is a breath of fresh air after the twisting, narrow streets of the old city.

The best place to begin is at the 174-foot Mirador de Colom, a monument to Christopher Columbus erected on the waterfront in 1888. Put the explorer at your back and head straight up the pedestrian walkway. It's a whirl of color with sidewalk cafés, newsstands, bookstalls, flower sellers, bird sellers, street musicians, panhandlers, human statues in every conceivable guise—and scores of visitors pointing their cameras and cellphones at the action.

About a third of the way up Les Rambles, a circular tile mosaic embedded in the pavement was designed by Catalan artist Joan Miró (see Chapters 90 and 97). It's a good place to make a short detour off the center strip and walk up the left-hand sidewalk to the Modernista jewel box of a pastry shop Escribá. Their *"lenguas de gats"* or "cats' tongues" of pure chocolate are good to eat while walking.

If you aren't already enamored of Barcelona, be sure to sip from the nineteenth-century Canaletes fountain near the end of Les Rambles. It's instantly recognizable by the four-armed streetlamp that rises above it. Legend says that anyone who drinks from the fountain will fall in love with the city and make many return visits.

Les Rambles officially ends at Plaça de Catalunya, a modern plaza with fountains and sculptures, a tourist information office, metro station, and stops for sightseeing buses. The plaza is also where the old city and the modern expansion of L'Eixample meet.

The orderly and refined city enlargement of the late nineteenth and early twentieth centuries is the home of the city's second great promenade, the Passeig de Gràcia. The once rural road was widened to 138 feet in 1827 and runs from Plaça de Catalunya to Carrer Gran de Gràcia—a distance of eight-tenths of a mile (1.3 km). Aristocrats once trotted up and down its length to show off their steeds and fine carriages. In the early twentieth century, Passeig de Gràcia was adorned with Modernista benches and street lights to signal its emergence as the most elegant street in the city's most elegant neighborhood. It is, as Hughes wrote, "one of the great promenades of the world, an expression of social consensus...."

That consensus achieves full bloom in the architecture. Of the neighborhood's three-dozen Modernista structures, several of the most famous dwellings are along Passeig de Gràcia (see chapter 84 for four that offer tours). Another, the 1905 Casa Lleó Morera, was designed by Lluís Domènich i Montaner. Since the mansion sits on a corner, he designed a striking double facade, which is almost a mirror image divided by a tower. Spain's famous maker of fine leather goods, Loewe, now occupies the ground level. If you're feeling whimsical, stop to examine their bags and coin purses shaped like elephants or pandas.

Preservationists lament the fact that the merchant did not retain Domènich i Montaner's interior design. But truth be told, the ethos of Passeig de Gràcia is shopping—note all the beautifully dressed women toting logo bags.

Barcelona took advantage of hosting the 1992 Summer Olympic Games to transform its once-funky waterfront into a huge civic amenity. It's best enjoyed on a breezy and beautiful (if somewhat disjointed) 1.8-mile (3-km) walk from the Mirador de Colom east to Port Olimpic.

The first stretch, the Moll de la Fusta, is equally popular with bicyclists and walkers. It's just slightly inland from the artificial islands that hold the high-tech aquarium and an American-style shopping and entertainment complex. The walkway features two delightfully playful pieces of public art—the gigantic fiberglass langostino that Xavier Mariscal built to advertise restaurant Gambrinus, and, at the foot of Via Laietana, pop artist Roy Lichtenstein's *Barcelona Head*.

A right turn here leads to Passeig de Joan de Borbó where you can admire the pleasure craft moored in the yacht basin and enjoy a plate of *arròs negre*—Catalan baked rice stained blue-black with squid ink—in one of the seafood restaurants that stand cheek-by-jowl on the land side. The street continues to the tip of the sand spit of Barceloneta, which was a fishermen's village before gentrification pushed the fishermen far up the coast. Now it's a trendy neighborhood of small flats, great casual restaurants, and some of the city's best swimming and sunning beaches.

Turn left on Carrer de l'Escar and walk to the end to reach the sandy strands of Platja de la Barceloneta, also known as Platja de San Sebastiá. Take off your shoes and let the sand squish between your toes until you reach the beachfront promenade at Passeig Maritim. At the end stands a great sculptural surprise, the 170-foot-long gold-colored, stainless steel abstract sculpture by Frank O. Gehry called *Peix* ("Fish"). Created for the 1992 Olympics, it is the de facto symbol of the rejuvenated waterfront.

## RECOMMENDED READING

*Barcelona* by Robert Hughes

# 86

## A Wedding and a Wine Bar

### BASÍLICA DE SANTA MARIA DEL MAR AND LA VINYA DEL SENYOR, BARCELONA

I've never had much luck practicing yoga or meditating as ways to relieve stress. But I do like the fairly undemanding coping strategy that calls for banishing unpleasant thoughts by visualizing a place where you were truly happy and at ease. More often than not, I relive an evening on the Plaça de Santa Maria in Barcelona.

Here's why. I always love stumbling on wedding parties when I'm in Spain. Everyone is in a buoyant mood—and so well dressed. That's especially true in Barcelona, where watching a wedding party can seem like a particularly lively fashion show, where each model is paired with a darkly handsome guy. One of the most reliable places to encounter a wedding in progress is at the Basílica de Santa Maria del Mar, a favorite for society nuptials. And the best seat on the show is from one of the few outdoor tables at La Vinya del Senyor, the wine bar that shares the Plaça de Santa María with the church.

❋ www.santamariadelmarbarcelona.org

The Basílica de la Sagrada Familia may be the most famous church in Barcelona, but Santa Maria del Mar, often called the "cathedral of La Ribera," is the people's church. In medieval times, this now gentrifying area adjacent to the Barri Gòtic was home to shipbuilders, merchants, and artisans. Those merchants donated the money to build a new church for their neighborhood. The people of the district literally put their backs into the project by carting stone from the quarries of Montjuïc and helping to erect the building. The cornerstone for Santa Maria del Mar was laid in 1329 and the church was consecrated in 1384. That lightning speed—at least for a church—means that the same architectural style was in vogue when the church was started as when it was finished. Santa Maria del Mar is practically the defining example of unadulterated Catalan Gothic style.

The church was built well. A 1936 fire destroyed a Baroque high altar and other ornamentation that had been added over the centuries, but left the bones intact. When it was rebuilt, the church fathers wisely chose to return the interior decoration to the Gothic era. Brides, I bet, have been thanking them ever since. With three soaring naves sitting atop tree-like columns that branch delicately as they extend to the ceilings and great ranks of stained glass windows that flood the church with light, it has a serene but solemn air that seems just right for exchanging wedding vows. And, it must be said, the clean and elegant lines of the interior are a perfect backdrop for brides in their gowns by designer extraordinaire Rosa Clara and their friends and relatives in new dresses from the boutiques of L'Eixample.

One Friday night, a wedding party had started to stream up the steps to the church when my husband and I passed La Vinya del Senyor and noticed that one of the few tables on the plaza had just been vacated. We took it as a sign and promptly sat down to watch the women in jewel-toned long dresses and the men in dark suits. Several of the ushers were hanging out at the bar and we followed their lead and ordered a couple of glasses of cava from the wine list. The sparkling wine seemed the only appropriately celebratory choice. When the bride and her father pulled up in a black

Mercedes, the ushers hustled inside and we could hear strains of organ music as the ceremony soon got underway.

We might have left at that point, but a guitarist and a saxophone player had just launched into a tune on the plaza and one glass of cava led to another. Before we knew it, the wedding party was bursting from the church in a shower of rose petals.

Traffic stopped as the revelers spilled into the street and onto the plaza. The musicians promptly joined the party—playing a long and lively rendition of "All of Me" while everyone ignored the churlish taxi driver who kept up a steady series of blasts from his horn. When they were good and ready, the wedding party moved on in a wonderful, colorful flurry of high spirits and high hopes. In their wake, they left a plaza full of rose petals, a couple of musicians with a hat full of tips, and a few empty cava bottles on the adjoining tables.

With apologies to Luis Buñuel and Pedro Almodóvar, when I think back on the scene I imagine that I am an extra in a Federico Fellini film. How could I not be happy?

# 87

## Portrait of the Artist as a Young Man

### PICASSO IN BARCELONA

"Give me a museum and I'll fill it," Pablo Picasso (1881-1973) once said. It was hardly an idle boast from the prolific genius who dominated the art world for most of the twentieth century. One of the artist's greatest works is in the collection of the Reina Sofía museum in Madrid (see Chapter 9) and, in Spain alone, two other museums mark way stations on his journey. In Málaga, a museum honors the city of Picasso's birth (see Chapter 68). In Barcelona, yet another museum celebrates the milieu where he broke from his academic training and began to invent the twentieth century.

Picasso and his family moved to Barcelona in 1895 when his father, José Ruiz Blasco, secured a teaching position at La Llotja art school, where young Picasso was also soon enrolled. His formal training was nearing its end, but the cosmopolitan city exposed Picasso to a broader artistic circle where he cultivated artist friends who would figure throughout his life. The group often gathered at Els Quatre Gats, a café modeled after Paris's Le Chat Noir and located in a landmark Modernista building. If you stop in for a drink or a bite to eat at the slightly renamed 4GATS, you'll probably encounter a reproduction of Picasso's design of a menu cover.

✳ www.4gats.com/en

By 1904, Picasso had succumbed to the lure of Paris, though he would occasionally return to Spain until the advent of the Civil War. In 1960, Jaume Sabartés, a friend from the Barcelona days and Picasso's personal secretary, raised the idea of a museum in Barcelona. The city council was enthusiastic—and so was Picasso—though the artist was to never set foot in the museum.

The Museu Picasso opened in 1963 in the Palau Aguilar, a venerable mansion in the city's Gothic quarter, with the nucleus of the collection donated by Sabartés himself. Artists such as Salvador Dalí, his wife Gala, and other collectors augmented the collection. Picasso and his family members, including his widow Jacqueline Roque, also made significant donations. The collection now numbers more than 4,200 works and the museum has spread into several adjoining old palaces. Visiting always reminds me of serial New England architecture, where rooms are strung together as each generation outgrows the old building; the art on the walls, of course, is much better in Barcelona.

❈ www.bcn.cat/museupicasso/en

The museum is particularly strong on Picasso's early works, such as a self-portrait and portraits of his mother and father, all painted in 1896. They show an artist beginning to break the bonds of formal academic training and gain confidence in his own technique and powers of observation. Of all the styles of Picasso's work, the Blue Period is most associated with his time in Barcelona. Many pieces in that melancholy hue were created here, including the 1903 *Motherhood*, a pastel and charcoal on paper depicting a mother and child, a favorite subject of the young Picasso.

Key pieces in the collection also reference some of the innovations that kept emerging from Picasso's studio. *The Offering*, a 1908 gouache on paper, was part of a series of studies on a subject that intrigued the artist: men observing a nude woman. It recalls

Picasso's groundbreaking composition in the 1907 *Les Demoiselles d'Avignon.* Considered one of the pivotal paintings of the twentieth century, Les Demoiselles refers to a nightlife street in Barcelona even though it was painted in Paris.

Picasso created Cubist set designs and costumes for Sergei Diaghilev's *Ballets Russes* and found himself back in Barcelona with the company for several months in 1917. Among the canvases he completed at that time was a portrait in oil of Blanquita Suárez, a variety star then singing at the Eldorado in Barcelona. Struck perhaps by the planes of her face in contrast to the curves of her body, Picasso deconstructed her coquettish pose in a work that was a treatise on using multiple points of view and contrasting color to render three-dimensional movement on a flat surface. Almost two decades later, Picasso was preoccupied with the mythological figure of the minotaur, with its body of a man and head of a bull. The 1935 etching *Minotauromachy* is considered one of his most accomplished pieces of graphic art. In addition, the figures, composition, and sense of tension in the piece suggest his great anti-war masterpiece, *Guernica*, of 1937, the highlight of the Reina Sofía.

When Sabartés died in 1968, Picasso made his most significant donation to the museum: the fifty-eight canvases of "Las Meninas." Picasso first saw the Diego Velázquez masterpiece at the Museo Nacional del Prado in 1895 while still an art student. (See Chapter 7 for a fuller description of the work that depicts Velázquez painting the Infanta María Margarita and her attendants as her parents, Felipe IV and Mariana de Austria, look on.)

Picasso was seventy-five years old when he painted the series in the south of France between August and December 1957. By measuring himself against one of the greatest painters of all time, he was both asserting his Spanish identity and boldly claiming his place in the artistic pantheon. In her book *Picasso's Variations on the Masters*, Susan Grace Galassi notes, "No painting in the history of art was more imbued with personal and historical meaning for Picasso than Velázquez's masterpiece, 'Las Meninas.'"

The ambiguity of the space, shifting perspectives, and fascinating group of characters in Velázquez's original gave Picasso multiple points of departure. The range of canvases shows how he dissected and recreated the work to make it his own. In studying the full scene or individual figures, Picasso sometimes changed the orientation of the canvas from vertical to horizontal; eliminated color in favor of shades of black, gray, and white; flattened the perspective; depicted characters with multi-faceted Cubist profiles; and diminished or even eliminated the image of the artist. In some versions he replaced the Infanta's massive Spanish mastiff with a portrait of his own dachshund, Lump.

Notably, of the whole series, at least fifteen paintings are variations on the Infanta. "Through this diminutive figure, one of the most enduring characters in the history of art," says Galassi, "Picasso reaches back through Goya to Velázquez, inscribing himself in the chain of great Spanish painters."

## RECOMMENDED READING

*Picasso's Variations on the Masters* by Susan Grace Galassi

# 88 _Dancing on the Plaza_

### BARCELONA'S BARRI GOTÍC ON SUNDAY

Pealing church bells that waken all but the soundest sleepers guarantee an early start to Sundays in Barcelona. That's a good thing, really, since Sunday is the best time to wander through the Barri Gotíc, or Gothic Quarter, still tucked within the defensive walls erected in the thirteenth century when Barcelona emerged as a sea power.

Much of the medieval street pattern persists in this oldest part of the city where construction of new buildings seems to have stopped after the fifteenth century. The quarter runs approximately from Les Rambles east to Via Laietana and from the waterfront north to Plaça de Catalunya. The best thing is to simply dive in and follow the narrow, often cobbled streets from plaza to plaza and from Gothic church to Gothic church.

Apart from those bells, Sunday mornings are so quiet that you might hear guitar music echoing off the stone buildings before you discover the musician seated in a tiny square with a box for coins in front of him. Nearby, someone else will likely be offering religious candles for sale.

The church of San Felipe Neri, on a pretty little plaza of the same name, is one of the exceptions to the quarter's dominant architectural style. It's one of the few Baroque-style buildings in Barcelona, but that is not its most remarkable feature. The walls of its rather austere facade still bear pockmarks from Nationalist bombs dropped on the city in January 1938. Forty-two people seeking shelter in the basement of the church's convent died in the attack, which took place almost exactly a year before Barcelona fell to Franco.

The proud Barcelonans suffered greatly under Franco's rule, when their language and many of their cultural traditions were outlawed. One look at city signage confirms that the Catalan language has made a resurgence—and so has the *sardana*, a popular folk dance that has become a symbol of Catalan unity.

The Barri Gotic's labyrinth of streets opens up in front of La Seu, as Barcelonans call their Catalan Gothic cathedral in their own language. If you arrive at the plaza out front around noon, you will likely encounter circles of dancers performing the mesmerizing *sardana*. A small orchestra of mixed woodwinds and brass instruments tunes up on the cathedral steps as people toss their belongings into a pile and form a circle. The *flabiol*, a nasal-sounding flute, plays a measure and the flautist strikes a drum. Then the other musicians join in with a measured, circular tune. The dancers hold hands down low and start—point-step-step-cross to the right, then to the left. They raise their arms and repeat the steps as more circles of dancers form.

My friend Corey Boniface, an accomplished dancer and past president of the Folk Arts Center of New England, checked an item off her bucket list when she joined one of the dance circles on an Easter Sunday. Corey still recalls how welcoming the dancers were when she threw her purse and jacket into the pile and clasped hands to join a circle.

"I was managing quite well and felt approval from the circle leader—until the tricky part of each tune. What began as baby steps and simple rhythm would periodically and unpredictably alter to a brief, complicated combination with which I struggled and tripped up, repeatedly," she says. During a break, the circle leader pulled her aside and helped her master the secret of the altered step.

"Thereafter, dancing under the blue sky on Easter, in the home turf of this authentic ethnic dance, to live music, with those patriotic Catalans who had kept the tradition alive through the Franco years—well, for a folkie, there is no greater joy," she says.

Even watching the ecstatic celebration of identity and cultural perseverance is enough to put an extra spring in your step as you leave the cathedral and delve deeper into the medieval streets and squares. If you're hungry, Plaça del Pi and its two contiguous plazas—Sant Josep Oriol and Placeta del Pi—are only about a five-minute walk toward Les Rambles. The shady squares are lined with café tables where you can order a cazuela of hot *butifarra* sausage and a cold beer. Once you're ready to relinquish your table, you can check out the wares of the artisans who assemble here on weekends.

During the summer, the church that gives the plaza its name, fourteenth-century Santa María del Pi, operates a series of concerts in its "Secret Garden." The church is a marvelous Gothic space to visit at any time of year—and the first thing every parishioner will point out is the gigantic rose window. The original was destroyed in the Civil War, along with much of the church. Barcelonans rallied and restored it all, starting with the window, the symbol of faith, in 1940, and finishing the last of the cosmetic fixes not long before Franco died.

# 89

## A Vision to Behold

### LA SAGRADA FAMILIA OF ANTONI GAUDÍ, BARCELONA

It's not often that you can see an already venerated landmark rising before your eyes. The Basilica de la Sagrada Família isn't slated for completion until 2026, but it's been the de facto symbol of Barcelona for decades—akin to the Eiffel Tower in Paris or the Statue of Liberty in New York. Since it is also a work in progress, all you have to do is purchase an admission ticket to do your part to support the construction.

The foundation for the church of the Holy Family was laid in 1882 and Antoni Gaudí (1852-1926) came on board as architect the following year. By 1914 the unquestioned genius of the Modernisme movement had given up all other commissions to devote himself to the project full-time. Already in his sixties, Gaudí knew he wouldn't live to see the building completed. But he didn't antici-pate his untimely death in 1926 after being struck by a trolley. (He is buried in a chapel on the lower level.)

Construction was slow and the church was less than 25 percent done when Gaudí died. But he did see the completion of the first bell tower and seemed to sense that his phantasmagoric building would dominate the skyline. "Look at the top! Is it not true that it seems to unite Heaven and Earth?" he is said to have exclaimed. "This burst of mosaics is the first thing that sailors will see when approaching Barcelona; it will be a radiant welcome."

Progress virtually halted during the Civil War and Gaudí's flamboyant architectural style has gone in and out of favor over the decades. But the building will not be denied. Since the 1980s, new construction materials and techniques have accelerated its progress. All work is funded by private donations and admissions.

Drawing from traditional models, Gaudí based his design on the Latin cross plan with five aisles, and envisioned a total of eighteen towers, and three elaborate facades. The Nativity facade was near completion at the time of his death and he considered it a model for other artists and architects who would come after him. It is a précis of the joyful opening stories of the New Testament—the Holy Trinity, the Immaculate Conception, the birth of Christ, the Star of Bethlehem, the wise men and shepherds, and a veritable zoo of creatures on the Tree of Life. It seems that every square inch is encrusted with a meaningful sculpture attesting to the faith of the architect and the donors who supported this expiatory temple as recompense for their sins.

Starting in 1986, sculptor Josep Maria Subirachs (1927-2014) worked for twenty-five years on the sculptural grouping for the more somber Passion facade that depicts Christ's crucifixion and resurrection. The style prompted immediate controversy, as Subirachs' simplified and angular forms bore more than a little similarity to the official Expressionist kitsch of Franco-era public sculpture.

Everyone is waiting to see the Glory facade, the largest of the three and the eventual entrance to the church. The walls were raised at the beginning of this century, and Gaudí planned a didactic imagery so ambitious that it would rival the carvings on a

Romanesque portal. It was to capture heaven and hell, the deadly sins and the heavenly virtues, and the Last Judgment, complete with demons, idols, and false gods on one hand, and angels and virtuous Christians on the other.

La Sagrada Familia was consecrated by Pope Benedict XVI in 2010 as a minor basilica and the stone and glass of the interior does seem to possess a certain ecstatic animism, as if the forms themselves were actively engaged in worship. Thousands of the human faithful fit inside, but they are dwarfed by the heroic scale of the church. Elaborate branching columns grow like tall trees from the ground, creating the impression of a lush forest. Joan Vila-Grau (born 1932) and his artisans are creating the stained glass windows that Gaudí specified to fill the space with color and light. Many of the portals are far from the floor of the church, so they are streamlined and geometric—and often elaborated in multiple shades of a single color.

As of October 2015, construction of the basilica was 70 percent complete. Plans call for the last six towers to be raised in 2026 to mark the centenary of Gaudí's death. They will also make La Sagrada Familia the tallest religious building in Europe at 564 feet—all the easier for those sailors to spot from out at sea.

✳ www.sagradafamilia.org/en

# 90 *The Magic Mountain*

## TREASURES OF MONTJUÏC, BARCELONA

The Roman poet Juvenal may have been the first to put forward the idea of "a sound mind in a sound body," but Barcelonans clearly took the concept to heart as they built on Montjuïc, the flat-topped hill southwest of the old city that used to be good for nothing but pastures, woodlots, and stone quarries. Even if you are only planning to visit Montjuïc's two great museums, wear walking shoes—and pack a bathing suit.

Surrounded by gardens and boasting expansive city and harbor views, Castell de Montjuïc, the eighteenth-century fortress at the top of the hill, is a favorite weekend picnic spot. But the modern makeover of the mountain began when it was selected as the site for the 1929 International Exposition. A flurry of construction gave the park several new buildings, including a replica Greek theater where a summer music and arts festival holds forth, and a sports stadium that was refurbished for the 1992 Summer Olympic Games.

The exposition also created a ceremonial entrance to the park, past the Font Màgica, the city's largest fountain. Always a delight on a hot day, the fountain was refurbished for the Olympic games. On many nights, synchronized lights and music accompany shows of dancing water jets.

The grand staircase behind the fountain ascends to the domed Palau Nacional, the Renaissance-style building created as the centerpiece of the 1929 festivities. Since 1934 it has housed the Museu Nacional d'Art de Catalunya (MNAC), which despite its regional focus is one of Spain's best art museums. In addition to Catalan art, it has a good selection of works by Spanish master painters such as Velázquez, Rivera, and Zurbarán and excellent displays of Modernisme design and furniture. Similar treasures can be found in other Spanish museums, but MNAC also has a unique and awe-inspiring collection of Romanesque Catalan art. The most thrilling pieces are the eleventh-to-thirteenth-century Romanesque murals rescued from abandoned ancient churches in the Pyrenees. They were saved from the clutches of wealthy art museums and collectors from abroad (a real threat in the early twentieth century), and assembled here in lovely, quiet, low-lit galleries.

✳ www.museunacional.cat/en

The vivid colors and powerful compositions speak across the ages without regard for the viewer's belief system. The pieces are simply great anonymous art that Catalans take as a birthright. Late in his life, Joan Miró (1893-1983) spoke of the impact of this work on his budding artistic sensibility. "Before I was ten years old," he recalled in a 1978 interview, "I was going by myself on Sunday mornings to the Museum of Romanesque Art...."

✳ www.fmirobcn.org/en

A Barcelona native, Miró has his own presence on Montjuïc. The Fundació Joan Miró is about an eight-minute walk uphill via Passeig de Santa Madrona from the Catalan museum. (Just keep in mind that adage about sound minds and sound bodies.) The foundation opened in 1975 in a building designed by Miró's friend, fellow Catalan Josep Lluís Sert, who also designed his studio on Mallorca. Miró himself donated many of the paintings, drawings, sculptures, and tapestries that fill Sert's light-infused galleries. It's a very simpatico space that reflects the meeting of the minds of two old friends. Always appreciated in his native Catalunya, Miró has risen to something of a cult status in the twenty-first century. His once radical surrealism of abstract forms and symbolic handling of primary and secondary colors has become as much a part of the Catalan visual vocabulary as the hooded-warrior chimney pots of Gaudí or the scaly curls of the

dragons slain by Sant Jordi. The museum building, by the way, has a rooftop sculpture garden and terrace with nice views of Barcelona below. (For Miró's home and studio on Mallorca, see Chapter 97.)

As you continue climbing, you'll pass the Anella Olímpica, or Olympic Ring. The so-called "nerve center" of the 1992 summer games includes the refurbished 1929 stadium, which now hosts European football matches; the ultra-modern domed Palau Sant Jordi, now a venue for sports events and concerts; and the 446-foot communications tower designed and sited by Spanish architect Santiago Calatrava so that its shadow turns the adjacent plaza into a sundial. Barcelonans most enjoy the Bernat Picornell swimming complex with indoor, outdoor, and diving pools, a terrace for sunbathing, and (once again) a stunning view of the city below. If you followed my advice and packed a bathing suit, you can end your day on Montjuïc right here.

Otherwise, keep walking another fifteen minutes uphill to the Jardí Botànic, which was established in 1930 and revamped in the 1990s. The 1,350 species of plants from countries with a Mediterranean climate struggle through the arid summer, soak up moisture in the autumn rains, store their energy over the winter, and finally burst into colorful bloom in the spring.

✳ www.museuciencies.cat/en

# 91 Temples of Food

## THE HEARTBEAT MARKETS OF BARCELONA

In Spain and other Mediterranean basin countries, the so-called "Mediterranean Diet" isn't just the latest fad for losing weight, cultivating a healthy heart, and living longer. Since 2013, UNESCO has celebrated the Mediterranean Diet as part of the "Intangible Cultural Heritage of Humanity," right up there with falconry, flamenco, and the gingerbread houses of Northern Croatia. (You can look it up.) The official international blessing honors the way food is grown, harvested, caught, prepared, and shared in all the countries surrounding the Mediterranean. Most of the people who live it probably don't think about it much. It's all they know.

I can't speak for Italy, Croatia or the other countries that UNESCO identified, but in Spain, the diet and foodways associated with it are celebrated first and foremost in the public food markets. No other city in Mediterranean Spain has quite the devotion to food as Barcelona, where one of the largest and certainly most celebrated food markets in the country sits right on Les Rambles. La Mercat de Sant Josep de la Boqueria—best known simply as La Boqueria—has been around since construction of the building began in 1840, and not much has changed since the metal roof was put on the train-station-sized hall in 1914.

✳ www.boqueria.info

But no one looks at the early Modernista structure. A glass of fresh juice in hand, they begin to choose from the boxes of perfect vegetables and fruits, the clear-eyed whole fish sprawled on crushed ice, the glass cases of cheeses and fresh meat, and the hanging displays of hams and sausages. With more than three hundred stalls, a handful of bars and restaurants around the perimeter, and even a demo kitchen that doubles for cooking classes, La Boqueria sells almost everything any self-respecting Mediterranean would  eat. And its vendors (when they can catch their breath) will go on and on about how to prepare whatever they're selling, how their mothers used to prepare it, and how their favorite famous chef (who naturally buys from them) prepares it. And you thought a *cep* was just another mushroom.

There are actually thirty-nine food markets distributed among the neighborhoods of the sprawling city. They range from traditional markets—a little damp and badly lit and usually running low on supplies by the time lunch arrives—to the poshly renovated and unrelentingly modern. What they all share is the love of food and the camaraderie of eating.

Some of the newest show how the old foodways are evolving. The Mercat Santa Caterina was Barcelona's second enclosed market, built five years after La Boqueria, and for decades served the working-class neighborhoods on the east side of the city. Following a thoughtful and artistic renovation in 2005—the roof is made of colorful mosaics representing fruits and vegetables—Santa Caterina has assumed a role of its own in Barcelona food culture. It has fewer fresh food stalls than La Boqueria (and maybe slightly lower prices, which I attribute to fewer tourists), but it also has first-rate restaurants (and one bakery café) serving simple dishes that give fresh meaning to "market cuisine." If you have a foodie friend in the city, you will almost certainly meet up here for lunch.

❋ www.mercatsantacaterina.com (Catalan only)

In keeping with a trend all over Spain, some markets are barely markets at all. They have evolved away from suppliers for DIY cuisine to something that more closely resembles the much maligned food court. Mind you, there's no room in these markets for American fast food chains, even though you'll often find at least one stand selling sliders and *frites*. The Mercat Princesa, not far from the Picasso Museum, was one of the first such markets I found in Barcelona. Seventeen stands are arrayed around the courtyard of a lovely fourteenth-century medieval palace. To be honest, they depart a little from the Mediterranean Diet, what with sashimi, sushi, pizza, and the aforementioned burgers and fries. But they also serve as a reminder that people eat well all over Spain, whether by the standards of the Med Diet or not. The fresh fish stall offers Andalucían-style fried fish as well as Galician octopus in a sweet pepper sauce. Txapela serves hot and cold pintxos, the Basque terms for tapas, with glasses of bracing txacoli wine. And you might think you're in Cádiz or Jerez if you belly up to the bar at La Xarcu to sip a sherry while a maestro with a long knife shaves paper-thin slices of Iberian ham to go with your plate of cheese.

❋ www.mercatprincesa.com/en

# 92

## The Most Important Meal of the Day

### FIVE BREAKFASTS IN BARCELONA

Spaniards love to eat, but the meal that often gets short shrift is breakfast. They grab a *café solo* and a roll as they hurry to work, secure in the knowledge that there will be plenty to eat—and snack on—throughout the day. Visitors, however, have no such time constraints and lingering over breakfast as you watch the day unfold is a lovely way to get to know a place. In Barcelona I have a few favorite spots, each of which places me at a good starting point for a day of exploration.

Star chef Carles Abellan of the much praised Bravo and el Suculent, is certainly doing his part to elevate breakfast in the eyes of his fellow Barcelonans. His modest little Tapas 24, located on the lower level of Carrer de la Diputació, 269 in L'Eixample, serves casual food all day. His signature breakfast is *estrellats*, a hearty plate of fried potatoes topped with a broken fried egg. Various sausages or Iberian ham can be added to the mix, but the ultimate treat is a serving of *estrellats* with foie gras, a favorite of Catalan chefs. A stool at the counter is the best place to watch the cooks as they move like clockwork in the kitchen. Modernista masterpiece Casa Battló (see Chapter 84) is just a block and a half up Passeig de Gràcia.

La Gardunya, a restaurant at the back of Barcelona's famed food market La Boqueria (see Chapter 91) practically defines "market cuisine." The fixed-price lunch and dinner menus are very popular, but the casual bar opens early and serves a few simple breakfast foods. Diners can take a table inside, but the tiny outdoor plaza behind the market building is the best place to watch vendors bringing in the meats, fish, and produce to stock the stalls. A small *tortilla Española*, or potato omelet, with fig confit and goat cheese, and a few slices of Barcelona's signature *pa amb tomaquet* (bread drizzled with olive oil and rubbed with fresh tomato) make a good introduction to the riches of the market.

Tucked away on Carrer Xucla, 4-6 off Les Rambles, Granja M. Viader was founded in 1870 as one of Barcelona's original "milk bars." Its signature chocolate milk, Cacaolat, is sold next to soft drinks in practically every shop in Barcelona, but it's more fun to sit down at one of the marble-topped tables in this little time capsule with tiled floors and walls covered with photos and awards. The coffee is strong and good, but most folks opt for hot chocolate and a light, flaky *ensaimada*. The sugar-covered pastry, which is a specialty of Mallorca, is quite popular here. This breakfast is the perfect calm preparation for strolling through the Fellini-esque carnival of Les Rambles.

Speaking of chocolate, Patisseria Brunells at the corner of calles Princesa and Montcada in the Barri Gòtic is one of the city's great old chocolatiers. It's a good place to stock up on chocolate bars as gifts for the folks back home. The small café at the back of the shop serves hot chocolate with churros, or with the more unusual *melindros*, slightly sweet oblong pastries with a heavy cake crumb. Many aficionados find them superior to fried churros for dunking in hot chocolate. From here, it's a short walk to the Museu Picasso (see Chapter 87). You will enjoy your breakfast without worry if you have purchased your admission on the web site so you can skip the long ticket line.

It's probably best to think of the morning meal at Xampu Xampany at Gran Vía de les Corts Catalanes, 702 in L'Eixample as brunch. Founded more than thirty years ago as a café, gourmet emporium, and wine store, Xampu specializes in the Catalan sparkling wine cava (see Chapter 83). The room is nothing special by morning light (it glitters with small soft lights at night), but there are usually a half dozen different cavas open and sitting on ice at any time of day. Italian-style coffees and freshly made pastries offer a more refined version of the typical hasty Spanish breakfast. Even better is a simple French-style omelet, rolled and tucked into a slice of baguette, with a glass or cava or, even better, cava mixed with fresh-squeezed orange juice in a Catalan take on a mimosa. You'll be in the right frame of mind to appreciate the celebratory excesses of La Sagrada Familia (see Chapter 89) a short walk away.

# 93

## *Hand of la Moreneta*

### THE SHRINE OF MONTSERRAT

In the fairly flat countryside northwest of Barcelona, the most peculiar mountain range suddenly springs out of the plain and shoots 4,055 feet almost straight up. It is called Montserrat, or "serrated mountain," in reference to the saw-toothed peaks that form its ridgeline like a swarthy version of the Italian Dolomites.

Never underestimate the allure of the strange. By some accounts, the Romans built a temple to Venus on one of this otherworldly mountain's many peaks, and since the twelfth century, pilgrims have flocked to the crags to pay their respects to "La Moreneta," as the 38-inch-high statue of Santa María de Montserrat is affectionately known in Catalan. The nickname means "the little dark-skinned one," as the statue is one of the most striking of the Romanesque "black Madonnas" found throughout Europe. It is also located in one of the most dramatic settings of all of Spain's pilgrimage sites.

Although hermits are known to have retreated to Montserrat as early as A.D. 800, the Benedictine Monestir de Montserrat was not constructed until 1025. Exactly when and how the venerated statue was discovered is up for debate, as the assorted miraculous tales all stretch credulity. But unlike the Holy Grail that Parsifal sought here in Wagner's opera named for the knight, the Virgen de Montserrat is a very real and striking artifact of faith. Ignatius of Loyola came here in 1512 to lay down his arms at her feet before he entered a phase of ascetic meditation that led to founding the Jesuit Order. Kings of Spain died clasping candles from the monastery to their breasts. So many pilgrims made their arduous way up the mountain that the monastery had to expand the church where the figure was kept. The grand basilica was consecrated in 1592. So widespread was devotion to La Moreneta that in 1881, Pope Leo XIII crowned her and declared Santa María de Montserrat the patroness of Catalunya.

Getting up the mountain is a lot easier than it was even in Pope Leo's day. The train from Barcelona's Plaça d'Espanya station stops at the station of the cable car, or Aeri, or continues on to the station of the less expensive but somewhat slower funicular rail. Less than ninety minutes after leaving Barcelona, either mode of transportation deposits pilgrims just outside the monastery's main plaza. Look downward from the windswept aerie for long vistas reaching almost to the sea—or up at the pink conglomerate of the mountain slope that wraps around the monastic community like a cloak.

Rebuilt after being heavily damaged by Napoleon's troops in the early nineteenth century, the basilica is a soaring Gothic church somewhat obscured by a twentieth-century facade. Once inside, pilgrims join the line to reach La Moreneta herself in her nook above and behind the main altar. The carved wooden statue is painted and partly gilded, and she affects the knowing serenity so common to Romanesque images of the Virgin. In this case, Santa María sits on the Throne of Wisdom with the Christ Child in her lap. The statue is surrounded by a clear protective shield of something like acrylic or Plexiglas, but her right hand, which holds a globe representing the temporal world, extends through an opening. (In the twelfth century, eastern Europe already knew

the world was round while western Europe still thought it was flat.)
Each pilgrim touches her, says a quick prayer, and moves on.

While the Montserrat statue depicts the Virgin in her role as
queen of the world, rather than the more tender and intimate
depiction of her as the mother of Christ, she clearly strikes a
familial chord with many Catalans. Among the faithful, a visit
to Montserrat is often one of the stops on their honeymoon, as
couples come to the Virgin for her blessing. Certainly many of
them name their daughters after La Moreneta—"Montserrat"
(often abbreviated as "Montse") is the second most common
woman's name in Catalunya.

✳ www.montserratvisita.com

# 94

## *Among the Legends*

### THE STORIED CITY OF GIRONA

Sitting on a hill above the Ríu Onyar, Girona is a city that seems marvelously comfortable with itself, its history, and its place in the Catalan hierarchy as the more laid-back, gentler-paced alternative to Barcelona.

Aiming to control the river crossing in these marches between the Pyrenees and the Costa Brava, the Romans built a walled city here in the first century B.C. Girona endured more than its share of strife: Beginning with Charlemagne in 785, it was besieged by enemy armies twenty-five times, prompting city leaders to build longer and higher walls during the Middle Ages. Walkways along the ramparts of those walls let you peer into the city on one side and across the countryside on the other. But even the stoutest fortifications didn't deter all the city's enemies. In 1809, Napoleon simply starved Girona into surrender.

Fortunately, the emperor's troops did not ravage the old city, so stately medieval buildings still stand on the Roman street plan. Approaching them, the first thing you'll see is a stretch of nineteenth-century houses along one bank of the river. They are painted in a rainbow of pastel colors and offer the first clue that Girona is a fanciful place.

The Sant Feliu pedestrian bridge over the river leads to the Plaça de Sant Feliu, one of Girona's main gathering places and the site of two of its many legends. There will almost certainly be someone around to explain that on returning from a journey, a Gironan must demonstrate loyalty to the city by kissing the hindquarters of the stone lion that climbs a column in the middle of the plaza. The locals, by the way, don't find the custom the least bit odd, though they do get a chuckle from tourists who follow suit.

The square is dominated by the Romanesqe Basilica de Sant Feliu, where Sant Narcís, a fourth-century martyr and the city's patron saint, is buried. He met his death on this spot, but managed to help defend the city a millennium later when it was besieged by the French in 1285. Tradition holds that giant *moscas*, or flies, escaped from his body and so spooked the French soldiers that they fled. Girona celebrates Sant Narcís on October 29 with some of the most flamboyant Catalan folkloric traditions, from processions of giant figures and towering human pyramids to the *correfoc*—a parade of devils dancing through the streets while spewing sparks and fire.

A gate from the early Roman walls leads from the plaza into the steep and compact old city. Gironans are literally a walking reminder of the value of cardiovascular exercise, but not all the fit people on the streets are local. The equally hilly terrain around the city is a favorite training base for elite cyclists getting ready for the Tour de France and other major races. The most gung-ho fitness buffs run up and down the "Stairway to Heaven," as the eighty-nine steps up to the entrance to the Catedral of Girona are called.

There is, of course, a legend associated with the cathedral. A woman considered to be a witch was caught in mid-curse, transformed into a stone gargoyle, and placed near the roof next to the Torre de Carlemany. Ever since, her mouth is washed out with a torrent of water every time it rains.

The cathedral was built between the eleventh and eighteenth centuries and boasts an ornate Baroque facade and a 75-foot Gothic nave that is the widest in the world. I often skip the treasure collections in Spain's great churches, but that would be a mistake in Girona. The cathedral museum displays the *Tapestry of Creation*, a magnificent twelfth-century embroidery. Anonymous stitchers depicted the creation of the heavens, the separation of the waters, and the creation of Adam and Eve and the animals in the Garden of Eden. Almost lost in the visual richness are portraits of some Girona citizens of the time, including prominent members of the Jewish community. It is one of the few portraits known of Jewish citizens in Spain.

It's hard to fathom why Isabel and Fernando expelled all Jews from the country in 1492. Like elsewhere in Spain, the Jewish citizens of Girona contributed greatly to the city's prosperity. During the twelfth century, the great rabbi Nahmanides and other scholars made Girona one of the most important centers of Kabbalistic mysticism in Europe.

The Jewish quarter, or "Call," evolved in the protective shadow of the cathedral and is a remarkably well-preserved remnant of a tight-knit community. A maze of narrow streets and pocket plazas surrounds the main street of the neighborhood, Carrer de la Força. Cyclist Lance Armstrong kept an apartment here during his training sessions, but the chief attraction is the Museu d'Història dels Jueus.

Spain went through a nationwide soul-searching in 1992 on the half-millennium anniversary of the expulsion of the Jews. No city took it more seriously than Girona, which made a real effort to recognize the Jewish contributions to its history and culture. The Museum of Jewish History was created to enlighten foreign and domestic visitors about Jewish traditions and community life and to explain a bit about the Jewish diaspora and the Spanish Inquisition. But the museum is most evocative when it is specific and local, highlighting Jewish artistic and cultural traditions in Catalunya. Beautiful carved sepulchers unearthed during excavations at the city's old Jewish cemetery recall the names of Girona's Jews incised in Hebrew script.

Time didn't stop with 1492, of course. Set in an eighteenth-century monastery building with second-century Roman cellars, the Museu d'Història de la Ciutat spans the centuries with artifacts from every era. It's best, I think, as it gets closer to our time, explaining Catalan traditions such as the *sardana* dance and the *cobla* band that accompanies the dancers, and highlighting the Catalan Renaissance. That artistic and intellectual bloom of the late nineteenth and early twentieth centuries led to Modernista buildings in the new city outside the old walls and the stubborn Catalan pride and identity that even Franco could not quash.

✳ www.girona.cat/turisme/eng

# 95 *Mad Love*

## SALVADOR AND GALA DALÍ, FIGUERES, CADAQUÉS, AND PÚBOL

By his own count, Surrealist artist Salvador Dalí (1904-1989) had twenty nicknames for his wife. Most people used "Gala" for the Russian-born Elena Ivanovna Diakonova (1894-1982). Ever the improviser, Dalí added the diminutive "Galuchka," "Olive" for her complexion and oval face, and "Lionette" for her fiery temper. But the name that fits her best is simply "The Muse."

Dalí and Gala were one of the most captivating couples of the mid-twentieth-century art world. His surreal imagery thrilled and perplexed viewers in equal measure and the couple moved with bravado through the high society of Europe and the United States. Regardless of whether her image actually appeared on the canvas, Dalí's obsession with Gala was often the subtext of his work. And Gala's skill at organizing their life—coupled with her thirst for fame and riches—largely drove his career.

Dalí was born in Figueres, an inland town about 87 miles (140 km) northeast of Barcelona, but spent childhood summers in the whitewashed fishing village of Cadaqués, 22 miles (36 km) east on the Cap de Creus. Throughout his life, he was drawn to the simple fishing life of the village and the "grandiose geological delirium," as he called the rocky coast of the cape.

In the summer of 1929, some of the most original artists of the time joined Dalí in Cadaqués. Among them were Belgian painter René Magritte and his wife Georgette Berger, Spanish filmmaker Luis Buñuel, and French poet Paul Éluard, his wife Gala, and their daughter Cécile. The group was heady with the possibilities of the nascent Surrealist movement to unleash the irrational forces of the psyche. Their cocktail chatter must have been a hoot.

One of the hallmarks of Surrealism is unexpected juxtapositions—and life certainly mimicked art when Gala and Dalí first met. In his autobiographical *The Secret Life of Salvador Dalí*, which he completed at age thirty-seven, Dalí recounted that Gala found that his pomaded hair and dandy dress gave him a "professional Argentine slickness." She was ten years older, had been married to Éluard for more than a decade, but routinely pursued other lovers. Dalí, who seems to have never become fully comfortable with sexual intimacy, was attracted to Gala's thin, rather boyish body. "I bore the ripening weight of a new-born love clutching my throat like a veritable octopus of solid gold sparkling with a thousand precious stones of anguish," he recalled.

However improbable, their relationship took hold. The couple married in 1934, about eighteen months after Gala and Éluard were divorced. Within a few years, Dalí began to sign his work "Gala-Salvador Dalí," giving The Muse top billing. The exact nature of their emotional and physical relationship will always remain a mystery. Alas, Gala's journal and the autobiography that she claimed to have written have never surfaced and Dalí, after all, was an artist who reveled in twisting reality. But two homes and a museum provide concrete touchstones of their lives—together and apart.

In 1930, they returned to Cadaqués and purchased a fisherman's shack in the even more isolated community of Port Lligat, about a twenty-minute walk from town. Lacking electricity and running water, it was ideal for what Dalí described as "a life of asceticism, of isolation." It was at Port Lligat, he wrote that "I learned to impoverish myself, to limit and file down my thinking in order that it might become effective as an ax...."

Now open to the public as the Casa Salvador Dalí, the property was expanded over the years. It's easy to see the serial architecture as it swelled from a humble abode into a Surrealist's sprawling summer house. The Dalís left Spain during the Civil War, but never relinquished the property. They usually arrived in April or May and left at the end of the year to reenter the social scene—and conduct business—in Paris and New York.

The couple seemed to have a penchant for crumbling buildings that they could remake to suit both their peculiar domestic arrangements and their self-image. In 1969, they purchased an eleventh-century castle in Púbol, 37 miles (60 km) from Port Lligat, and transformed it into Gala's private retreat. Here she entertained her significantly younger lovers and permitted Dalí to visit only on her written invitation.

Now called Gala Dalí Castle Púbol, it is a flamboyant goof on medieval courtly love, romantic in its own way while being simultaneously ironic. (Ever the good Surrealist, Dalí always had to have it both ways.) On one hand it is a solid old ruin, a stony keep in the countryside typical of the medieval Latin world. On the other, it is a study in bourgeois decadence with its faux Baroque draperies, voluptuously overstuffed furniture, and visual follies and trompe l'oeil wall paintings. Playing Michelangelo, Dalí made the grand gesture of painting the ceiling of the Great Hall. At the same time, he painted a finely detailed landscape on the golden Throne of Gala, which is a literal throne on a pedestal.

By the time Gala retreated to her castle, Dalí had his own distraction. Work began on the Teatro-Museo Dalí in Figueres in

1970. The artist was intent on converting the Teatro Principal, where he had first seen stage shows and had first exhibited his work, into the largest Surrealist object in the world.

✳ www.salvador-dali.org/museus

Dalí's ode to himself opened in 1974. It is less an art museum than a chance to meander the twisted corridors of Salvador Dalí's memory, from the old Cadillac where it rains inside the car to the sofa-sized lips of Marilyn Monroe. Yet there are constant sweet nods to his not-so-sweet wife. A number of paintings trace Dalí's infatuation with Gala from the 1934 *Portrait of Gala with Two Lamb Chops in Equilibrium upon Her Shoulder* to *The Three Glorious Enigmas of Gala*, painted in 1982. That same year, The Muse died at Port Lligat and was buried at Púbol.

Dalí never returned to Port Lligat and lived at Púbol until 1984 when he moved to the Torre Galatea, a medieval tower adjacent to the Teatro-Museo. After his death in January 1989, Dalí was buried at his museum, beneath the massively magnified eye of a fly painted on the great dome of the theater. The ceiling also features a dual portrait of Gala and himself as seen from below ground. (The soles of their feet form the foreground.)

In his art, at least, they are together for eternity.

## RECOMMENDED READING

*The Secret Life of Salvador Dalí* by Salvador Dalí
*The Shameful Life of Salvador Dalí* by Ian Gibson

# 96 *Running Without the Bulls*

## WOMEN'S MARATHON IN PALMA DE MALLORCA

The grassy band of Parc de la Mar in Palma, Mallorca's sprawling capital city, makes a gorgeous—perhaps even inspirational—starting point for a foot race. Runners bend and stretch, loosening up under the watchful gaze of the city's Catalan Gothic cathedral which sits just above them on a rocky shelf between the narrow streets of the old city and the glistening harbor below. It is as if the church were offering a blessing to the assembled runners as they try to banish their starting-line jitters and focus on the course ahead.

Lisa Jackson, a London-based clinical hypnotherapist and author of *Your Pace or Mine? What Running Taught Me About Life, Laughter and Coming Last*, participated in the first race in 2014. "Everyone on the start line in the shadow of the cathedral was exceptionally excited," she recalls. "We knew we were making history."

They were, in fact, the first runners in the first all-female marathon in Europe. The race was launched with the backing of Kathrine Switzer, the woman who challenged the gender barrier of the Boston Marathon in 1967. Although Switzer is no longer involved, the 261 Women's Marathon is named for the bib number she wore on the April day in Boston when she finished the course despite the attempts of officials to stop her. Palma's event is held in March or April, when the daily high temperatures of early spring only reach 60-65 degrees Fahrenheit. That means it's cool enough for comfortable running, and that tourists have not yet arrived en masse. As a result, it's also a great time of year to see the city sights.

✳ 261wm.com/en

By the second year, the 261 Women's Marathon, which also features a 10K run, had attracted more than eight hundred runners, most of whom ran the 10K. But ever since the race started, organizers have been fine-tuning the course with an eye to giving women a good, fast route that will also delight them with all the best features of Palma. Starting in 2016, the organizers added a half marathon option for those looking for more of a challenge than the 10K race, but who were not ready to commit to the full marathon. Men, by the way, are permitted to run to support a woman runner, though few women have felt the need for any encouragement beyond the strong sisterhood around them.

The camaraderie of the runners was, in fact, one of the things that most impressed Jackson. "It was my fifty-second marathon," she says "but my first women-only one, and I was blown away by the feeling of sisterhood and solidarity. Most of my fellow competitors spoke Spanish rather than English, but they never failed to wave or give a thumbs-up on the switchbacks. Even the leading runners patted me on the back as they sped by."

Departing from the large green park, marathon runners complete four laps on the loop course. First they head uphill just west of the old wall into the heart of the city to the lovely eighteenth-century Baroque palace of Casal Solleric before looping back down to the waterfront. The next stage of the route passes the yacht harbor before turning around near the ferry docks to retrace the long, flat, and gently curving path along the shore. As the city's name suggests, palms rustle in the cooling saltwater breezes.

The variety of the course is a boon to runners. "A stretch along the promenade gave us invigorating lungfuls of sea-spray-scented air," says Jackson. "Then we plunged into the heart of Palma's old town, full of quaint little shops, before heading out to the port, past hundreds of yachts bobbing in the bay. Having to do this section several times meant getting a good look at Palma's architectural treasures, including its monumental cathedral. It also gave the runners a chance to cheer each other on."

The finish line, by the way, is covered with pink carpet. The winners get no big purses, but every runner, whatever her time, receives a small pearl pendant. Palma is a city known for its style, and the island is famous for its lustrous man-made pearls—the perfect industry on an island in the middle of the Mediterranean Sea.

"I wore my pendant for several weeks because I'd had such a memorable race experience," says Jackson. She spent her final lap running alongside a friend who got a severe cramp and was in danger of not finishing. "I'd tried to distract her from the pain by telling her funny stories. She was just one of many women who faced their fears and achieved what they'd once thought was impossible," Jackson says. "For me the pendant symbolized not only my own joy at finishing, but their joy too."

# 97 *Keeper of the Gate, Keeper of the Flame*

## THE PILAR AND JOAN MIRÓ FOUNDATION, MALLORCA

It took nearly two decades, but Catalan artist Joan Miró (1893-1983) finally occupied the studio that he had first described in a 1938 article in a Paris magazine. "My dream, once I am able to settle down somewhere," he said, "is to have a very large studio, not so much for reasons of brightness, northern light, and so on, which I don't care about, but in order to have enough room to hold many canvases, because the more I work, the more I want to work."

In 1956, Miró moved into just such a studio in Son Abrines, just uphill from the early Mallorca resort district of Cala Major on the west side of Palma. The person who largely made his dream come true was his wife Pilar Juncosa (1904-1995).

Wed for more than fifty years, the couple's harmonious union was a far cry from the more tumultuous relationships of such Miró contemporaries as Pablo Picasso (see Chapters 68 and 87) and Salvador Dalí (see Chapter 95). The Mirós may have seemed hopelessly old-fashioned in the heady art world of the early twentieth century, but their marriage attests that creativity can thrive in harmony as well as in discord. In a century where modern art was characterized by experimentation and abstraction, Miró always worked on the cutting edge of both fronts, producing a refined art that translated as unalloyed sensuality. Although little was written about Juncosa, she exercised considerable influence on her husband's art throughout his career and jealously protected him from distractions.

Born in Barcelona, Miró developed an early affinity for the island that would become his home for the last quarter-century of his life. His mother and his maternal grandparents, in fact, were Mallorcan. From the age of seven, he spent part of each summer on the island, where he began to develop his love of untamed scenery. Later, he also fell in love with island native Pilar Juncosa. The couple married in 1929 and their only child, Maria Dolors Miró Juncosa, was born the following year.

Miró was drawn to the Paris art scene in the 1920s, although he returned frequently to Spain. In exile during the Spanish Civil War, the couple spent most of their time in France until they had to flee the Nazis in 1940. They found a safe haven with Juncosa's family on Mallorca, where Miró was known as "the husband of Pilar Juncosa."

In 1954, when the couple decided to settle permanently on Mallorca, Pilar Juncosa asked Miró's friend and fellow Catalan Josep Lluís Sert (1902-1983) to design a studio for her husband. Completed in 1956, the concrete building slides into the terraced hillside almost like a kitchen drawer into a cabinet. From the outside, it is a happy building with doors and shutters painted in the red, blue, and yellow primaries that Miró so favored. The roofline is curved like gull wings to funnel rainfall into cascades. Inside, it's all business with big windows on one wall, a tiled floor, and another wall of rough stone. The two-story construction provides room for both work and storage. Miró liked to put pieces out of sight, then take a fresh look before resuming work on them. Indeed, many unfinished works stand on easels awaiting the brushstrokes that will never come.

As the artist had predicted, the space and the hillside setting overlooking the water launched a fertile new period in his work. Again, Juncosa played her role, acting as a gatekeeper to ensure that her husband could work undisturbed. Miró was so productive, in fact, that in 1959 he purchased an adjacent late eighteenth-century house, Son Boter, to use as his studio for large-scale sculpture and canvases. His energy was so unbridled that he even covered the walls with charcoal drawings and later used the space as a print workshop as well.

Connecting the two studios, a narrow stone path along a ridgeline affords scenic views of rooftops as they ripple down to the sea like so many terracotta steps. Outside Son Boter, a table sits in the shade beneath a big pine tree. I like to picture Juncosa walking the path to meet her husband at the table for lunch. They might discuss his work, look out to sea, or simply enjoy the silence and intimacy of a long life together.

In 1981, they established the Pilar and Joan Miró Foundation and donated the studios and all art works, documents, and objects in them. In doing so, they preserved not just Miró's life's work, but the environment that they had created together to make it possible. Miró died in 1983 and three years later Juncosa donated the adjacent land for a new building to hold galleries and a library. Some of her personal collection was auctioned at Sotheby's to cover the building costs. Now the main building of the complex, it was designed by Spanish architect Rafael Moneo and opened in 1992. Its galleries contain changing exhibitions, which vary from photographs of the artist's printing plates, to assemblages of found objects that gave him delight, to selections from periods or conceptual streams of his work. The building also contains the inevitable gift shop and a café where many museum visitors nurse a coffee, sketch in a notebook, or simply sit and soak in the sense of place.

✳ miro.palmademallorca.es

Juncosa was dedicated to preserving her husband's legacy, but she also looked forward to the frontiers of art. Four foundation grants are named for Juncosa, with awards for serial art, visual arts education, and for research projects about Miró. Finally, one grant is for an artistic project in the foundation gardens—an affirmation of the bond between nature and creativity as espoused by the artist who liked to refer to himself as "a gardener." Writing about his process in 1959, he explained, "The leaves have to be cut so the vegetables can grow. At a certain moment you must prune."

## RECOMMENDED READING

*Miró* by Walter Erben

# 98

## *Suffering for Art, Like Good Romantics*

### GEORGE SAND AND FRÉDÉRIC CHOPIN IN VALLDEMOSSA, MALLORCA

It turns out that Spain may not be for every woman. At the very least, Romantic rebel and writer George Sand (1804-1876) certainly did not hit it off with Mallorca, the largest island in the Balearic archipelago east of Valencia and Barcelona. The cigar-smoking iconoclast who dressed in men's clothing was equally at home among the leading artists of Parisian society or at her bucolic country estate in central France. But the rustic mountains and country people of Mallorca tested her mettle and ultimately sent her packing.

In *Winter in Mallorca*, Sand describes the fifty-six days she spent in an abandoned Carthusian monastery in the town of Valldemossa with her lover Frédéric Chopin (1810-1849) and her children, fifteen-year-old Maurice and eight-year-old Solange. The little group lived in Cell 4 in the Real Cartuja de Valldemossa from December 20, 1838 to February 13, 1839. They left in some haste, but have hardly been forgotten. The cell is now a small museum dedicated to the couple.

They started the adventure with high hopes. Sand recalled in her book, "I fancied once again that I should find some faraway quiet retreat where there would be no notes to write, no newspapers to peruse, no callers to entertain...." Perhaps more importantly, she imagined there would be no prying eyes to look askance at the couple's affair. Sand, who was 34 at the time, had legally separated from her husband about three years earlier. Chopin was not her first lover. The composer, who was already suffering from tuberculosis, was 28.

The couple reached their "faraway quiet retreat" in an arduous drive in a small carriage that bumped and twisted over the rough terrain. These days, the MA-1110 highway runs due north from Palma to Valldemossa, taking about a half hour by automobile. Even if you take the slower, more scenic coastal and mountain route (MA-1 to MA-10), as I did, the trip via endless switchbacks takes only a couple of hours. And those couple of hours are a visual delight: The cliffside road is alternately flanked by pine trees and naked rock. Along the stretch between Andratx and Estellencs, tiny turnouts mark trailheads for hiking paths best suited for the wild mountain goats. As the road approaches Bañalbufur before turning inland, the slopes toward the ocean have been cleared of their pine forest and are terraced into vineyards. In the village, bright morning glories climb every otherwise unadorned pole.

Valldemossa itself is a handsome market town tucked into a bowl between mountain ranges, just a few miles inland from Mallorca's north coast. The Carthusian monastery, which was seized by the Spanish government (like most properties of the Roman Catholic Church) about three years before the couple arrived, remains a sturdy and imposing building that squats on a slight rise above town. I didn't know quite what to expect as I entered through a big wooden door and walked down a wide tiled hallway past a lovely central courtyard with a fountain and orange trees.

In my mind's eye, the couple's cell consisted of one small room with a lone window high on the wall and a hard palette on the floor. On the contrary, it turned out to be rather charming, especially on a sunny autumn afternoon. From a small entry, the cell opens into three good-sized rooms: a kitchen with fireplace, a central living area, and a bedroom large enough to section off a sleeping area for the children and still hold the piano that was delivered to Chopin once he arrived. The rooms look out on a big courtyard filled with flowers and trees. In Sand's time, it was probably more of a kitchen garden, but the view across the valley and to the mountains was the same. Even Sand was delighted at first, calling the cell "the most romantic dwelling place in the world" and thanking God "who hast given me good eyes" to appreciate the majesty of the setting.

Praises to God aside, the religious origin of their quarters soon began to weigh her down. "Why attempt to deny that sinister abodes like these, dedicated to an even more sinister religious cult, have some effect on the imagination?" she wrote. "I would challenge the calmest and coolest brain to preserve perfect sanity here over a long period."

Apart from any lingering odor of sanctity, the little group did endure a number of hardships. They did not realize that winter in the mountains is cold and rainy and that the big stone building would hold in the chill. On top of that, the townspeople feared Chopin's illness and generally disapproved of the couple's living arrangement. Sand considered the locals "dreary and poor" and fettered to their religion. What they said about her was not recorded for posterity.

The prolific Sand, who authored about sixty novels as well as nonfiction and plays, found but small inspiration at Valldemossa. (Later in 1839, she published a horror novel, *Spiridion,* set in a creepy monastery.) Chopin, on the other hand, had significant bursts of creativity despite his illness. He composed some of his most popular works here, including "Raindrop" (Prelude in D-flat Major), as well as Polanaise No. 4 in C-minor, Ballade No. 2 in F, and Scherzo No. 3 in C-sharp Minor. Alternately brooding and warmly reflective, Chopin's music plays as a soundtrack and it's easy to imagine the composer at his piano, bringing the space to life as he worked out the melodies and counterpoints.

Sand's time in the contemplative setting of the monastery, however, did not go for naught. She seems to have come to know herself better. "Now the moral of this tale, childish perhaps, but heartfelt," she wrote at the end of her book, "seems to be that man is not made to live with trees, stones, the clear sky, the azure sea, flowers and mountains, but with his fellow-men."

✳ www.celdadechopin.es (Spanish only)

## RECOMMENDED READING

*Winter in Mallorca* by George Sand

# 99

## Mallorca's Literary Love Nest

### CA N'ALLUNY, THE HOME OF LAURA RIDING AND ROBERT GRAVES

The brilliant American poet and uncompromising intellect Laura Riding (1901-1991) spent only fourteen years with English poet and novelist Robert Graves (1895-1985), but it was in many ways the most incandescent period in both their lives.

The two escaped to Europe in 1929, hoping to, as Riding put it, "live untroubled." In truth, they were trying to extricate themselves from the scandal caused by their tangled relationships. They sought refuge first with their friend Gertrude Stein, who suggested that Mallorca might suit the couple's needs. It's a "paradise—if you can stand it," she told them.

Graves and Riding were up to it. Rejecting the capital city of Palma as too worldly, they settled in the little mountain village of Deià, nestled between the Sierra de Tramuntana range and the sea. It's really no surprise that Graves and Riding craved the quiet and anonymity of this then-primitive village. Riding was an up-and-coming poet when Graves invited her in 1925 to join him in England to work on a book about modern poetry. Soon they were involved in what Riding described as a "three-life" with Graves's wife, the artist Nancy Nicholson, with whom he had four children. The already complicated relationship became a "four-life" with the arrival of Irish poet Geoffrey Phibbs in 1928. Distraught that Phibbs preferred Nicholson to her, Riding threw herself from a fourth floor window. Graves rushed down the stairs to her aid, but equally distraught at the thought of losing her, instead threw himself from a third floor window.

Really.

Graves, who had survived a devastating shell wound in World War I, was not seriously injured. Riding, on the other hand, suffered a fractured spine. When she was well enough to travel, the couple left England. By November 1929, Graves wrote to a friend from Mallorca that, "It is very good to be here and we intend to stay a long time. Sun. Olives, figs, oranges, fish, quiet."

After renting a house for a couple of years, Riding and Graves bought a lot that received plenty of sun to nourish a garden. It was also close enough to town so that they could walk in to pick up their mail, socialize in a café, or meet friends at the bus stop. Riding designed the house, which was completed in 1932. In a letter to his friend T. E. Lawrence, Graves pronounced it "a great success, inside and out." The two story limestone structure with tile roof and

green shutters seemed to blend seamlessly into the landscape and was surrounded by olive, carob, and citrus trees that provided cool shade for several terraces.

Inside, the whitewashed rooms have floors of yellow tile that Riding particularly favored. Perhaps most tellingly, the couple had separate bedrooms. Riding apparently renounced the physical part of their relationship the same year they moved in, preferring to nurture the intimacy of sublimation. Riding and Graves also had their own studies. His was on the first floor. Several bookcases give it a bit of an old-school feel. Directly above it, Riding's studio is more spare. She generally worked at night, while Graves was an early riser.

The house opened as a museum in 2006 and recreates the period of the Riding/Graves residency. Visits begin with a video that borrows from BBC interviews with Graves to put the importance of the house—and of his relationship with Riding—in his own words. "I was infatuated by her," he said. "I wrote the books she wanted me to write. The villagers took me as her manservant." For her part, Riding adopted traditional dress and loved to wear the jewelry that she and Graves searched out in island shops.

✳ www.lacasaderobertgraves.org/en

They both poured themselves into their work. During the couple's time in Deià, Graves completed his popular novels *I, Claudius* (1934) and *Claudius the God* (1935) and wrote some of his most fervent love poems. His *Collected Poems* (1938) helped establish his reputation as a major poet. Riding was less well recognized than Graves, but her *Collected Poems*, also 1938, became her poetic legacy. In 1975, the *New York Review of Books* noted that, "At an age when most poets are just beginning to come into their own, she had already reached maturity."

Recalling the time for the BBC, Graves maintained that, "The outside world did not exist. It was the end of history."

The couple gathered like-minded friends around them and, by force of personality and intellect, Riding was the sun around which the others revolved. But, alas, the outside world did exist. In July 1936, reactionary Nationalist forces took over the Balearic Islands. Riding and Graves left Mallorca in haste in early August, carrying but one suitcase each. It was like turning out a light on a brilliant period of their lives. Their hopes for a quick return were not to be. They settled in London and spent time in Switzerland and the United States. Unable to overcome the distance that had been creeping into their relationship, each soon found partners they would stick with for the long haul.

Riding relinquished her ownership in Ca n'Alluny, asking only that Graves "burn all papers of mine found there." Graves returned to Mallorca in May 1946 with new wife Beryl and three children. Their fourth child was born on the island. Mallorca continued to suit Graves, who lived and worked here the rest of his life. He is buried in the Deià cemetery, the highest point in town.

In 1941 Riding married poet and critic Schuyler B. Jackson. By then, she had renounced poetry and turned her attention to essays, fiction, and lexicography. Riding never returned to Mallorca. But her study, once converted to a children's bedroom, has been restored to the way she intended it. Her simple wooden desk and chair rest on a straw mat. Her bodice lies draped across the chair, as if her fierce apparition could at any moment quicken the golden air.

## RECOMMENDED READING

*In Extremis: The Life of Laura Riding* by Deborah Baker

*A Mannered Grace: The Life of Laura (Riding) Jackson* by Elizabeth Friedman

*Robert Graves: The Years With Laura, 1926-1940* by Richard Perceval Graves

# 100

*Sun on the Skin*

## NUDE BEACHES IN SPAIN

There was a time not so long ago when you risked being rushed by the Guardia Civil if you dared remove your bikini top at the beach. But now the Spanish Constitution guarantees you the right to dress however you wish—or not dress at all—as long as you aren't creating a public nuisance. Seemingly daring topless beaches of a generation

ago have given way to beaches all over Spain where you can happily go with nothing between you and the Spanish sun except a good covering of sunblock. The naturist movement began in Germany and Scandinavia, but warm temperatures and abundant sunshine make the 5,000 miles (8,000 km) of Spanish coastline an even more logical place to shed your clothes and your inhibitions. In fact, the national tourist office estimates that 1.5 million visitors (mostly Europeans) flock to Spain each year to lie on the beaches *au naturel* and that another half million Spaniards join them.

Recognizing that not everyone wants to see their fellow vacationers in the buff, many communities have clearly marked certain beach areas as nude, or at least clothing-optional. But even in those areas without "official" nude beaches, nudity is often tolerated at one end of the beach that nudists share with "textiles." Look around and you'll quickly see which end. In practice, you'll also find many beaches where some people are topless, some nude, and some covered up. The days of having to sneak off to secluded coves to sun and swim nude are over, and many nude beaches now have showers and *chiringuitos*. On the other hand, access to the nude area might require a bit of a walk from the parking lot, and some of the more spectacular nude beaches are, in fact, wild and remote.

Here are a few places where a woman can feel comfortable in her own skin:

## Playa de El Puntal, Santander

This sandy point in the middle of the bay of Santander has more than a mile of golden-sand beach and is historically one of the most popular beaches—textile or nude—on the Cantabrian coast. It's about a ten-minute ferry ride across the bay from downtown Santander (catch the boat at the Botin Center pier) and El Puntal *chiringuito* is one of the most famous beach bars in Spain. Nudists tend to cluster between the beach bar and the rolling dunes. Be careful with the strong waves, which are particularly good for body surfing.

## Playa de El Chorrito, Bolonia

The stunning Costa de la Luz between Cádiz and Tarifa is lined with sandy shores, though not all of them are accessible. Bolonia, one of the more popular beach towns, is located between Zahara de los Atunes (a famous tuna fishing port) and Tarifa. It's a little more sheltered than Tarifa, which makes it less suitable for wind- and kite-surfing but better for sunbathing and swimming without winds to whip up the sand. The central beach is very family-oriented and jammed with beach bars and restaurants, but if you walk south, you'll come to the nudist strand of El Chorrito. (It's nudist in practice, though not by regulation.) If you keep going to the cliffs, you'll find an area with seams of gray mud where you can muck up for a mud bath.

## Playa de Cuesta de Maneli, Doñana National Park

You'll be sharing the sands of Playa de Cuesta de Maneli—a two-mile stretch of sand backed by sandstone cliffs and scrub forest—with sea and shore birds from nearby Africa, and with a certain number of textiles toting binoculars to spy on the birdlife. Getting there is a little tricky—watch for signs to Cuesta de Maneli between km38 and km39 on the A-494 highway, halfway between Mazagón and Matalascañas, south of Huelva in Andalucía. A mile-long boardwalk through the dunes and scrub pines leads to the beach. When you get there, turn left and pass the *zona naturista* sign before you start disrobing.

## Playa Naturista de Playa Marina, Mijas Costa

The Costa del Sol was Spain's first sun-and-sand getaway, developed in the middle of the twentieth century and still being developed wherever builders can find an uncovered square inch. With all the high-rise condos and apartment buildings, beaches can get more crowded than most nude sunbathers find comfortable. One escape from the blanket-paved beaches of Torremolinos, Fuengirola, and Benalmadena is this 1,000-foot sandy cove designated by Mijas as its nudist beach. There's a prominent sign on the A7, but note that parking is across the highway from the beach, with a footbridge overpass to get to the sands. If you're looking for it with GPS, it's in Urbanización Playa Marina near the Los Amigos Golf Club.

## Platja de Els Balmins, Sitges

Just a little south of Barcelona, Sitges has been out as Spain's gay resort for decades, and its beaches have long been nude-friendly for gay and straight alike. While most Sitges beaches are clothing-optional, a few are, by tradition, more nudist than others. Platja de Els Balmins, a little over a half mile east from the main beach at the center of town, snuggles up to the rocks by the breakwater that defines the Aiguadolç pleasure boat marina. A rocky point divides Els Balmins between nude and textile, and both have great views of the Baluart outcrop with the church of Sant Bartolomeu towering over the sea. Like most Sitges beaches, Els Balmins enters the sea at a very shallow angle, so you will have to walk out a fair distance to reach a good depth for swimming.

## Platja Es Trenc, Mallorca

This pristine beach was one of the first unofficial nude beaches in Spain, going back even to the cover-up-and-blush years of Franco. Roughly a mile and a half of fine, pale golden sand is framed by grassy dunes, and the crystalline turquoise waters are quiet—no motorboats or jet skis. Protected as part of a regional park, Es Trenc is free of all hotels and the few restaurants and bars are across the access highway. Several small parking lots dot the highway, and while many beachgoers wear swimsuits, much of the beach is nude. Perhaps because it lacks bars and restaurants, Es Trenc is one of the most tranquil, least commercial beaches on Mallorca.

# *Index*

261 Women's Marathon  337

accommodations
   Hostal Dos Reis Católicos  136
   Hotel de Áliva  123
   Hotel de la Reconquista  125
   Hotel Marqués de Riscal  83
   La Hostería del Laurel  204
   La Hostería de San Millán  99
   Marbella Club  233
   Monasterio de Santa María  165
   Parador de Cardona  164
   Parador de Guadalupe  165
   Parador de Olite  165
   Parador de Orepesa  164
   Parador de Úbeda  165
   parador system  163
A Coruña  127
Acueducto de los Milagros  168
Aire de Sevilla  207
Alameda del Tajo  231
Albaicín  262
Alcázar  196
Alfaro  87
Algodonales  226
Alhambra  254
Alicante  277
Altamira cave  117
Ambar  21
Amfiteatre Ròma  288
Andalucía  206
Anella Olímpica  318
Antonio Pérez Foundation  158
Antonio Saura Foundation  157
Aqueduct of Segovia  58

Arbo  141
Archeological Museum  44
Arcos de la Frontera  228
Arriondas  121
Arzak  111
Askuna Zentroa  106
Ávila  55

Baja de Guía  219
Barcelona  299, 303, 306, 310, 313,
   320, 323
Barri Gotíc  310
Barrio de Las Letras  16
Basilica de la Macarena  183
Basilica de la Sagrada Família  313
Basilica de Nuestra Señora de
   Covadonga  121
Basilica de Nuestra Señora del
   Prado  154
Basilica de San Isidoro  75
Basílica de Santa Maria del Mar  303
Basilica de Sant Feliu  330
Bay of Biscay  143
beaches  219, 222, 234, 278, 302,
   352, 353, 354, 355
   Playa La Caleta  222
   Venus Beach  234
Bernat Picornell  318
Bilbao  103
Bilbao Fine Arts Museum  105
birdwatching  87
Bistro 1860  85
Bodegas Barbadillo  218
Bodegas Elias Mora  64
Bodegas José Pariente  71

Bodegas Tradición 212
Bolonia 353
Botanical Garden 35
Bubión 269
Buenavista Palace 241
bullfighting 230
Burgos 76

Cabo Fisterra 138
Cadaqués 333
Cádiz 221
Café Iruña 96
Calderería Nueva 261
Calderería Vieja 261
Caligae Muestrarios 20
Camino de Santiago 130
Camino Frances 73
Ca n'Alluny 348
Cangas de Onís 121
canoeing 142
Cantabria 117
Cantabrian Mountains 120
Capileira 269
Casa Amatller 296
Casa Battló 297
Casa Gonzalez 42
Casa Lleó Morera 301
Casa Milà 297
Casa Museo de María Pita 128
Casa Patas 48
Casa Salvador Dalí 335
Casa Zavala 157
Casco Antiguo 235
Castell de Montjuïc 316
Catedral de León 73
Catedral de San Salvador 126
Catedral de Santa María 78
Catedral de Santiago de
    Compostela 134
Catedral de Sevilla 171
Catedral Nueva 224

Catedral of Girona 330
Catedral Vieja 62
cave tours 118
Centre Pompidou 238
Centro Cerámica Triana 194
Ceramica Rocio-Triana 195
Cerámica Santa Ana 194
ceramics 152, 194
chocolate 324
Chocolatería San Ginés 10
Chocolats 42
Chueca 19
churches
    Basilica de la Sagrada Família 313
    Basilica de Nuestra Señora de
        Covadonga 121
    Basilica de San Isidoro 75
    Basílica de Santa Maria
        del Mar 303
    Basilica de Sant Feliu 330
    Catedral de León 73
    Catedral de San Salvador 126
    Catedral de Santa María 78
    Catedral de Santiago de
        Compostela 134
    Catedral de Sevilla 171
    Catedral Nueva 224
    Catedral of Girona 330
    Catedral Vieja 62
    Convent of Santa Teresa 56
    Iglesia Colegiata de San
        Miguel 87
    Iglesia del Valle 191
    Iglesia de Santiago 240
    Iglesia de Santo Tomé 150
    La Colegiata 67
    La Mezquita 251
    La Seu 311
    Monestir de Montserrat 326
    Nuestra Señora de la Cabeza 269
    Oratorio de Santa Cueva 223

Royal Chapel 54
San Felipe Neri 311
San Miguel del Lillo 126
San Pedro Church 275
Santa Iglesia Catedral
    de Córdoba 251
Santa María del Naranco 126
Santa María del Pi 312
Santa María la Mayor 67
Tarragona Catedral 289
Toledo Cathedral 53
Circ Romà 288
Codorníu Winery 293
Coleción del Museo Ruso 237
Consuegra 160
Convento de las Dueñas 63
Convento de Santo Domingo 148
Convent of Santa Teresa 56
Córdoba 54, 248, 251
Córdoba Courtyard Festival 248
Costa Blanca 277
Costa Daurada 288
Costa del Sol 232, 236
Courtyard of the Maidens 197
Covadonga 121
Cristóbal Balenciaga Museoa 100
Cuenca 155
Cueva de María la Canastera 264
cuisine 40, 75, 111, 114, 122, 157,
    160, 180, 269, 278, 280,
    320, 323
culinary tours 40
cycling 282

Deià 348
Descent of the Sella 142
Doñana National Park 354
El Castillo 118
Elche 279
El Generalife 257
Elias Mora Winery 64
El Maestro Sierra 212

El Paraje Natural Torcal de
    Antequera 246
El Postiguet 278
El Retiro 33
Els Quatre Gats 306
Emerita Augusta 167
equestrian ballet 215
Escribá 300

Fallas Festival 284
fashion 20, 100, 107, 108
Fiesta de la Rosa del Azafrán 160
Fiesta de los Patios de Córdoba 248
Fiesta de San Fermín 93
Fisterra 138
flamenco 48, 177, 193, 264
Font Màgica 316
Fountain of Seven Pipes 122
Fuente Dé 122
Fundació Joan Miró 317, 342
Fundación Real Escuela Andaluza del
    Arte Ecuestre 214

Gala Dalí Castle Púbol 335
Ganbara Bar-Asador 116
Gastrofestival Madrid 28
Gernika 31, 32
Getaria 100
Gibralfaro 237
Girona 329
González Byass 211
Granada 54, 254, 259, 261, 264
Granja M. Viader 324
Grazalema 227
Grazalema Mountains Natural
    Park 227
Guadalupe 165
Guggenheim Bilbao 103

Hall of Monarchs 53
hammam 206
hiking 123, 130, 247, 267

Hostal Dos Reis Católicos 136
Hotel de Áliva 123
Hotel de la Reconquista 125
Hotel Marqués de Riscal 83
Huerta de San Vicente 259

Iglesia Colegiata de San Miguel 87
Iglesia del Valle 191
Iglesia de Santiago 240
Iglesia de Santo Tomé 150
In Vino Veritas 99

Jardí Botànic 318
Jerez de la Frontera 209, 214
Juan Foronda 186
Judería 249

kitesurfing 144

La Alhambra 254
La Alpujarra 267
La Boqueria 320
La Casa de Robert Graves 350
La Colegiata 67
La Concepción Festival 90
La Fontanilla 234
La Fuente de los Siete Caños 122
La Gardunya 324
La Giralda 172
La Hostería del Laurel 204
La Hostería de San Millán 99
La Mancha 159
La Mercat de Sant Josep de la
    Boqueria 320
La Mezquita 251
La Moreneta 326
La Palmera 279
La Pepica 280
La Plaza de Toros de Ronda 230
La Rioja 83
Las Arenas de Cabrales 122
La Seu 311

La Taberna del Gourmet 278
La Vinya del Senyor 303
La Xarcu 322
L'Eixample 296
León 73
Les Rambles 299
Loewe 301

Madrid 3, 6, 10, 13, 16, 19, 30,
    33, 37
Madrid Food Tours 40
Madrid Fusion 28
Madrid Río 35
Málaga 236, 239, 244
Mallorca 341, 344, 355
Mantecería de A Cabello 42
marathon 337
Marbella 232
Marbella Club 233
Mare Shoes 19
Marqués de Riscal 84
Mercado Antón Martín 43
Mercado de San Miguel 5
Mercado de Triana 193
Mercat Central 281
Mercat Princesa 322
Mercat Santa Caterina 321
Mérida 168
Mijas Costa 354
Monasterio de Las Descalzas
    Reales 13
Monasterio de San Juan de los
    Reyes 149
Monasterio de Santa María 165
Monasterio de Suso 97
Monasterio de Yuso 98
Monastery of San José 57
Monestir de Montserrat 326
Monte Benacantil 277
Monte Facho 139
Monte Naranco 126
Montjuïc 316

Mont San Lorenzo 97
Montserrat 326
Mundaka 143
Museo Arqueológico 201
Museo Arqueológico y de
  Historia 279
Museo Carmen Thyssen 243
Museo Casa Natal 239
Museo Cuevas del Sacromonte 266
Museo de Altamira 117
Museo de Artes y Costumbres
  Populares 201
Museo de Bellas Artes de
  Asturias 126
Museo de Cádiz 223
Museo del Baile Flamenco 177
Museo del Greco 149
Museo de Santa Cruz 150
Museo des Peregrinacións 136
Museo Nacional Centro de Arte
  Reina Sofía 30
Museo Nacional de Arte
  Romano 168
Museo Nacional del Prado 23
Museo Picasso Málaga 241
Museo Ruiz de Luna 153
Museo Sefardí 149
Museo Thyssen-Bornemisza 6
Museu d'Història dels Jueus 331
Museum of Jewish History 331
Museum of Pilgrimages 136
Museum of Spanish Abstract Art 156
Museu Nacional Arqueològic de
  Tarragona 289
Museu Nacional d'Art de
  Catalunya 317
Museu Picasso 307
museums
  Antonio Pérez Foundation 158
  Antonio Saura Foundation 157
  Archeological Museum 44
  Bilbao Fine Arts Museum 105

Casa Museo de María Pita 128
Castillo San Jorge 193
Centre Pompidou 238
Centro Cerámica Triana 194
Coleción del Museo Ruso 237
Convent of Santa Teresa 56
Cristóbal Balenciaga Museoa 100
Fundació Joan Miró 317
Guggenheim Bilbao 103
Huerta de San Vicente 259
La Casa de Robert Graves 350
Monastery of San José 57
Museo Arqueológico 201
Museo Arqueológico Nacional 44
Museo Arqueológico y de
  Historia 279
Museo Carmen Thyssen 243
Museo Casa Natal 239
Museo Cuevas del Sacromonte 266
Museo de Altamira 117
Museo de Artes y Costumbres
  Populares 201
Museo de Bellas Artes de
  Asturias 126
Museo de Cádiz 223
Museo del Baile Flamenco 177
Museo del Greco 149
Museo de Santa Cruz 150
Museo des Peregrinacións 136
Museo Nacional Centro de Arte
  Reina Sofía 30
Museo Nacional de Arte
  Romano 168
Museo Nacional del Prado 23
Museo Picasso Málaga 241
Museo Ruiz de Luna 153
Museo Sefardí 149
Museo Thyssen-Bornemisza 6
Museu d'Història dels Jueus 331
Museu Nacional Arqueològic de
  Tarragona 289

Museu Nacional d'Art de
Catalunya 317
Museu Picasso 307
Museum of Jewish History 331
Museum of Pilgrimages 136
Museum of Spanish Abstract
Art 156
National Museum of Roman
Art 168
Pilar and Joan Miró
Foundation 342
Prado Museum 23
Reina Sofia Museum 30
Russian Museum 238

Nasrid Palace 255
National Museum of Roman Art 168
Nuestra Señora de la Cabeza 269

Oleo-le 181
Olite 166
Olive Oil Workshop 181
opera 174–176
Oratorio de Santa Cueva 223
Oropesa 164
Oviedo 124

Palacio de Cristal 34
Palacio de las Dueñas 190
Palacio de San Telmo 200
Palacio Nazaries 255
Palau Aguilar 307
Palau de la Musica Catalana 291
Palau de la Música Catalana 291
Palau Güell 295
Palau Nacional 317
Palau Sant Jordi 318
Palma 337
Palmeral de las Sorpresas 237
Palm Garden of Surprises 237
Pampaneira 268
Pamplona 93

Parador de Cardona 164
Parador de Guadalupe 165
Parador de Olite 165
Parador de Orepesa 164
Parador de Úbeda 165
parador system 163
Parc de la Mar 337
Parque del Buen Retiro 33
Parque de María Luisa 199
Parque Natural de L'Albufera 282
Passeig de Gràcia 300
Passeig de Joan de Borbó 301
Passeig Maritim 302
Patio de las Doncellas 197
Patio del Mexuar 255
Patio de los Leones 256
Patisseria Brunells 324
Picos de Europa 120
Pilar and Joan Miró Foundation 342
pilgrimage 130–132, 138–140
Plaça de Santa Maria 303
Plaça de Sant Feliu 329
Platja de Els Balmins 355
Platja de la Barceloneta 302
Platja de San Sebastiá 302
Platja Es Trenc 355
Playa Artola 234
Playa de Cuesta de Maneli 354
Playa de El Chorrito 353
Playa de El Puntal 353
Playa de la Concha 110
Playa de San Juan 278
Playa La Caleta 222
Playa Naturista de Playa Marina 354
Plaza de América 201
Plaza de España 201
Plaza de las Palomas 201
Plaza del Ayuntamiento 285
Plaza de los Naranjos 235
Plaza de los Refinadores 204
Plaza de Mío Cid 76
Plaza de San Juan de Dios 224

Plaza Mayor 3
Pons Quintana 20
Poqueira Gorge 268
Port Lligat 334
Praza de Obradoiro 134
prehistoric cave paintings 117
Púbol 335
Puente de Alamillo 192
Puente Nuevo 231
Puente Romano 168
Puerta de las Palomas 227

Queen Isabel I 51

Real Fábrica de Tapices 37
Real Jardín Botánico 35
Rebeca Sanver 21
Restaurante Bernardo Etxea 116
Restaurante Gandarias 116
Restaurant Marqués de Riscal 85
restaurants
    Arzak 111
    Bistro 1860 85
    Casa Patas 48
    Chocolatería San Ginés 10
    Chocolats 42
    Els Quatre Gats 306
    Granja M. Viader 324
    In Vino Veritas 99
    La Gardunya 324
    La Pepica 280
    La Taberna del Gourmet 278
    Patisseria Brunells 324
    Restaurante Bernardo Etxea 116
    Restaurante Gandarias 116
    Restaurant Marqués de Riscal 85
    Tapas 24 323
    Xampu Xampany 325
Río Miño 141
Río Sella 142
road trip 225

Ronda 229
Royal Chapel 54
Royal Tapestry Factory 37
Royal Tobacco Factory 175
Rúa da Raína 136
Rúa do Franco 136
Rúa do Vilar 136
Rueda 70
Rue St. Honoré 21
running 337
Running of the Bulls 93
Russian Museum 238
Ruta de los Pueblos Blancos 225

Sacromonte 266
Saffron Rose Festival 160
Sala de los Abencerrajes 256
Salamanca 61
Sala Puig Cava Bar 293
Salón de los Embajadores 255
San Felipe Neri 311
Sanlúcar de la Barrameda 217
San Miguel del Lillo 126
San Millán de la Cogolla 97
San Pedro Church 275
San Román de Hornija 65
San Sebastián 110, 114
Santa Iglesia Catedral de
    Córdoba 251
Santa María del Naranco 126
Santa María del Pi 312
Santa María la Mayor 67
Santander 353
Santiago de Compostela 130, 134
Santillana del Mar 117
Santo Domingo de la Calzada 90
Sant Sadurní d'Anoia 293
Segovia 52, 58
Sevilla 171, 174, 180, 183, 186, 196,
    199, 203
sherry 209, 217

Sherry Triangle 210, 217
shopping 108, 136, 186, 261, 279,
   281, 320, 321, 322
   Ambar 21
   Caligae Muestrarios 20
   Casa Gonzalez 42
   Cerámica Santa Ana 194
   Loewe 301
   Mantecería de A Cabello 42
   Mare Shoes 19
   Mercado Antón Martín 43
   Mercado de San Miguel 5
   Mercado de Triana 193
   Pons Quintana 20
   Rebeca Sanver 21
   Rue St. Honoré 21
Sinagoga del Tránsito 149
Sitges 355
Son Abrines 340
Son Boter 342
Sotres 122
spas 85, 206, 207
Spa Vinothérapie Caudalie 85
surfing 143
swimming 318, 352–355
Talavera de la Reina 152
Tapas 24 323
Tarifa 143
Tarraco 287
Tarragona 287

Tarragona Catedral 289
Teatro y Anfiteatro Romano 169
Temple of Diana 168
Teresa of Ávila 55
Teruel 273
thermal bath 206
Toledo 147
Toledo Cathedral 53
Toro 64, 67
Torre Tavira 223
Trevélez 269
Triana 192

University of Salamanca 61

Valencia 280, 284
Valldemossa 344
Virgin Kitesurf World
   Championship 144

water sports 141
whitewater rafting 141
windsurfing 143
wineries 64, 71, 84, 210, 218, 293
wine tours 211, 218, 293

Xampu Xampany 325

Zahara de la Sierra 226

# Acknowledgments

There are two people without whom this book would have been impossible. I am forever indebted to my high school Spanish teacher, Señor Sirbursky, whose enthusiasm opened my teenage eyes to the Hispanic world through the door of language. I owe an equal debt to the redoubtable Pilar Vico, who took me under her wing as an adult and pushed me to explore more and more of her native country until it became my second home.

Many thanks to Marcia DeSanctis for introducing me to Larry Habegger and James O'Reilly and for setting such a high standard with her own captivating book about France. Larry and James have long recognized the life-affirming value of travelers' stories, and I'm pleased that they were receptive to mine. I am grateful to them and to all the staff at Travelers' Tales who shaped my manuscript into a book and brought it to the public.

I cannot express my gratitude enough to the women who shared their own stories with me. The book is far richer for their multiple points of view. Thank you to Mare Espinal, Lauren Aloise, Victoria Benavides, Victoria Pariente, Patti Nickell, Riley J. Ford, Elena Arzak, Ana Intxausti, Ann Kirkland, Alexis Kerner, Talia Baiocchi, Corey Boniface, and Lisa Jackson.

Many people in various Spanish tourism offices have been of immeasurable assistance over the years, often interceding to cut through red tape or formalities peculiar to the Spanish way of doing things. Among them, I am deeply appreciative of Rosa Pavón in Sevilla, Estafania Gómez in Madrid, and the crew at the national tourist office in New York: Tomás Rodríguez, Patricia Sotes, and Jesús Pérez. Special thanks as well are due to Ana Rojo and Laura Cuenca Castellanos in Madrid and Carmen Sanchez on Mallorca.

I cannot thank enough my family members who stepped up in a pinch so that I could keep writing and traveling, and my mother, who told me in no uncertain terms not to come home. Finally, thank you to my strongest, most unwavering supporter, my husband and often fellow traveler, David Lyon.

# About the Author

Patricia Harris travels the world researching and writing about travel, food, and the arts for a variety of U.S. and British publications. But she returns again and again to Spain, partly because she likes the person she becomes there—the one who stays out late at flamenco clubs, walks windswept beaches, dances the *sardana* in front of Barcelona's cathedral, and eats a thousand delicacies she probably wouldn't try at home.

A former arts administrator who handled funding for literature, theater, dance, and the visual arts, she loves the anguished angular faces of Catalan Gothic saints, the enigma of pure color on a Miró canvas, the pulsing rhythms of flamenco song and dance, the buffoonery of *zarzuela,* and the poignant passion of *Carmen.* Her kitchen cabinets are full of smoked Spanish paprika, Spanish saffron, and bags of a special sea salt from the Costa Brava that she buys in Spanish supermarkets for less than one euro per kilo. She lives in Cambridge, Massachusetts.